Computer Simulation

Computer Simulation

A Practical Perspective

Roger McHaney

ACADEMIC PRESS, INC.

Harcourt Brace Jovanovich, Publishers

San Diego   New York   Boston   London

Sydney   Tokyo   Toronto

Copyright © 1991 by ACADEMIC PRESS, INC.

All Rights Reserved.

No part of this publication may be reproduced or transmitted in any form or by any means, electronic or mechanical, including photocopy, recording, or any information storage and retrieval system, without permission in writing from the publisher.

Turbo Pascal is a registered trademark of Borland International. Graph-in-the-Box is a registered trademark of New England Software. LOTUS 1-2-3 is a registered trademark of LOTUS Development Corporation. IBM, IBM PC, GPSS/V are registered trademarks of International Business Machines. Microsoft, MS-DOS, GW-BASIC are registered trademarks of Microsoft Corporation. VAX is a registered trademark of Digital Equipment Corporation. GPSS/PC, GPSS/PC ANIMATOR are registered trademarks of Minuteman Software. Operations Plannner is a registered trademark of Palladian Software, Inc. Manuplan is a registered trademark of Network Dynamics, Inc. SIMAN, SIMAN IV, CINEMA are registered trademarks of Systems Modeling Corporation. GPSS/H, GPSS/H 386, Proof are registered trademarks of Wolverine Software Corporation. AutoMod, AutoGram, AutoMod II are registered trademarks of AutoSimulations, Inc. SIMSCRIPT, SIMSCRIPT II.5, SIMFACTORY, PC SIMSCRIPT II.5, SIMGRAPHICS are registered trademarks of CACI, Inc. TESS, SLAM, SLAM II, XCELL+ are registered trademarks of Pritsker Corporation. SEEWHY, WITNESS are registered trademarks of Istel, Inc. AutoCad is a registered trademark of AutoDesk, Inc.

Academic Press, Inc.
San Diego, California 92101

United Kingdom Edition published by
Academic Press Limited
24–28 Oval Road, London NW1 7DX

Library of Congress Cataloging-in-Publication Data

McHaney, Roger.
    Computer simulation : a practical perspective / Roger McHaney.
        p.   cm.
    Includes bibliographical references and index.
    ISBN 0-12-484140-6
    1. Digital computer simulation.   I. Title.
QA76.9.C65M395   1991
003'.3--dc20   90-28865
                                                         CIP

PRINTED IN THE UNITED STATES OF AMERICA
91   92   93   94   9   8   7   6   5   4   3   2   1

For Annette
my partner, my friend, my wife

This book exists because of your patience and understanding.

Contents

CHAPTER 3

Simulation in the Real World   **34**

CHAPTER 4

Six Symptoms of a Sick Simulation   **55**

CHAPTER 5

The Professional Simulation Analyst   **63**

CHAPTER 6

Building a Simulation the Right Way   **74**

CHAPTER 7

Learning a Simulation Language   **114**

CHAPTER 11

Applying the Process: Part II **242**

Index **271**

Foreword

Simulation is a rich and complex subject; complex to the point that at least one university offers a master's degree in simulation, with rumors that others may follow suit, and with Ph.D. dissertations frequently addressing themselves to one or another simulation research frontier. At the same time, simulation is an extremely important tool for operations researchers, management scientists, and decision makers. Surveys indicate that both practitioners and academics now rank simulation as the second most important quantitative modeling technique (Harpell et al., 1989), and informed opinion otherwise attests to its significance (Wagner, 1988). The practice of simulation requires operational knowledge of a range of topics, including a detailed understanding of the situation to be modeled, insights into the modeling process, skills in correctly representing a model in computer-processable terms, data collection and analysis, design and conduct of experiments, analysis of output, and interpretation of results in the context of the situation that was modeled. In addition, if a simulation-based project is to come to fruition, the project must be bought into by the client (the one or ones on whose behalf the project is being conducted in the first place), and the resulting findings must not only be firmly and confidently believed by the client but also must be put into practice by the client.

All of this leads to the need for differing levels of insight and knowledge on the part of simulation practitioners on the one hand and of their clients on the other hand. Practitioners must not only be skilled in the technical aspects of simulation, but they must also be adept at successfully marketing themselves and their work to their clients. This requires a willingness and ability on the part of practitioners to understand and adapt to the perspective of the client from time to time, and it also presupposes practitioner aptitudes for communicating ideas in terms with which the client is familiar and comfortable. In their turn, simulation clients must have an understanding of simulation in broad-based terms, should have some knowledge of the sequence of steps involved and the time and resources required to conduct a balanced and complete simulation study, and should be sensitive to the needs of the practitioner if a simulation project is to be supported and conducted successfully.

It is against this background that Roger McHaney has written *Computer Simulation: A Practical Perspective*. McHaney is a simulation practitioner who has had many successful experiences in marketing himself and his work to clients both internal and external to his organization. And he himself has played the role of client (an unusually well-informed client at that) relative to other simulation practitioners in his organization. Given his skills, experience, and motivation, he is in an admirable position to write a book presenting practical perspectives on computer simulation.

McHaney's book provides a relevant spectrum of information for simulation practitioners and clients alike. In the first of three sections of the book (Chapters 1 and 2), the concepts of modeling and simulation are described. The second section (Chapters 3 through 9) expands on these concepts and discusses their practical consequences when they are brought to bear in realistic settings. The third and last section (Chapters 10 and 11) brings together material from the first two sections to illustrate comprehensively how the simulation process is applied in practice.

Practitioners and clients of simulation (as well as would-be practitioners and would-be clients) would do well to go through this entire book. Most practitioners probably can browse through the early chapters but should then slow down in their reading and absorb details in later chapters. In contrast, most clients probably should read the earlier chapters in detail and then strive for the bigger picture in later chapters without necessarily trying to assimilate all the details. If a practitioner and client are both appropriately familiar with the contents of this book, it should support practitioner–client dialog nicely and substantially improve the probability that the simulation project that brings them together will be successful.

Thomas J. Schriber
Professor of Computer and Information Systems
The University of Michigan
Ann Arbor, Michigan

Harpell, John L., Michael S. Lane, and Ali H. Mansour (1989). Operations research in practice: a longitudinal study. *Interfaces* **19**(3), 65–74, May–June 1989.
Wagner, Harvey M. (1988). Operations research: a global language for business strategy. *Operations Research* **36**(5), 797–803, September–October 1988.

Preface

A fundamental goal of simulation is the reduction of risk and uncertainty associated with a given system. Simulation is used to study and to predict the performance of new systems or analyze changes to existing systems. It is used to play relatively inexpensive "what if" games and to test new ideas without a real world implementation. During my tenure as a simulation analyst, I have adapted much of the methodology used in model development and applied it to other areas. The structure and composition of *Computer Simulation: A Practical Perspective* is an example of this application.

My goals in writing this book are threefold:

1. To give readers who are unfamiliar with computer simulation a basic understanding of what it is, how it is being used, and how it can be used in their applications. (In other words, to reduce the risk of investing in computer simulation.)
2. To give the existing community of simulation analysts a chance to evaluate their use of computer simulation and to provide some ideas that might enhance their modeling practices.
3. To provide readers with a detailed look at a specific simulation language and the development of application programs.

It is my sincere hope, in this role as author, that I am able to convey my enthusiasm for computer simulation to all readers, whether they be seasoned professionals, novices, or those with academic interests in the field. Starting with this book, I encourage them to explore (or continue exploring) the dynamic field of computer simulation.

Comments, inquiries, or to order ASCII Source Code for all example programs in this book, send $10 (check or money order) to: Roger McHaney, P.O. Box 206, Pickford, Michigan 49774.

Acknowledgments

Computer Simulation: A Practical Perspective resulted from the efforts of many individuals. It is difficult to put into words the feelings of gratitude I have for my friends and colleagues who put forth so much to make this book a reality.

I would first like to thank my wife Annette for the many hours she spent researching, proofreading, and critiquing; and for the time she spent watching our two young boys, Mark and Matthew, so that I could work uninterrupted.

My appreciation and thanks go out to my parents Bob and Pat McHaney for the encouragement they provided throughout the project. I would also like to thank my father-in-law and mother-in-law James and Prudy Allen for lending support to my work.

A number of other individuals unselfishly gave of their time and talents. Among these are

- Tom Schriber, Ph.D., University of Michigan Graduate School of Business, for taking time to review the manuscript and write the book's foreword.
- Dan Brunner, Jim Henriksen, Bob Crain, and Nancy Earle of Wolverine Software for proofreading and reviewing the manuscript and providing me with a temporary license to use GPSS/H.
- Timothy Thomasma, Ph.D., University of Michigan, Dearborn, for encouraging my simulation work and lending support to the project.
- Lee Wightman (formerly of Wolverine Software) for proofreading several chapters.
- Colleagues at Control Engineering Company who work (or have worked) in the Simulation Department, including Dan McClure, Jeff Ebert, Cheryl Gray, and Mike Carson.
- Managers and supervisors at Control Engineering Company who have encouraged my activity and education in the simulation field, including Frank

Gregg, Parke Groat, George Melke, Gerry Chilson, Don Allerding, Jim Shoemaker, and Dick Vokes.
- Marshall Ellis whose engineering philosophies have provided much food for thought.
- Don Gerrie, Director of Lake Superior State University MBA program, for encouraging my interest in computer simulation through special topics courses.
- Richard Crandall, Ph.D., Lake Superior State University, for teaching me how to perform effective research.
- My brother-in-law Neil Harrison, who has always been a role model in the computer and engineering fields.
- My sister Sue Harrison, who inspired me to write this book.
- My sister Tish Walker and her husband Tom for giving good advice.
- Kathy Kangas and Dean Irey of Academic Press for their patience, suggestions, and professionalism throughout this project.
- Thomas M. and Pamela A. Piljac for kindly allowing me to reprint their illustration of Mackinac Island.

Thank you everyone.

Simulation Overview

As the world continues to grow more technical and complex, the margin for error continues to shrink. Business, industry, and government can no longer afford to make educated guesses concerning complicated system designs and policy formulations. Reliable analysis techniques are required to avoid costly mistakes and changes. One such technique is computer simulation.

Computer Simulation : A Practical Perspective is a book intended for the professional, scientific, and engineering community. Its primary focus is on discrete event simulation and the value of this expanding field to industry and business. To highlight this value, special attention is given to the development of a wide variety of simulation programming applications.

This book has been specifically designed to fill a gap in existing simulation literature. Prior to its publication, very few practical discrete event simulation books were available. Several good academic-style textbooks were in existence, as were some well-written product specific user manuals. These categories of books exist at opposite ends of the literary spectrum, one group being intense with high-level statistics and theory and the other being narrow in scope and limited to the capabilities of a particular simulation product. *Computer Simulation : A Practical Perspective* has been designed to appeal to people wishing to either get involved with coding a model or to managers who wish to set up a simulation group in their work environment (Figure 1.1). Targeting these interest groups has necessitated the inclusion of many new topics in simulation such as transfer methodology, generic models, simulators, automatic code generation, and graphic animation.

This book has been divided into three sections. The first section is tailored to educate newcomers and provide the old hands with a solid review of modeling. It includes an introduction to simulation and its history and current state. The

Figure 1.1 Simulation book spectrum.

second section deals with simulation in the real world. Perfect textbook viewpoints are pushed aside and replaced with a realistic approach to successful modeling. The third section of the book has been dedicated specifically to the development of application programs. All steps in the simulation process, from gathering input data to communicating output reports, are carefully discussed.

1.1 What Is Simulation?

Simulation is the use of a model to develop conclusions that provide insight on the behavior of any real world elements. Computer simulation uses the same concept but requires that the model be created through programming on a computer. Although this field is relatively young in practice, its most common function of forecasting the behavior of an entity that does not yet exist has roots that run quite deep.

Since ancient times people have tried to foretell the future. Kings employed wizards and soothsayers. Various religions used prophets. Astrologers tried to make predictions based on birthdates and the stars. Crystal balls, bones, and cards were all used as tools to probe the future. In the same way that the modern chemist bears a relationship to the ancient alchemist, the modern simulation practitioner has a relationship with the ancient prophet. It is safe to say that the methodology of modern simulation shares little similarity with the prediction methods used in ancient times, but the goals of both do have common elements. Each sought to take the risk out of a future event or behavior, thereby reducing uncertainty. The prophet tried to accomplish this with magic and the simulation analyst through mathematical principles, experimentation, and statistics.

1.2 The Nature of Computer Simulation

Computer simulation is a branch of applied mathematics that has been gaining popularity in recent years due to the availability of computers and improvements in simulation programming languages. The process of describing many complex real world systems using only analytical or mathematical models can be difficult or even impossible in some cases. This often necessitates the employment of a more sophisticated tool such as computer simulation. Using a computer to imitate or simulate the operations of a real world process or facility requires that a set of assumptions taking the form of logical or mathematical relationships be developed and shaped into a model. This model can then be manipulated to help the simulation analyst gain an understanding of the dynamics at work in the system. The simulation program is typically evaluated numerically over a period of time, and data is gathered to estimate the true characteristics of the actual system. The collected data is generally interpreted with statistics, as are the results of any experiment.

1.3 Usage

Computer simulation can be an expensive and complicated problem-solving technique. Therefore, it should be used only under certain circumstances. Some situations warranting its use are:

1. The real system does not exist and it is too costly, time-consuming, hazardous, or simply impossible to build a prototype. Some examples might be an airplane, an economic system, or a nuclear reactor.

2. The real system exists but experimentation is expensive, hazardous, or seriously disruptive. Some examples might be a materials handling system, a military unit, or a transportation system.

3. A forecasting model is required that would analyze long periods of time in a compressed format. Examples would be population growth, forest fire spread, or urbanization studies.

4. Mathematical modeling of the system has no practical analytical or numeric solutions. This might occur in stochastic problems or in nonlinear differential equations.

1.4 Developing a Grasp of Simulation Terminology

An important part of any discipline is developing a grasp of the terminology commonly used by its practitioners. Listed below are a few words and phrases with special meaning in the simulation field. For readers who are exploring this area for the first time, the following list will help accelerate learning and reduce misunderstanding. For the more experienced reader, it will serve as a review and insure that we are speaking a common language.

Animation Using computer graphics to dynamically display simulated entities and their activities as represented by a model.

Animator Another name for an animation software package.

Attributes Data values that characterize the entities used in a model.

Clock A device used by simulation languages for modeling the passage of time (also known as a simulated clock).

Customers Entities that compete for resources in a simulation model.

Debugger A highly desirable interactive debugging facility provided in conjunction with several simulation software products. Use of such a tool provides the modeler with the ability to control program execution for the purpose of locating run time errors.

Deterministic A deterministic system is the opposite of a stochastic system. All variables and elements contain known values and no random elements are present. Only one possible output exists for each set of input data.

Dynamic A model that changes with simulated time is defined as being dynamic. Most discrete event simulations are of a dynamic nature.

Entity An individual object or subsystem within the model. A general term used to refer to both system resources and customers.

Face Validity The degree of confidence, felt by the model user, that the model is valid.

Model A simplified representation of a system. A model is built to provide the modeler and others with an understanding of how a proposed or existing system is to perform (Figure 1.2).

Queue A line of entities waiting to be serviced. A large percentage of simulation work deals with the allocation of limited resources and the study of the causes and remedies for congestion. The analysis of queues is an important part of this.

Resource A permanent entity in a simulation that has a limited capacity.

Server Another name for a resource.

Simulation The process of defining, creating, and studying a model with the intention of drawing inferences and forming conclusions as to the behavior of the actual system. Simulation not only includes model development but also experimentation with that model.

Simulation Language This class of simulation software consists of versatile general purpose languages that can be used for a multitude of different applications. These languages are comparable to FORTRAN, BASIC, or Pascal but have statistic gathering and other simulation specific features. Some ex-

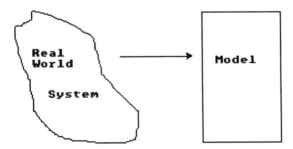

Figure 1.2 Model representing real world system.

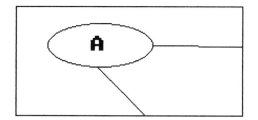

Figure 1.3 Subsystem: one part viewed in isolation.

amples of these simulation languages are GPSS (Henriksen and Crain, 1989;
Schriber, 1988), SLAM (O'Reilly and Lilegdon, 1988), SIMSCRIPT (Russell, 1988), and SIMAN (Davis and Pegden, 1988).

Simulator Originally this term was used to define the person performing the
simulation work. In the context of this book, its newer definition will be used.
A simulator is one class of simulation software packages. These packages are
prewritten, user friendly, and usually application specific. An example is a set
of prewritten software modules that simplify the modeling of manufacturing
facilities.

Static A static simulation model is the representation of a system at a particular
point in time. Monte Carlo simulations are usually static in nature.

Stochastic Simulation models that incorporate random behavior are defined as
being stochastic. This random behavior can take the form of input variables,
each with its own probability distribution. Since this input data is random, the
model outputs are also random estimates of the true characteristics of the
model and need to be dealt with statistically.

Subsystem A component or element of the total system that can be viewed
either independently or as a part of the overall system. In terms of a manufacturing plant system example, a representative subsystem is the inventory system. It can be viewed as both an independent system and as part of the whole
(Figure 1.3).

System A set of components or elements that are related to each other in such a
manner as to create a connected whole. For example, a manufacturing plant
consists of many components including assembly lines, conveyors, workers,
materials handling facilities, computers, work in process, and inventory.
Therefore, a manufacturing plant system is comprised of all elements needed
for the production of a finished product (Figure 1.4).

Validation The process of making sure the working simulation model accurately
represents the system being modeled.

Verification The process of making sure that the simulation model matches the
simulation analyst's concept of the system. (Debugging is a big part of this.)

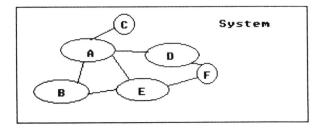

Figure 1.4   System: a whole consisting of interconnected parts.

1.5   Benefits

The main advantage in using simulation is the reduction of risk involved with implementing a new system or modifying an existing one (Figure 1.5). General feasibility studies can be conducted using "what if" scenarios constructed into a computer model. Several alternatives can be tested, and the one that gives the best results can be chosen. Proposed solutions to problems discovered with simulation can be analyzed in less time than real world observations. In addition, better control over experimental conditions can be maintained in a simulation. This insures that only valid comparisons between different solutions are made.

Another benefit often realized during the construction of a computer simulation is the requirement that designers must carefully determine and document how a proposed system will work. The process of creating the logical relationships to be embedded in a simulation will bring to light problems or oversights. Diverse sources of information are often brought together for the first time in this situation. The knowledge gained during the simulation phase will be of great value throughout the entire lifetime of a project.

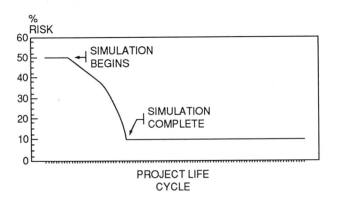

Figure 1.5   Simulation reduces risk.

1.6   Limitations

There are also a few disadvantages inherent with the use of computer simulation. Simulation is neither an art nor a science but a combination of both. Simulations can be expensive to run and time-consuming to develop. Modeling only yields approximate answers. Since it relies on random number generators to produce results, there is some uncertainty associated with the output that must be dealt with statistically.

Simulation is not an optimization tool. Answers to questions can be provided but these answers will not always be the optimal solutions.

Another major limitation experienced in many simulation studies is the problem with model validation. With systems that do not yet exist, this can become a formidable task.

1.7   Different Types of Simulation

The three most common types of computer simulation are discrete event, continuous, and Monte Carlo. Although many authorities consider discrete event simulation to be a form of Monte Carlo simulation, the two will be evaluated separately in this book (Figure 1.6).

1.7.1 Monte Carlo Simulation

The name Monte Carlo invokes thoughts of gambling, roulette, and chance. John Von Neumann used the code name Monte Carlo for his experiments based on the use of random numbers conducted at Los Alamos (during development of the atomic bomb). The name has stuck. Now Monte Carlo simulations are defined as "a scheme employing random numbers that is used for solving certain stochastic or deterministic problems where the passage of time plays no role" (Law and Kelton, 1982). The last part of this definition (i.e., passage of time) is what distinguishes Monte Carlo from discrete event simulation. In discrete event models time plays a significant role.

Monte Carlo simulations have features that allow random events to be generated internally. In IBM PC BASIC, the RND command will return a random

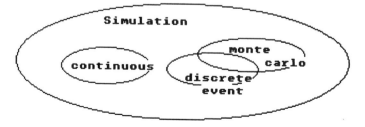

Figure 1.6   Set of simulation types.

number. This feature enables a model to be written and run on a microcomputer. Consider the following IBM PC BASIC military model based on research conducted by Frederick Lanchester (1916).

This model predicts the number of green soldiers to survive a battle between green and blue armies of given initial sizes. The following assumptions have been made to keep the problem relatively simple:

1. Combat is waged by archers. Any archer can hit a randomly chosen opponent with equal ease.
2. No two archers ever select the same target.
3. The battle is fought until one side is completely wiped out.
4. Every arrow shot is lethal.
5. In the context of a Monte Carlo simulation, the entire battle takes place in zero simulated time.
6. The probability of *"which side shoots next"* is based on the percentages of green and blue archers who are currently alive.
7. The initial army sizes will be 45 blue and 100 green.
8. The number of survivors will be based on an average derived from 100 battles.

Figure 1.7 contains a source code listing for this Monte Carlo simulation. Running this model gives the following results (Figure 1.8).

If the model were allowed to run for 1,000 or 10,000 battles, the average number of survivors would converge closer to an exact solution which in this case can be mathematically evaluated as 89.02. A few minutes work on a microcomputer gives an answer that would be nearly impossible to evaluate in a real life situation. Another advantage inherent in this simulation is the ease with which parameters can be altered and different experiments run. Table 1.1 was

```
100   ' Battle Program
130 LET BLUE=45
140 LET GREEN=100
150 LET DEAD=GREEN/(BLUE+GREEN)
160 SHOT=RND
180 IF SHOT < DEAD THEN GOTO 210
190 GREEN = GREEN-1
200 GOTO 220
210 BLUE = BLUE-1
220 IF (BLUE = 0) OR (GREEN=0) THEN GOTO 230 ELSE GOTO 150
230 LET N=N+1
240 LET TOTAL=GREEN+BLUE+TOTAL
255 IF N>100 THEN GOTO 270
260 GOTO 130
270 PRINT "AVERAGE NUMBER OF GREEN SURVIVORS AFTER 100
    BATTLES IS ";TOTAL/N
280 END
```

Figure 1.7 Source code for Monte Carlo battle simulation.

AVERAGE NUMBER OF GREEN SURVIVORS AFTER 100 BATTLES IS
89.14851

Figure 1.8 Model output.

TABLE 1.1
Summary of Additional Runs of Military Model

Initial Green Archers	Initial Blue Archers	Average Green Survivors
100	90	43.089
100	80	59.109
100	70	71.129
100	60	79.653
100	50	86.050
100	40	91.069
100	30	94.941
100	20	98.158
100	10	99.500

generated by altering the initial conditions of the simulation. Figure 1.9 graphically illustrates the same data.

1.7.2 Continuous Simulation

Continuous simulation is concerned with modeling a set of equations that represent a system over time. This system may consist of algebraic, differential or difference equations set up to change continuously with time. An example of a continuous simulation is a model of a four-wheel drive suspension system in

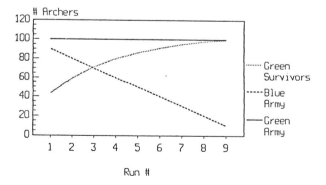

Figure 1.9 Military model additional runs.

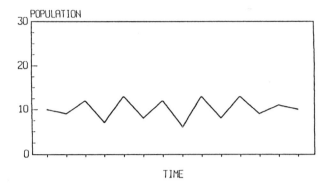

Figure 1.10 Predator–prey model illustrative output.

which the dynamics of running over different types of terrain can be examined. Continuous simulations are sometimes used in conjunction with computer aided drafting (CAD) systems.

Another example of a continuous simulation is a model of competition between two populations. Biological models of this type are known as predator–prey models. The environment consists of two populations that interact with each other. The predators depend on the prey as a source of food. If the number of predators grows too fast, the available prey will decrease, causing the predators to starve. If the number of predators drop, the number of prey will increase. This relationship can be analyzed with a continuous simulation using partial derivatives. The mathematics of this two species system was worked out by the noted theorist Vito Volterra. He demonstrated that with no outside interference, a fluctuating relationship similar to the graph shown in Figure 1.10 would result.

1.7.3 Discrete Event Simulation

Discrete event simulation is characterized by the passage of blocks of time during which nothing happens and is punctuated by events that change the state of the system. An example is a simple queuing system consisting of bank customers arriving at an automatic teller machine (ATM). Customers arrive, wait for service if the machine is in use, receive service, and depart (Figure 1.11). A model ATM using these assumptions follows:

1. Arriving customers wait in front of the ATM (if it is in use) in a single queue.
2. The time between customer arrivals is as follows (Figure 1.12):

1 min	5% of arrivals
2 min	7% of arrivals
3 min	8% of arrivals
4 min	10% of arrivals
5 min	20% of arrivals

      6 min   20% of arrivals
      7 min   10% of arrivals
      8 min   8% of arrivals
      9 min   7% of arrivals
     10 min   5% of arrivals

3. The time ATM service takes is as follows (Figure 1.13):
      1 min   10% of arrivals

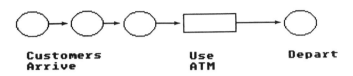

Customers   **Use**   **Depart**
Arrive   **ATM**

Figure 1.11 Bank customers using an ATM.

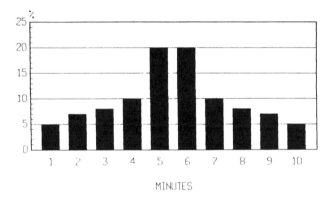

Figure 1.12 Time between ATM customer arrivals.

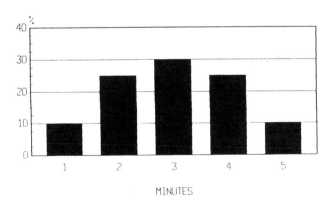

Figure 1.13 ATM service time.

```
        SIMULATE

*================================================================*
*                   FUNCTION DEFINITIONS                         *
*================================================================*

*
* A FUNCTION THAT GIVES CUSTOMER ARRIVAL RATES
        ARRIVE FUNCTION    RN2,D10
        0.05,1/0.12,2/0.20,3/0.30,4
        0.50,5/0.70,6/0.80,7/0.88,8
        0.95,9/1.0,10
*
* A FUNCTION THAT GIVES ATM SERVICE TIMES
        SERVE  FUNCTION    RN3,D5
        0.10,2/0.35,3/0.55,4/0.80,5
        1.0,6
*================================================================*
*                    MAIN PROGRAM                                *
*================================================================*
*
        GENERATE    1,0,1,1          CREATE CUSTOMERS FOR ATM
*
*
CREATE  ADVANCE     FN$ARRIVE        CUSTOMER WAITS FOR
*                                    ARRIVAL TIME TO ELAPSE
*
        SPLIT       1,ATM            CUSTOMER SENT TO ATM
*
*
        TRANSFER    ,CREATE          TRANSACTION RETURNS TO
*                                    CREATE NEXT CUSTOMER
*
ATM     QUEUE       WAIT             WAIT IN LINE FOR ATM
*
*
        SEIZE       MACHINE          ATM IS AVAILABLE
*                                    SO USE IT
*
        DEPART      WAIT             CUSTOMER IS NO LONGER
*                                    WAITING IN LINE
*
        ADVANCE     FN$SERVE         ATM SERVICE TIME PASSES BY
*
        RELEASE     MACHINE          ATM IS RELINQUISHED
*
        TERMINATE                    CUSTOMER LEAVES SYSTEM

*================================================================*
*                    TIMING SEGMENT                              *
*================================================================*
*
        GENERATE    60               TIME UNIT IS IN MINUTES
        TERMINATE   1
*
*
        START       1000             SIMULATION LASTS FOR 1000
*                                    HOURS OF SIMULATED TIME
        END
*================================================================*
```

Figure 1.14 GPSS/H source code.

2 min	25% of arrivals
3 min	30% of arrivals
4 min	25% of arrivals
5 min	10% of arrivals

4. The simulation is written using GPSS/H, a discrete event simulation language from Wolverine Software (Henriksen and Crain, 1989).
5. The purpose of this simulation is to determine the maximum customer queue length, the average wait time for service, and the percentage of time that the ATM is in use. (Other statistics will also be gathered.)
6. The simulation will be run for 1000 hours of simulated time.

Figure 1.14 contains the GPSS/H source code for the simulation. The GPSS/H model produces the standard output shown in Figure 1.15.

By observing the queue statistics, the maximum number of customers waiting in line was five. The average wait for the ATM was 1.453 minutes and it was in use 76.4% of the time. The average number of customers waiting in line was 0.264 people. The machine was used 10,915 times, and 10,916 customers entered the system.

A simulation such as this might be based on the customer arrival rates and service times observed at an actual ATM. If the simulated ATM *average customer wait time* was above an acceptable level, a decision might be made to purchase an additional machine.

This simulation could also be modified to represent what would happen during peak usage times. For instance, if Friday is payday at a large, nearby plant, a surge of users could be expected to use the ATM after work that afternoon. Data representing this surge could be entered into the simulation model and analyzed to see what the resulting effects would be on machine utilization and waiting line times.

1.8 Discussion

Chapter 1 has defined and illustrated computer simulation. Although simulation can be broken into three distinct areas (continuous, discrete, and Monte Carlo),

1	QUEUE	MAXIMUM CONTENTS	AVERAGE CONTENTS	TOTAL ENTRIES	AVERAGE TIME/UNIT
	WAIT	5	.264	10916	1.453

FACILITY	TOTAL TIME	ENTRIES	AVERAGE TIME/XACT
MACHINE	.764	10915	4.201

Figure 1.15 Standard GPSS/H output for ATM model.

the remainder of this book will be limited in scope to the discussion of discrete event modeling and its applications. Discrete event simulation is widely practiced throughout business and industry and enjoys its greatest usage as an engineering design or process analysis tool.

References and Reading

Davis, D., and C. D. Pegden. 1988. "Introduction to SIMAN." *Proc. 1988 Winter Simulation Conf.* (San Diego, Dec. 12–14). SCS, San Diego, pp. 61–70.

Henriksen, James O. 1988. "One System, Several Perspectives, Many Models." *Proc. 1988 Winter Simulation Conf.* (San Diego, Dec. 12–14). SCS, San Diego, pp. 352–356.

Henriksen, James O. 1989. "Alternative Modeling Perspectives: Finding the Creative Spark." *Proc. 1989 Winter Simulation Conf.* (Washington, D.C., Dec. 4–6). SCS, San Diego, pp. 648–652.

Henriksen, J. O., and R. C. Crain. 1989. *GPSS/H Reference Manual,* Third Edition. Wolverine Software Corporation, Annandale, Virginia.

Keating, Barry. 1985. "Simulations : Put the Real World in Your Computer." *Creative Computing* (Nov.): 56–64.

Lanchester, Frederick W. 1916. "Mathematics in Warfare." Reprinted in *The World of Mathematics* (James R. Newman, ed.). Simon & Shuster, New York.

Law, Averill M., and W. David Kelton. 1982. *Simulation Modeling and Analysis.* McGraw-Hill, New York.

McHaney, Roger. 1989. "Discrete-Event Simulators Optimize Industrial Operations." *Personal Engineering & Instrumentation News* (Aug.): 57–62.

O' Reilly, J., and W. Lilegdon. 1988. "SLAM II Tutorial." *Proc. 1988 Winter Simulation Conf.* (San Diego, Dec. 12–14). SCS, San Diego, pp. 85–89.

Russell, E. C. 1988. "SIMSCRIPT II.5 and SIMGRAPHICS : A Tutorial." *Proc. 1988 Winter Simulation Conf.* (San Diego, Dec. 12–14). SCS, San Diego, pp. 115–124.

Schriber, Thomas J. 1988. "Perspectives on Simulation Using GPSS." *Proc. 1988 Winter Simulation Conf.* (San Diego, Dec. 12–14). SCS, San Diego, pp. 71–84.

Evolution of Modern Computer Simulation

Chapter 2 is designed to provide the reader with a historical perspective on modern computer simulation including its roots, present state, and possible future trends. The development of and distinctions between simulation languages, simulators, and integrated simulation environments also form topics for this chapter. In addition, computer hardware, trends in animation software, and the use of microcomputers as platforms for simulation are also covered.

2.1 Historical View of Computer Simulation

As mentioned in the beginning of Chapter 1, computer simulation has developed in response to people's natural inclination and desire to take the risk out of the decision-making process. In ancient times, the rulers of nations often relied on fortune tellers to provide insight on the outcome of a military action. In modern times, sophisticated military models are created by computer scientists on powerful computers to provide the same information the ancients sought. *"What will the outcome of this battle be? Will we win if. . . .?"* The methodology of developing solutions has changed but the questions needing answers remain the same. No one wants to take unnecessary and costly risks.

In recent history, people have come to the conclusion that the future cannot be clearly or reliably predicted through supernatural or any other methods. This disheartening "discovery" prompted the development of alternative methods of reducing risk. Some of these methods included using mathematics, statistics, and other analytical tools.

As time progressed, analytical methods became more accurate and sophisticated. Techniques were developed to take into account the stochastic nature of many events. With the advent of the computer age came a tool with which models of complicated processes could be developed and exercised.

In the 1950s, computer simulations were programmed in machine code, assembly language, or higher level languages such as FORTRAN. Simulation work was severely constrained by prohibitive hardware costs, the general scarcity of computers, and the lack of software tools. Models ran slowly and computing machinery was prone to breaking down. But the value of these models was becoming apparent, and this prompted a search for better methods of modeling.

The first breakthrough toward making the concept of a computer simulation practical occurred in 1961 when Geoffrey Gordon of IBM introduced a language called GPSS (General Purpose Simulation System). GPSS was being used at IBM to analyze systems that could not easily be described analytically (Gordon, 1961). Norden, the Air Force, Boeing, Martin Marietta, Hughes Aircraft, and General Dynamics, to name a few, took an immediate interest in the power that this product had to offer.

In 1962, shortly after the introduction of GPSS, Rand Corporation announced that Harry Markowitz, Bernard Hausner, and Herbert Karr had developed a simulation language called SIMSCRIPT. The Air Force used this product as an inventory analysis tool. During this same time period, Norwegian scientists O. Dahl and K. Nygaard produced yet another simulation language called SIMULA. Many other new simulation languages also emerged as computing power continued to become more readily available.

With the development of different simulation languages and the many different approaches to modeling came a realization that formal communication mechanisms were needed. These mechanisms would help insure that the knowledge being gained by the disparate groups of simulation practitioners was not lost. In response to this realization, several workshops, organizations, and conferences were created. The first of these was the Workshop on Simulation Languages at Stanford University in March of 1964. In 1967, a Conference on Applications of Simulation Using GPSS was organized by the IBM "SHARE" users group, ACM, and IEEE. (This yearly conference still continues under the name of the Winter Simulation Conference.) In 1968, what is now known as the Society for Computer Simulation (SCS) became an official sponsor of this conference and gained widespread popularity as a leading organization for simulation practitioners.

At the Third Simulation Conference in 1969, a paper describing the general purpose simulation language GASP was presented. GASP would eventually evolve into the present day SLAM family of languages.

As technology progressed into the 1970s, computing power increased and costs continued to decrease. This encouraged the development of new simulation software products as well as variations of and improvements to existing ones.

During the early 1970s, the number of fields using applications of simulation and the number of available professional publications, training sessions, conferences, and journals continued to grow.

In 1977, James O. Henriksen announced a new and improved version of GPSS called GPSS/H. It was designed to run faster and more efficiently than existing versions of GPSS. It also incorporated features to give the language added power and make it easier to use.

In the 1980s, the simulation field continued its phenomenal growth, both in terms of the number of companies using the technology and the number of simulation products offered.

The early 1980s provided a backdrop for the introduction of two new major simulation languages. Nineteen-eighty marked the release of the language SLAM by Pritsker and Associates (now Pritsker Corporation, West Lafayette, Indiana). In 1983, Systems Modeling Corporation (State College, Pennsylvania) entered a language called SIMAN into the simulation arena (Pegden, 1987).

In 1982, a powerful materials handling environment simulator named Automod (AutoSimulations, Inc., Bountiful, Utah) became available as a commercial product. This simulator, which compiled into GPSS/H code, was developed to facilitate modeling complex materials handling equipment and other factory processes. After the model was written, the simulated system could be viewed with an animation package called AutoGram running on a graphics workstation.

During the mid-to-late 1980s, many new simulation languages and simulator packages were developed and marketed. At the same time, established simulation software companies continued to expand their product lines with animation packages, simulation development toolkits, simulator modules, and enhancements to their languages. Nearly all of the software products were modified to run on the 286 and 386 personal computers that gained widespread acceptance throughout the industry.

By the end of the 1980s, a diverse and actively growing simulation software marketplace was in existence. An October 1988 issue of *Simulation Magazine* listed nearly 200 different simulation software packages (not including simulators). This number continues to change as the simulation software market grows very rapidly.

Figure 2.1 provides a summary of simulation product introduction times.

2.2 Simulation Languages

Chapter 1 defines a simulation language to be a versatile, general purpose class of simulation software that can be used in a multitude of different modeling applications. These languages are comparable to FORTRAN, BASIC, or Pascal but have specific features built in to facilitate the modeling process. Some examples of modern simulation languages are GPSS/H, SLAM II, SIMSCRIPT II.5, and SIMAN IV.

Year	Software Product	Vendor/Developer
1961	GPSS	IBM (Gordon)
1962	SIMSCRIPT	Rand Corporation
1963		
1964		
1965		
1966	SIMULA	Dahl & Nygaard
1967		
1968		
1969	GASP	
1970	GPSS V	IBM
1971		
1972		
1973		
1974		
1975		
1976		
1977	GPSS/H	Wolverine Software / Henriksen
1978		
1979		
1980	SLAM	Pritsker & Associates
	SEEWHY	ISTEL Inc.
1981	SLAM II	Pritsker & Associates
1982	AutoMod/AutoGram	AutoSimulations, Inc.
	SIMAN	Systems Modeling Corporation
1983		
1984	GPSS/PC	Minuteman Software
1985	Cinema	Systems Modeling Corporation
1986		
1987		
1988	AutoMod II	AutoSimulations, Inc.
1989		
1990	Proof	Wolverine Software Corporation

Figure 2.1   Simulation product time line.

2.2.1 Simulation Language Features

Several specialized features usually differentiate a simulation language from other more general programming languages. The function of these features is to free the simulation analyst from the drudgery of creating certain software tools and procedures that need to be used by virtually all modeling applications. Not only would the development of these tools be time-consuming and difficult, but without them the consistency of methodology used by modelers would vary to an even greater extent than it does now. Among the tools provided by most simulation languages are the following:

1. Simulation clock or a mechanism for advancing simulated time.
2. Methods to schedule the occurrence of events.
3. Tools to aid in the collection and analysis of statistics concerning the usage of various resources and entities.
4. Methods of representing constrained resources and the entities using these resources.
5. Tools for reporting results.

6. Debugging and error detection facilities.
7. Random number generators and related sets of tools.
8. General frameworks for model creation.

2.2.2 Comparison to Traditional Languages

Although many models are written using simulation languages, some analysts prefer to rely on traditional programming languages such as BASIC, Pascal, FORTRAN, or C. The primary reasons motivating a decision to use a general purpose language are:

1. Programmers are already familiar with a general purpose programming language. They may not have the time or inclination to learn a simulation language.
2. Programming languages are usually more flexible, giving the modeler freedom to create the model using the preferred methodology.
3. Programming language software is usually more accessible and far less expensive than specific simulation software. For example, a C compiler may cost only one-twentieth of the price commanded by a leading simulation language package.
4. General purpose software may be available on any hardware platform, while some simulation languages may require special machines and memory configurations.
5. The analyst lacks knowledge on the advantages of using a simulation language package.

Although traditional languages do offer some advantages, most of these are outweighed by features standard to many simulation languages. In a typical modeling application, the programmer or analyst will find that the initial investment in a simulation language will more than pay off. A simulation language will provide savings in the following areas:

1. Model coding time.
2. Debugging time.
3. Having access to the tools described in Section 2.2.1 of this chapter.
4. Reduction of model size.

2.2.3 Specific Simulation Languages

The next four sections of this chapter briefly discuss four specific simulation languages including GPSS, SLAM II, SIMSCRIPT II.5, and SIMAN IV.

GPSS

General Purpose Simulation System (GPSS) is a multi-vendor simulation software language (Schriber, 1988). It enjoys widespread popularity because of the ease with which it can be learned and the power that it has to offer. GPSS is most often used to model systems that consist of customer entities that compete for constrained or scarce resources. GPSS models are structured as networks of blocks. Temporary entities called transactions are created and allowed to move through these networks that have been organized in a manner that is representative of the system being simulated. Statistics are collected to report on the use of various entities during the time period simulated. This data is made available for analysis at the end of a production run.

Presently three major vendors offer versions of GPSS for sale or lease in the U.S. and Canada.

1. Wolverine Software produces GPSS/H, a state-of-the-art version of GPSS that runs on many mainframes, minicomputers, and microcomputers. A popular feature of GPSS/H is its interactive debugger that facilitates the programming effort. Proof is a high-performance animation program offered by Wolverine Software that runs in conjunction with GPSS/H and other simulation languages. A new addition to Wolverine's product line is GPSS/H 386, a full-power microcomputer version of their software.

> Wolverine Software Corporation
> 4115 Annandale Road, Suite 200
> Annandale, VA 22003–2500

2. Minuteman Software produces a user friendly GPSS simulation environment that runs on the IBM PC. It features special model development tools and several graphics options.

> Minuteman Software Inc.
> P.O. Box 171
> Stow, MA 01775

3. Simulation Software Limited produces several implementations of GPSS that run on computers, including many VAX machines and the IBM PC.

> Simulation Software Ltd.
> 760 Headley Drive
> London, Ontario, Canada N6H 3V8

Chapter 7 provides more information about GPSS, specifically GPSS/H, that will be used throughout the text to illustrate the model development process.

SLAM II

Simulation Language for Alternative Modeling (SLAM) is a FORTRAN-based language that will run on any supermini or mainframe computer that supports an ANSI standard FORTRAN compiler. Adding to the list of potential hardware platforms is a PC version of SLAM II that was first released in 1984. SLAM II is distributed by:

> Pritsker Corporation
> 1305 Cumberland Avenue

P.O. Box 2413
West Lafayette, Indiana 47906

SLAM II was the first language to allow modelers to approach a problem from a discrete event, continuous, or network viewpoint or from any combination of these three world views. This integrated approach to modeling allows the simulation analyst to take advantage of the simplicity of creating a network model, to add in discrete event elements if the network approach becomes too restrictive, and to utilize continuous variables for representation of various system elements in the discrete event or network portions of the model (O'Reilly et al., 1988). This ability to combine discrete event, continuous, and network elements results in a very versatile and powerful tool for modeling.

Since SLAM II is FORTRAN-based, it is possible to "custom" design a subroutine that is called and used by the simulation. This adds to the language's flexibility and the range of tasks that SLAM II can address.

SIMSCRIPT II.5

SIMSCRIPT II.5 is a direct descendant of the original SIMSCRIPT language produced at Rand Corporation in the 1960s. SIMSCRIPT II.5 is not FORTRAN dependent as was its precursor. Instead, it is supported by a compiler that translates SIMSCRIPT code into assembly language. SIMSCRIPT II.5 runs on a wide variety of computers, including those produced by IBM, CDC, Honeywell, Digital, and NCR. A recent addition to the SIMSCRIPT family is PC SIMSCRIPT II.5, which is specifically designed to run on IBM PC compatible hardware (Hughes and Benton, 1985).

The SIMSCRIPT II.5 language has constructs that allow a modeler to approach a problem from either a process- or event-oriented world view (see Chapter 3). In addition, continuous elements may be introduced through an extension called C-SIMSCRIPT (Delfosse, 1976).

SIMSCRIPT II.5 offers some unique features that add to its appeal. Included among these are a free-form, English-like syntax. This syntax allows the code in the system to become a good form of documentation. Model components can be programmed clearly enough to provide an excellent representation of the organization and logic of the system being simulated (Russell, 1988).

SIMSCRIPT II.5 is maintained and distributed by:

CACI Products Co.
2011 San Vicente Blvd.
Los Angeles, CA 90049

SIMAN IV

SIMAN IV (SIMulation ANalysis program), like SLAM II, allows systems having process-oriented, event-oriented, and continuous components to be integrated in a single system model. A SIMAN IV model typically consists of model code and a series of statements best described as being a framework for conducting experiments.

The SIMAN IV language runs on mainframes, minicomputers, and microcomputers with all versions being completely compatible. SIMAN IV incorporates a graphic interface to the CINEMA animation system. Models can be displayed while execution occurs. Another feature making SIMAN IV a popular tool is its interactive debugger. It allows errors to be located and corrected during the execution of a simulation.

Systems Modeling Corporation produces both SIMAN IV and CINEMA (Davis and Pegden, 1988).

> Systems Modeling Corporation
> The Park Building
> 504 Beaver Street
> Sewickley, PA 15143

2.3 Simulators

A recent product development in the simulation field is the simulator. A simulator is defined as a user friendly software package that will develop a model for a particular application. These models are created by the person who is not a simulation analyst or programmer but still wishes to analyze a system. For example, the person who is an automation expert (rather than a computer programming expert) is able to model a conveyor system with pull-down menus and user friendly interface tools. SIMFACTORY, XCELL+, and WITNESS are all examples of simulator software packages.

Simulators are often characterized by "buzz phrases" (Brunner, 1988) such as:

> *"No programming"*
> *"Graphical model building interface"*
> *"Model any system in just a few hours"*
> *"Any manager can use it"*
> *"Anyone on the shop floor can use it"*

2.3.1 Advantages and Disadvantages of Simulators

Simulators offer some definite advantages such as:

1. *Ease of Use.* Simulators are designed specifically for the nonprogrammer. They typically have user friendly features such as pull-down command menus and special tools to simplify model construction. Many simulators are marketed with more emphasis on their user friendliness than on their underlying system modeling capability.

2. *Quick Model Development.* Many simulators are set up to provide a fast method of constructing a model. This development speed is gained since the underlying system model has already been created, and the user of the simulator

is only changing parameters through a user interface program. The user interface may be set up to allow model construction through the piecing together of graphic icons, with a series of questions, or with the construction of a mini-language.

3. *Base System Simulation Already Complete.* At the center of all simulators is a model that has already been constructed. In theory the user of the simulator does not need to be concerned with fully understanding and analyzing the system to be modeled. As long as several key attributes of the system can be identified, the simulator will do the work. This saves time, energy, and frustration on the part of the model builder.

4. *Framework for Analysis of a Particular Type of System.* Most simulators have been used many times and therefore are constructed to provide a logical method of analyzing a particular type of system. This structure or experimental framework has evolved from repeated use and in many cases is superior to what a first time simulation analyst could devise. This framework is another time-saving feature.

Although simulators may sound too good to be true, they offer a world of knowledge in return for very little effort. When used in the proper context, they can be a very helpful tool. But when misused they can provide misleading results. Some of the pitfalls of simulators are the following:

1. *Oversimplification.* Simulators tend to oversimplify system representation. In order to sell a simulator, a vendor must be able to apply the product to many similar systems. This means that a generic approach to these systems must be taken. The resulting simulator may have simplifying assumptions built in. An automatic guided vehicle vendor evaluated several simulator packages only to discover the simplifying assumptions would not allow them to take advantage of their advanced design concepts. So instead of displaying their edge over the competition, simulator models would make them just one of the pack.

2. *Inflexible System Representation.* Simulators can be somewhat inflexible. The base model has already been built and with it are some general, unchangeable, underlying assumptions. A comment was once heard from an engineer concerning the use of a simulator to aid in system design. "I'm not going to throw out my concept because the simulator can't be changed to show how it will work."

3. *Encourages Jumping the Gun.* Due to the nature of simulators and the ease with which models can be created, the modeler is often tempted to skip intermediate steps in the model creation process (see Chapter 6) and immediately begin performing a quick analysis. This temptation is sometimes hard to overcome and can lead to the construction of invalid or shoddy models.

4. *Visual Component May Create a False Sense of Credibility.* Most simulators, especially personal computer based simulators, rely heavily on the use of graphics for model creation and output displays. This visual component may give

the model users a "warm, fuzzy feeling" but it should not be unconditionally accepted as valid. All models should be analyzed using proper validation and verification techniques.

2.4 Comparison : Simulators versus Simulation Languages

The following questions come to mind after the preceding discussion about simulators.

"When should simulators be used?"
"Should simulators ever be used?"
"How do simulators compare to simulation languages?"

In answer to these questions, the following observations can be made.

1. Commercially available simulators should not be used for leading edge or specialty systems. In most cases, simulators are created for broad and general applications. If a modeler wants a simulation that exploits all specific attributes of the system to gain a competitive edge, a simulator should not be used.

2. Simulators can make excellent "concept modeling tools." Chapter 6 discusses the steps in the modeling process. One of these steps is to create a rough cut or concept model. Simulators can be used to build quick models for feasibility studies.

3. Simulators can be used as an estimating tool. The company that wishes to purchase a conveyor, for example, can use a simulator to provide a general estimate of what will be needed. A simulator will provide a good idea without actually getting too specific.

4. Use of a simulator does not automatically eliminate all work. Simulators reduce the time involved in model construction. The other steps in the simulation process will still require time and expertise.

Table 2.1 makes a general comparison between simulators and simulation languages. Depending on the application, either a simulator or simulation language

TABLE 2.1
Simulators versus Simulation Languages

Attribute	Simulator	Simulation Language
Flexibility	Limited	Unlimited
Development Speed	Fast	Slow
Applications	Specific	Unlimited
Detail of System Definition	Predefined	Unlimited
Ability to Change Model	Limited	Unlimited
Required Skill Level of Modeler	Low	High

TABLE 2.2

Examples of Simulator and Simulation Language Applications

Application	Tool Chosen	Reason for Choice
Monorail Vendor's Proposed System	Simulation Language	To take advantage of specific vendor attributes
Monorail Purchaser's Proposed System	Simulator	Vendor still unknown, quick general model desired
Concept Simulation of an Assembly Line	Simulator	Fast nondetailed model desired
State-of-the-Art Automotive Plant	Simulation Language	Simulators not detailed or specific enough
Patented Process for Producing Plastic	Simulation Language	Simulator unable to duplicate process

should be used. Table 2.2 provides a few specific examples of users selecting a simulator or simulation language based on their application.

2.5 Integrated Environments

Integrated environments are collections of software tools for designing, writing, verifying, running, and analyzing models. Software environments of this type are just starting to appear in the simulation market. TESS (The Extended Simulation System; Standridge, 1985) was one of the first integrated simulation environments to be offered. TESS originally ran in conjunction with several simulation languages and provided data bases, graphics, and other integrated support features. GPSS/PC (Cox, 1984) produced by Minuteman Software (Stow, Massachusetts), is an example of a simulation language that has been incorporated as part of an integrated environment approach to modeling. This GPSS software package includes facilities for creation, debugging, verifying, running, analyzing, and animating a model.

Integrated environments allow the simulation analyst to easily move from one step in the simulation process to the next without much of the unproductive housekeeping work required by nonintegrated simulation tools.

2.6 Automatic Code Generators

Another method to aid in the creation of a simulation is the use of automatic code generators (Rich and Waters, 1988). Simulation source code can be created directly from plant layout drawings, programmable logic controller (PLC) ladder logic, or existing data bases. In its original release, the AutoMod simulation language was set up as a form of automatic code generator. AutoMod statements were translated into the simulation language GPSS/H. The resulting model, together with a prewritten GPSS/H simulation library, could be run and the system analyzed.

An automatic code generator is nothing more than a processor program that will input the existing source information (CAD drawing, ladder logic, digitizer data, etc.), digest it, and create simulation language–based output. This output can be combined with existing simulation libraries and then run as a model.

An automatic simulation code generator can help debug existing data or help determine if certain control logic is viable (Thomasma et al., 1989).

2.7 Hardware

Computer hardware technology has advanced tremendously in the past few decades. The computing power once found only in a room-sized mainframe can now be carried in a small pocket-sized computer. Execution speeds have increased, sizes have decreased, and computer availability is continuing to grow. All of these factors have helped to produce an environment well-suited to modeling applications.

Simulation software can be found for nearly any type of computer system. Mainframes, minicomputers, workstations, and microcomputers all support versions of modeling software. The trend among many simulation software vendors has been to produce packages that offer the most power while operating on inexpensive hardware platforms. In some cases, execution speed ends up being sacrificed for the ability to create larger models.

For the simulation analyst that expects to create large models, mainframes and more powerful minicomputers offer the lowest execution times and provide an overall time savings. For the analyst doing small models, the convenience of PC-based modeling packages is hard to bypass.

2.8 Microcomputer Use in Simulation

During the 1980s, personal computers (PCs) moved from hobby shops into the mainstream of American and international businesses. PCs have grown so popular that they can be found in nearly any business, factory, or office and in many homes. Their memory capabilities, power, speed, and graphic resolution have soared while their price has plummeted.

Because of this widespread appeal and availability, microcomputers are fast becoming the tool of choice among people performing simulations. Many simulation analysts either use or are actively planning to use PCs for future applications of simulation.

PCs offer the ability to share simulation libraries through networks, produce high-resolution graphics, and run large simulation programs. In addition, the availability of other software such as spreadsheets, statistical analysis packages, and standard programming languages gives the simulation analyst a wide variety of other tools for manipulating input data, analyzing output data, and performing other tasks in the modeling process.

2.9 Animation

The use of computer graphics to dynamically display simulation entities and their activities is defined as animation. Because of the increased availability of micro-computers and the widespread use of graphics in many different application areas, a demand for the same capabilities in the simulation field has been steadily increasing. This demand for animation by both simulation analysts and users has resulted in the release of graphic tools by most major simulation software vendors. Some of the more notable of these packages are AutoMod II, CINEMA, GPSS/PC ANIMATOR, and Proof. Two examples of animating a computer simulation using Proof are shown in Figure 2.2.

AutoMod II/AutoGram AutoSimulation, Inc. helped to pioneer the simulation animation field with its three-dimensional CAD-like AutoGram package. AutoGram software animated the output of AutoMod, their industrial model creation language. AutoSimulations, Inc. has combined the features of AutoGram into its AutoMod II language. AutoMod II runs on Silicon Graphics 31xx and 4D/xx, Intergraph Clipper 3xx and 3xxx, Sun-4, DEC VAXstation 3200 and 3500, microVAX GPX, and several Apple Macintosh machines.

CINEMA CINEMA is the companion animation package to the SIMAN language. It provides an easy-to-operate user interface that employs pull-down menus. CINEMA was specifically designed to allow nonprogrammers to quickly develop realistic animations. Users build an animation background and define dynamic symbols that change during the simulation. CINEMA runs either on PC compatible machines or in a special high-resolution mode using a graphics controller card and 19-inch monitor. CINEMA can run either real time or in the post-processor mode.

GPSS/PC ANIMATOR Minuteman Software offers both a CAD-based post-processing animator and a real time character graphics animator. These animators run in conjunction with GPSS/PC. The CAD-based animator uses AutoCad to create high-resolution wire frame style drawings. The character graphics mode animation was designed as a quick graphics display that can be used by the simulation analyst as a debugging tool. Both packages run on personal computers (Cox, 1988).

Proof Wolverine Software Corporation offers a low-priced, high-performance animation program called Proof. This animator runs on any IBM PC, AT, PS/2, or compatible machine having an EGA or VGA display and a math coprocessor chip. Proof was released as a general purpose animator that will work in conjunction with all major simulation languages or with any other software that produces an ASCII output file (Brunner, 1990).

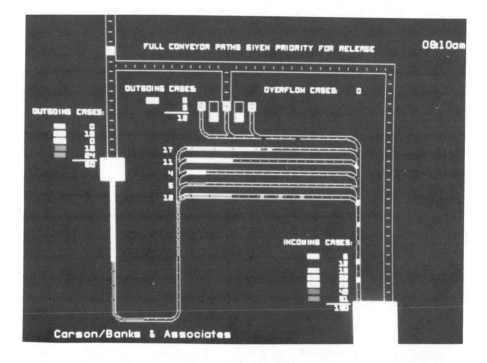

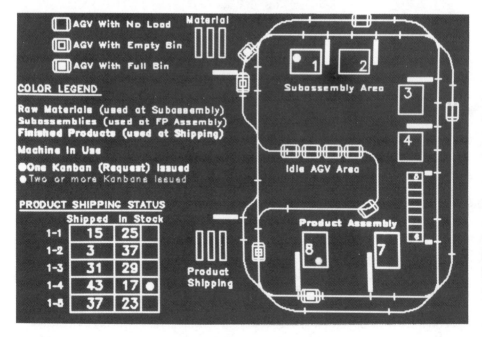

Figure 2.2 Examples of animating a computer simulation using Wolverine Software's Proof. Black and white reproduction is from a color original; please disregard reference to color in the figure. (Courtesy of Wolverine Software Corporation.)

2.9.1 Using Animation in the Proper Context

Animation is used for several general reasons. Among these are the following (Brunner and Henriksen, 1989):

Produces User Friendly Output For the nontechnical person, an animation will be much easier to comprehend than a statistical printout. By watching simulated entities move about on the screen, the observer can become familiar with the system's operation and with the logic embedded by the analyst.

Validation Technique When the simulation analyst is working with a system expert, animation provides a method of communicating information concerning the construction of the model. The expert can visually examine the model as a means of validating its operation.

Tool for Debugging The simulation analyst can use an animation as a debugging aid. Subtle inconsistencies can sometimes be detected visually on the graphics screen more easily than through statistics. The analyst is able to verify that the actual model matches the conceptual design. Animation will make all errors and problems obvious, thereby eliminating the temptation to say, "*It's such a rare problem that it's not worth fixing.*" No matter how rare or inconsequential the problem may be, if an observer can see it happen during an animation, it has to be dealt with or the face validity of the model will be destroyed.

Visual Impact/Sales Tool One of the most popular reasons for using animation is the visual impact or sense of reality that it brings to the modeling process. It is much easier to sell a system that can be seen on the screen of a personal computer than it is to sell a system that is represented by a stack of paper covered with numerical data. Most vendors of industrial equipment rely heavily on animation as a tool that can be used by its sales force when trying to "sell" a concept to a customer. Seeing is believing, and seeing an animation is no exception to that precept.

2.9.2 Misuse of Animation

James O. Henriksen of Wolverine Software (GPSS/H, Proof) was quoted by *Business Week* magazine (August 17,1987) as saying, "Watching cartoons on a screen is no substitute for good statistical work." Like all good things, animation can be misused. It is not a cure-all and does have a downside. Animation should be used to supplement a simulation study rather than to drive it. The following pitfalls are common when animation is used:

Creation of Overconfidence A model is still only a model and is only as accurate as the data and assumptions it uses. Animation tends to make model users and creators forget some of the underlying assumptions and techniques that were incorporated during the model building stage. It is easy to think that if it looks realistic on the screen, then the system must be modeled properly. This is not necessarily always the case.

Unwise Time Spent on Animation Rather than spending time building the actual model, undue time is spent trying to build a "pretty" animation screen. The animation should be used as a supplement to the simulation, not as its focal point.

Substitute for Good Statistical Work Rather than spending time to perform a proper analysis on the results of a simulation study, the decision makers base their opinions on a short period of observed animation. The animated portion of the simulation observed might not be representative of the system's true behavior. It is very important not to jump the gun and draw conclusions only on the basis of an animation.

2.9.3 Animation Attributes

Animation software may be structured in different ways, depending on the application. For instance, most personal computer animators are two-dimensional, exhibiting graphics with height and width. Workstation animators such as Auto-Mod II usually provide three-dimensional graphics. A depth dimension is added to enhance the picture.

A CAD-like three-dimensional animation is an exciting and wonderful sales tool but it does have a few problems. For instance, if the animation runs on special hardware, a customer must be brought to the computer (unless he or she owns the same minicomputer with graphics hardware which is unlikely) or the animation must be videotaped and replayed at the customer's site.

Personal computer–based animations, although generally two-dimensional and not quite as detailed (the level of PC version animators is beginning to approach that of workstations), easily can be transported to customer sites and run on in-house PCs. This facilitates communication and makes presentation easier. In addition, initial hardware cost is much lower.

Another attribute of animation software is that it runs real time or in the post-processor mode. The term *real time* is used to indicate that the animation runs on the computer screen while the simulation program is executing. The disadvantages of this type of animator are loss of speed, corruption of statistics,[1] and the necessity to run the simulation when the animation is to be viewed.

The post-processor mode means that the animation is displayed after the simulation run is complete. The simulation creates a data file that is used as an input to the animation program. A post-processor offers many advantages such as the ability to fast forward, reverse, speed up, or slow down a viewing. The animation can be easily transported requiring only the animator software and data file. And since the animation is run from a data file, multiple copies can be running at one time without needing additional copies of the simulation program.

2.10 Future Trends

Simulation is still a young discipline. It is growing fast and has not yet entered all the areas that can use what it has to offer. Over the next few years, simulation

---

[1]Some animation packages allow model parameters to be changed on the fly. This can result in the corruption of output statistics.

tools can be expected to continue evolving into forms that offer more power, greater flexibility, and added user friendliness. The following trends will more than likely have an impact on the simulation tools of the future.

- The development of artificial intelligence tools and applications.
- Languages that allow new block statements to be created by users. (See Chapter 7 for definition of block statements in a simulation language.)
- Simulation language development kits may be available to allow simulation analysts to easily create their own simulator software packages.
- More PC implementations, better graphics and a movement away from the mainframe applications (Klein, 1988).
- Advances in the area of automatic simulation code generators.
- Advanced and more flexible commercially available simulators.
- More modelers will be creating simulation-based tools for nontechnical users.
- Better links to the real world, before and after the simulation effort, will be engineered.
- On-line control in factories will be linked to the simulation effort more closely.
- Simulators and simulation languages will have embedded expert systems for statistical analysis and model coding.

All of these trends add up to a dynamic and exciting future for the field of computer simulation.

2.11 Summary

Computer simulation has its roots in the desires of all people to reduce risk and to know what is unknown. This desire sparked a revolution that began with clumsy analysis techniques on large, slow computer systems. It then moved to better machines running sophisticated software and is now beginning to employ artificial intelligence and fast, exciting computer graphics to enhance the modeling process.

References and Reading

AutoSimulations, Inc. 1984. *AutoMod Users Manual*. AutoSimulations, Inc., Bountiful, Utah.

Brunner, Daniel T. 1990. *Proof Documentation (Final Alpha: Draft 5.3)*. Wolverine Software Corporation, Annandale, Virginia.

Brunner, Daniel T., and James O. Henriksen. 1989. "A General Purpose Animator." *Proc. 1989 Winter Simulation Conf.* (Washington, D.C., Dec. 4–6). SCS, San Diego, pp. 155–163.

Brunner, Daniel T. (Chair). 1988. "Easy to Use Simulation Packages: What Can You Really Model?" (Panel Discussion). *Proc. 1988 Winter Simulation Conf.* (San Diego, Dec. 12–14). SCS, San Diego, pp. 887–891.

Bryan, Otis F. 1989. "Productivity Tools in Simulation: SIMSCRIPT II.5 and SIMGRAPHICS." *Proc. 1989 Winter Simulation Conf.* (Washington, D.C., Dec. 4–6). SCS, San Diego, pp. 164–171.

"Catalog of Simulation Software." 1988. *Simulation* (Oct.): 136–156.

Conway, Richard, and William Maxwell. 1987." *Proc. 1987 Winter Simulation Conf.* (Atlanta, Dec. 14–16). SCS, San Diego, pp. 202–206.

Cox, Springer. 1984. *GPSS/PC.* Minuteman Software, Stow, Massachusetts.

Cox, Springer W. 1988. "GPSS/PC Graphics and Animation." *Proc. 1988 Winter Simulation Conf.* (San Diego, Dec. 12–14). SCS, San Diego, pp. 129–135.

Dahl, O., and K. Nygaard. 1963. "SIMULA—An ALGOL-Based Simulation Language." *CACM* **9**(9) : 671–678.

Davis, Deborah A., and C. Dennis Pegden. 1988. "Introduction to SIMAN." *Proc. 1988 Winter Simulation Conf.* (San Diego, Dec. 12–14). SCS, San Diego, pp. 61–70.

Delfosse, C. M. 1976. *Continuous Simulation and Combined Simulation in SIMSCRIPT II.5.* CACI, Inc., Arlington, Virginia.

"Directory of Vendors of Simulators, Specific Components, and Related Services." 1989. *Simulation* (Dec.): 259–275.

Gilman, Andrew B., and Claire Billingham. 1989. "A Tutorial on SEE WHY and WITNESS." *Proc. 1989 Winter Simulation Conf.* (Washington, D.C., Dec. 4–6). SCS, San Diego, pp. 192–200.

Gordon, Geoffrey. 1961. "A General Purpose Systems Simulator." *Proc. EJCC, Washington D.C.* Macmillian, New York, pp. 87–104.

Grant, John W., and Steven A. Weiner. 1986. "Factors To Consider in Choosing a Graphically Animated Simulation System." *Industrial Engineering* (Aug.): 37–40, 65–68.

Grant, Mary E., and Darrell W. Starks. 1988. "A Tutorial on Tess : The Extended Simulation Support System." *Proc. 1988 Winter Simulation Conf.* (San Diego, Dec. 12–14). SCS, San Diego, pp. 136–140.

Henriksen, James O. 1977. "An Improved Events List Algorithm." *Proc. 1977 Winter Simulation Conf.* (Gaithersburg, Maryland, Dec.). SCS, San Diego, pp. 546–557.

Henriksen, James O., and Robert C. Crain. 1983. *GPSS/H User's Manual.* Wolverine Software Corporation, Annandale, Virginia.

Hughes, William R., and Mohamed Benton. 1985. *PC SIMSCRIPT II.5 Introduction and User's Manual.* CACI, Los Angeles.

Klein, Arthur. 1988. "Factory Simulation Comes of Age." *Managing Automation* (Aug.): 24–29.

Law, Averill M., and Christopher S. Larmey. 1984. *An Introduction to Simulation Using SIMSCRIPT II.5.* CACI, Los Angeles.

Markowitz, Harry M., Bernard Hausner, and Herbert Karr. 1963. *SIMSCRIPT–A Simulation Programming Language.* Prentice-Hall, Englewood Cliffs, New Jersey.

McLeod, John (editor). 1988. *Proc. 1988 Conf.: Pioneers & Peers.* (Orlando, April 18–21). SCS, San Diego.

O'Keefe, Robert M. 1987. "What is Visual Interactive Simulation? (And is There a Methodology for Doing it Right?)." *Proc. 1987 Winter Simulation Conf.* (Atlanta, Dec. 14–16). SCS, San Diego, pp. 461–464.

O'Reilly, Jean J., and William R. Lilegdon. 1988. "SLAM II Tutorial." *Proc. 1988 Winter Simulation Conf.* (San Diego, Dec. 12–14). SCS, San Diego, pp. 85–89.

O'Reilly, Jean J., and Kristen C. Nordlund. 1989. "Introduction to SLAM II and SLAMSYSTEM." *Proc. 1989 Winter Simulation Conf.* (Washington, D.C., Dec. 4–6). SCS, San Diego, pp. 178–183.

Pegden, C. Dennis. 1987. *Introduction to SIMAN.* Systems Modeling Corporation, State College, Pennsylvania.

Poorte, Jacob O., and Deborah A. Davis. 1989. "Computer Animation with CINEMA." *Proc. 1989 Winter Simulation Conf.* (Washington, D.C., Dec. 4–6). SCS, San Diego, pp. 147–154.

Pritsker Corporation. 1990. *SLAM II Quick Reference Manual.* Pritsker Corporation, West Lafayette, Indiana.

Reitman, Julian. 1988. "A Concise History of the Ups and Downs of Simulation." *Proc. 1988 Winter Simulation Conf.* (San Diego, Dec. 12–14). SCS, San Diego, pp. 1–6.

Rich, Charles, and Richard C. Waters. 1988. "Automatic Programming : Myths and Prospects." *Computer* **21** (8): 40–51.

Rohrbough, Mark C. 1989. "Introduction to SIMFACTORY II.5." *Proc. 1989 Winter Simulation Conf.* (Washington, D.C., Dec. 4–6). SCS, San Diego, pp. 201–204.

Russell, Edward C. 1988. "SIMSCRIPT II.5 and SIMGRAPHICS: A Tutorial." *Proc. 1988 Winter Simulation Conf.* (San Diego, Dec. 12–14). SCS, San Diego, pp. 115–124.

Schriber, Thomas. 1988. "Perspectives on Simulation Using GPSS." *Proc. 1988 Winter Simulation Conf.* (San Diego, Dec. 12–14). SCS, San Diego, pp. 71–84.

Schroer, Bernard J. 1989. "A Simulation Assistant for Modeling Manufacturing Systems." *Simulation* (Nov.): 200–206.

SIMSCRIPT II.5 Programming Language. 1983. CACI, Los Angeles.

Standridge, C. 1985. "A Tutorial on TESS : The Extended Simulation System." *Proc. 1985 Winter Simulation Conf.* (San Francisco, Dec.). SCS, San Diego, pp. 73–79.

Thomasma, Timothy, Onur M. Ulgen, and Youyi Mao. 1989. "Tools for Designing Material Handling Control Logic." *Proc. 1989 Western Simulation Multiconference* (San Diego, Jan. 17–19). SCS, San Diego, pp. 19–22.

Thompson, Michael B. 1989. "AutoMod II : The System Builder." *Proc. 1989 Winter Simulation Conf.* (Washington, D.C., Dec. 4–6). SCS, San Diego, pp. 235–242.

Wild Jr., William G., and Otis Port. 1987. "This Video Game Is Saving Manufacturers Millions." *Business Week* (Aug. 17): 82–84.

CHAPTER 3

Simulation in the Real World

The purpose of this chapter is to take simulation out of its textbook setting and provide insight into how it is being used in the real world (Figure 3.1). The uses and misuses of simulation and its good and bad points are covered using examples drawn from actual experience.

3.1 Why Simulation Has Become Such a Popular Tool

In the last three decades, simulation has progressed from research and development centers and academia to widespread use in a variety of diverse industries and businesses. There are many reasons for this rapid growth. Included among them are the following:

1. *Improvements in Computers.* The first simulations were done on large room-sized mainframe computers. These computers relied on card decks and operated most often in the batch mode. Not many people had access to these

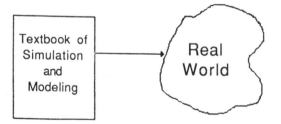

Figure 3.1 Real world approach to simulation.

mammoth devices. Present day computers have been reduced considerably in size and cost. Equivalents of the mainframes that previously occupied large rooms are now carried around in briefcase-sized packages. Computers have moved out of the research laboratory and can now be found on practically every desk in all industries. The computing power of a single chip is fast becoming all that is necessary to run the most sophisticated commercial simulation software. This widespread availability and reduction in cost of computers has enabled simulation to prosper.

2. *Improvements in Simulation Products.* Originally, most simulation work was done using assembly language, FORTRAN, or other high-level languages. Development time was much greater. Debugging and statistic tabulation as well as the results were less reliable. This situation began to change with the advent of GPSS in 1961. Since that time, a multitude of simulation languages, analysis programs, animators, and preprogrammed simulators have become available. Much of the development time required to create a model has been eliminated through standard features found in these products. In addition to performing the necessary simulation functions, varying degrees of user friendliness are available. Simulation languages such as SIMAN and GPSS/H are appealing to people who are more computer programming–oriented while nonprogrammers can enjoy the mouse-driven menus found in many application specific simulators.

3. *New Opportunities for Simulation Education.* Until recently, very few universities offered discrete event simulation classes. Today, nearly every college and university offers simulation classes in both engineering and business departments. In addition to the collegiate setting, many private seminars and training sessions are available. These sessions are sponsored by simulation software vendors, consultants, and corporations that have a simulation program in place. Other sources of simulation education are trade magazines, academic publications, conferences, societies, and books such as this one. All these items have become commonplace and readily available to interested persons.

4. *Increasingly Complex and Technical Work Environments.* The average work environment has changed from simple manual assembly lines to complex automated systems. Many repetitive human tasks have been replaced with robots and factory automation equipment. Conveyors, forklift trucks, storage and retrieval racks, as well as many other factory floor items are now routinely automated with programmable logic controllers or computers. This new complexity has made factory output rates very difficult to predict and manage. The need for better analysis tools arose. New simulation techniques evolved to satisfy this demand and were able to remove much of the guesswork and uncertainty in the workplace.

5. *Greater Computer Literacy among Analysts and Engineers.* Thirty years ago computers were still mysterious. Highly trained specialists were the only people qualified to use them. Computers fueled the imagination of many science fiction writers and represented the future. At the present time, computer literacy is increasing by leaps and bounds. Everyone has the ability to receive some type

of computer training. Most high schools and colleges require students to take at least one computer class. In the workplace, computers are used by the entire spectrum of personnel, from engineers to secretaries and clerks. Many corporations have entire departments dedicated to training employees on the use of in-house computers and software. This new age of computer literacy has given the simulation field fertile grounds upon which to take root and grow.

6. *Overseas Competition and Tightening Budgets.* Another factor adding to growth in the use of simulation is the increasing emphasis on lowering overhead costs, reducing labor requirements, and streamlining operations. Much of this has come about because of the foreign competition now facing domestic manufacturers. At one time, U.S. markets (particularly the automotive and steel industries) were under no type of external competitive threats. Today that has all changed. Many of the industries that were nearly wiped out are rebounding. Some of this recovery can be attributed to better planning and the use of simulation techniques.

7. *Realization of the Benefits Offered by Simulation.* Only recently have the true benefits of simulation been completely recognized by industries. For many years computer modeling was considered to be a nice toy but was not fully trusted as a planning tool. As its economic advantages continue to become more apparent, many companies are investing time and resources into developing their simulation capacity. Payoffs are high, and much of the risk is removed from exploring innovative solutions to problems. Equipment purchases can be functionally tested using modeling techniques prior to making large capital expenditures. In other words, simulation has provided a method of looking before leaping. Costly errors are avoided. Benefits such as these cannot be ignored any longer.

8. *Industrial Peer Pressure.* Once simulation departments and resources were in place in many companies, those without the ability to create models found themselves at a competitive disadvantage. This was most apparent in industries such as materials handling, where a simulation study accompanying a quotation would lend credibility to a proposed system and often become a determining factor when the contract was awarded. A situation of industrial peer pressure was created. Purchasers would inquire why simulation was not being used by their vendors and demand that some type of throughput guarantee be given. Rather than fight, many companies chose to go along with the crowd and develop the ability to generate simulations. Presently, most materials handling system request-for-quotations require that some type of modeling be performed prior to purchase. This has been a major force in popularizing simulation.

9. *Warm, Fuzzy Feeling It Creates.* Many companies have developed internal simulation groups to model in-house problems, proposed systems, and existing manufacturing processes. Presentation materials such as simulation animation packages have helped to sell internal proposals to management and create a corporate warm, fuzzy feeling. Seeing is believing, and many simulation packages available today place an emphasis on graphics and output.

10. *Part of an Effort to Increase Quality.* Another recent wave that has been rocketing through U.S. industry is a renewed committment to quality. The success of these philosophies (see Chapter 5) have been demonstrated in Japan with large productivity gains and high profits. As this phenomenon continues to catch on, its relationship to simulation will continue to strengthen and popularize modeling. One of the major precepts of quality is "doing it right the first time" (Crosby, 1985). By creating a model of what is to be designed, purchased, or installed, costly mistakes can be avoided, and the process can be done right the first time.

These ten points help illustrate why the field of simulation and modeling has grown from the laboratory to widespread real world use in such a short time. Presently, the market is still expanding and as all the factors listed continue to impact society, simulation will continue to grow more and more popular.

3.2 Art/Science of Simulation

There has been a long-running debate that concentrates on trying to decide whether simulation should be defined as an art or a science. Those who believe it to be a science feel that statistics, mathematics, and computer science comprise its foundation and are the basis for this classification. Others feel that the skill of the modeling team, the creativity involved in developing the model, and the interpretation of the results all add up to an individualized art. In this author's opinion, there is no real way to scientifically structure a simulation to guarantee that its results are valid. Instead, after the model has been coded and run, the outputs can be studied and compared with corresponding known values to determine suitability. If no known values exist, then the modeler must rely on instincts and the judgment of experts to make this determination.

The creativity and instincts used are akin to an art. Much of the methodology involved in model creation and analysis are based on computer science and mathematical principles. Therefore, elements of both art and science exist in modeling. Simulation can best be defined as a "soft-science" (Bobillier et al., 1976). Figure 3.2 depicts the spectrum extending from art to science and simulation's place.

In recent years simulation has been moving along the spectrum more toward the science end. Improvements in simulation languages and the advent of simulators have removed some of the need to be creative and innovative. Much of the uncertainty in model creation has also been eliminated through the development of application specific languages such as AutoMod (AutoSimulations, 1984).

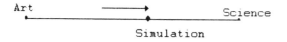

Figure 3.2 Art versus science: simulation's category.

3.3   Questions Answered by Simulation

Depending on the area of application, simulation can be used for many different purposes and to answer a variety of questions. It is important to know what information the simulation is required to provide at an early stage in its development. This insures that sufficient detail is incorporated into the program and helps to prevent the running of inappropriately designed models that will not produce any useful output data (Thesen and Travis, 1988).

Besides the area of application, the stage in the simulation process may also determine what questions should be asked. For example, early in the study answers to broad-scale questions may be sought. General feasibilty is often determined with a simplified version of the model. If the system seems to perform as desired in this stage of the project, more detail can be added and different types of information can be sought. Simulations of the preliminary nature are often performed with spreadsheet programs such as Lotus 1-2-3 or rapid-modeling tools such as Manuplan (Suri and Tomsicek, 1988).

Listed below are some examples of questions that may be posed at different stages in the simulation process.

1. Preliminary Stages (global questions of feasibility)
   Do we have sufficient plant capacity?
   Is this type of system feasible for use in our application?
2. General Strategy Questions
   Would an automatic guided vehicle system or monorail be more appropriate?
   Should a just-in-time inventory scheme be employed?
3. Specific Design Questions
   Can the chosen conveyor move enough parts to station A per unit time?
   Are these workcycle times fast enough to keep up with the product flow?
   Should four queues feed the four stations or should one queue feed all four?
4. Fine Tuning
   What is the optimum number of automatic guided vehicles to run the system?
   How may queue positions would be best at this workstation?
   Should the coffee breaks be staggered?

Questions such as these are both application specific and project stage dependent. It is important to know the purpose for the simulation and to keep sight of the goals throughout the process. This will insure that costly runs providing little useful information are avoided.

3.4   Types of Simulation

The previous section states that in order to build an appropriate simulation, it is important to be aware of two major factors: information being sought and stages in the simulation process. During the early stages of a simulation process when broad conceptual questions are being investigated, it is advantageous to use fast, less detailed modeling techniques. When these global concerns are resolved, the model can be refined with more detail until a complete understanding of the problem is gained.

3.4.1 Concept Simulation

A less detailed first run simulation is commonly called a concept simulation (Trunk, 1989), rough cut simulation, rapid model, or handsim. All these names evolved to describe the different benefits this modeling practice provides.

Concept simulation The phrase *concept simulation* is beginning to replace the other three as accepted terminology for early stage simulation work. Its name implies that overall concepts are being tested without the addition of final stage detail.

Rough cut simulation Just as a diamond is rough cut prior to its finish cut and polishing, early stage simulations are rough and lacking the final luster. One advantage experienced when using rough cut models lies in their ability to provide fast answers to "what if" questions without having to invest the time that detailed modeling requires (Smith, 1989).

Rapid model Rapid modeling is another name used to describe up-front simulation work. Development speed is gained by omitting the finer details.

Handsim This term evolved from techniques in place during the days when computers were not yet in widespread usage. In order to determine materials handling equipment requirements, extensive mathematical calculations, called hand simulations, were utilized. These calculations were eventually incorporated into spreadsheet programs but the name handsim stuck.

Not only does concept simulation save time, it also gives the modeler insight as to what problems can be expected during a more detailed analysis. Model simplifications often make it possible for changes to be completed faster and with less effort. This allows different alternatives to be tested in a short amount of time.

It is important to understand that concept simulation does have some potential pitfalls. In order to simplify the model, some detail is sacrificed. This means that the results can be inaccurate. Depending on what simplifications are made, models can become completely invalid. It is important to prevent crucial factors from being oversimplified.

Concept simulation is most applicable in situations where similar systems are modeled frequently. For example, the manufacturer of monorails might use concept simulation to provide potential customers with a general system picture. Since this particular vendor has simulated and built many monorails in the past, he/she can be fairly confident that the system has not been detrimentally oversimplified. A budget price can then be calculated without ever performing a detailed simulation. If the customer likes the concept and the price, the simulation can move to a new stage of development where additional detail is added.

3.4.2 Detailed Simulation

After the completion of a concept simulation, the model is ready for the addition of finer details. There are two ways of accomplishing this. The first method is to modify the existing concept simulation. The second is to develop an entirely new model using what was learned with the concept simulation. Most commonly the second alternative is chosen for several reasons. The concept simulation in many cases is written using a determinist spreadsheet or rapid-modeling package such as Manuplan (Suri and Tomsicek, 1988). The development of a more detailed model will often require that a simulation language or simulator be employed. This will provide the modeler with the necessary flexibility to enhance the simulation.

In this phase of the modeling process, the simulation analyst works very closely with engineers or system designers. Actual measured distances, workcycle times, and scheduling algorithms are utilized. Realistic stochastic probability distributions replace the estimated deterministic times used in the concept simulation. Machinery downtimes, repair rates, and other system inefficiencies are added. The model is run, tested, and either compared to an existing similar system or examined by experts for correctness. By the time the detailed simulation is complete, the entire system being modeled has been defined.

3.4.3 Operational Changes and Follow-Up

Although design is complete and the simulation considered to be done, it is very likely that when the system is installed, some estimated parameters will change. For instance, a manual assembly operation that in theory was expected to take three minutes may actually take four minutes. It is important to update the simulation as theoretical values are replaced with actual ones. If the model is maintained in this way, it can be used in the future to test the impact of desired (or undesired) changes to the system, to estimate daily production, or as part of a larger overall simulation.

3.4.4 Common Simulation Methodology
Used in Manufacturing

In the manufacturing sector, a specific simulation methodology incorporating both concept and detailed simulation has developed to facilitate the design, selling, and installation of materials handling equipment. This methodology can be summarized in the following six steps (Cox, 1989):

Step 1: Concept Simulation The creation of alternate models to test the most promising of the possible materials handling solutions.

Step 2: Acceptance of Concept The prospective customer accepts what is felt to be the best alternative. Price, functionality, and throughput requirements are all considered.

Step 3: Engineering Design The simulation is redone by adding details and final design parameters.

Step 4: Operational Changes Final changes are made to accommodate the changing requirements of the customers. These changes are then simulated and tested for cost-effectiveness.

Step 5: Simulation Report A final simulation report is provided along with an animation, if desired.

Step 6: Maintenance If desired, the simulation is maintained throughout installation of the system. Any changes or required modifications are incorporated into the model, and the impact on the system is tested.

3.5 Forcing Completion of Design with Simulation

Simulation is typically used as a design tool. For this reason, a simulation study will be among the first few activities slated for completion in the life cycle of a project. Simulation is a process that requires that all aspects of a system be thought out and planned. To create a model, information must be gathered from diverse sources and compiled for use (Figure 3.3). This gathering process will often bring different people and ideas together for the first time. Communication between persons with responsibility for the different parts of the system is facilitated. Subsystem interface points will be discussed and obvious problems will be eliminated. Common goals will be set. Aspects of the system that were not previously considered may come to light. The formulation of creative solutions and innovative ideas may evolve. By the time the simulation is ready to be coded, very few unknown variables will remain.

3.6 Advantages of Simulation

Using computer simulation for analysis has many advantages over other design techniques. Seven of these advantages are the following.

1. *Allows Experimentation without Disruptions to Existing Systems.* In systems that already exist, the testing of new ideas may be difficult, costly, or impossible. For example, an automotive assembly line may be running 24 hours

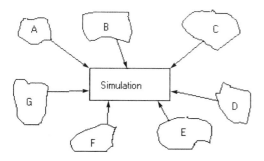

Figure 3.3 Diverse sources of model's information.

a day, 7 days a week. To shut the line down to put in a temporary modification that may or may not speed up the process and then resume production would be very expensive. Another example would be adding a piece of equipment to the same assembly line. Unless the machinery was already purchased, the process of adding it to the line and trying it out firsthand would be impossible. In these types of situations, simulation provides a great advantage. A model can be developed, compared to the system, and fine-tuned. This insures that it was constructed realistically. Any desired modifications can be made to the model first, the impact on the system examined, and then the decision to implement the changes in the real world system can be made.

2. *Concept Can Be Tested Prior to Installation.* For the design of new systems, a computer simulation will allow concepts to be tested prior to installation. This testing may reveal unforeseen design flaws and give the designers a tool for improvement. If the same flaws were discovered after installation, changes to the system might end up being very costly or even impossible to implement. An example of this situation can be illustrated by the purchase of a large automatic storage and retrieval system (ASRS). Engineers in a medium-sized company decide to replace an existing warehouse system with an ASRS. After stretching their tight budget to its outer limits, the equipment was procured and installed. Several months usage revealed that the new system was unable to keep up with the demands for pallets being entered and removed from the racks. Their assembly line process began to bog down because material was not arriving from storage in a timely fashion. The budget was gone and upper management told manufacturing to live with their decision. The entire situation could have been avoided by simulating the ASRS prior to equipment purchase.

3. *Detection of Unforeseen Problems or Bugs.* When a system is simulated prior to installation and found to work in concept, the model is often refined to include finer details. The detailed simulation may reveal problems or bugs that exist in the system's design. By discovering these problems prior to installation, debugging time and rework costs can be avoided. In addition, improvements to system operation may be discovered. An example of a traffic light simulation can be used. Analysts were running data through the model of a new traffic light to be installed near a busy industrial park. Traffic seemed to flow smoothly most of the time but one exception existed. On the average, daily traffic flows were heaviest from east to west. However, the largest factory had a shift change at 3:30 P.M. and that caused traffic to run heavier in the north and south directions. By detecting this fact, analysts were able to produce a recommendation that would lengthen the north and south green light times between 3:00 and 4:00 P.M. Traffic would run smoother and congestion would be eased.

4. *Gain in System Knowledge.* A primary benefit that is a direct result of the simulation process is the increase in overall system knowledge. At the start of a simulation project, especially in the modeling of complex systems, knowledge is often dispersed among many different people. Each individual is an expert in a particular area. In order to develop a working simulation, all this information needs to be gathered together and woven into a complete picture. This process of

bringing all the pieces together ends up being of great value by providing those involved with an education on the overall system. The simulation analyst acts as a sleuth seeking out information from various sources and producing a finished picture. In the situation where simulations are done on a regular basis, channels for the information-gathering process need to be established. This will speed up the process considerably and allow data to flow from individual experts to simulation.

5. *Speed in Analysis.* After a model has been developed, it is possible to run the simulated system at speeds much greater than would be attainable in the real world. With many simulation languages, multiple experiments can be set up and completed in one run, adding to the time savings. A finished model can take anywhere from fractions of seconds to hours of run time to produce results. But these results can represent minutes, hours, days, or even years of system time. Many manufacturing plants keep a simulation of their assembly processes on hand. Each morning before production begins, they enter the anticipated system inputs into their model and predict how long the daily operations will take.

6. *Forces System Definition.* In order to produce a valid working model of a system, it is important that all aspects of the system be known. If incorrect or incomplete definitions exist, the model will be inaccurate and should not be used as an analysis tool. Therefore, development of a simulation forces users of a system to fully define all parameters pertinent to its operation. If certain facts cannot be determined with complete certainty, a safe figure should be calculated for use. If this figure is found to cause a system bottleneck when the model is run, careful investigation and additional research time are indicated as being necessary.

7. *Enhances Creativity.* Having a simulation on hand can enhance creativity in the design of a system. For instance, an engineer may conceive two possible solutions that would put an end to a particular problem on the factory floor. One solution is guaranteed to work but is more expensive. The second solution is a new technology that is less expensive but somewhat risky. Without any means of analyzing the two possible courses of action, the more conservative solution will probably be chosen. If a simulation of the system is in existence, both potential solutions can be tried and compared. If the less expensive solution were found to perform as desired, the creativity of the engineer could be exercised without the risk of failure.

All seven advantages of using simulation for an analysis tool have a point in common: *the reduction of risk.* Simulation is a risk reduction method. Uncertainty is removed and replaced with certainty about the expected operation of a new system or about the effects of changes to an existing system.

3.7 Disadvantages of Simulation

Simulation is not a perfect cure-all that works in every case to remove risk from all uncertain decisions. It has limitations and disadvantages. Some of these disadvantages are the following.

1. *Expensive.* The creation of a computer model can often be an expensive method of analysis. Although lower priced simulation packages are beginning to enter the market (Cox, 1987), most large-scale simulation languages and their environments represent a major investment. Examples are GPSS/H (Henriksen and Crain, 1989), SIMSCRIPT (Russell, 1988), SIMAN (Davis and Pegden, 1988), and SLAM (O'Reilly and Lilegdon, 1988). In addition to the software, hardware must either be available or purchased. If animation is going to be used, this cost must include a graphics monitor. The current trend in simulation is a move toward microcomputer-based products. However, many large applications still run better in a mainframe environment. This means that CPU usage is another cost that must be considered in many projects. In addition to hardware and software costs, labor expenses can often be quite high. Major simulation projects can represent years of effort. The first time use of simulation in a company can include extra costs to cover personnel training, learning curve expenses, and set-up time.

2. *Time Consuming.* Modeling is not generally set up to produce quick answers to questions. In most cases, data collection, model development, analysis, and report generation will require considerable amounts of time. The simulation process can be speeded up through two methods: reduction of detail and use of generic code libraries. By reducing the level of detail, general concept questions can be answered much faster. However, caution should be exercised when using this approach. Model accuracy can also be affected by eliminating key details. In situations where many similar simulations will be run, a generic simulation or code library can be created. This reusable resource will prevent "reinventing the wheel" for each simulation project. It will also reduce development costs (Figure 3.4).

3. *Yields Only Approximate Answers.* Discrete event simulation relies on the use of random number generators to provide model input. Since the input has a

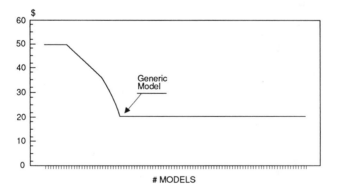

Figure 3.4 Simulation cost per number of models.

random element, some uncertainty is also associated with the output. In order to produce meaningful results, statistics must be used as a tool for interpreting output. All outputs are only estimates of the true behavior of the system. It is important to recognize this fact and treat simulation results as close approximations.

4. *Difficult to Validate.* Validation is the process of making sure the computer model accurately represents the system being studied. When the system does not yet exist, this can become a formidable task. The opinions of experts and intuition must be relied on to insure that the model runs in the same way the system will. Any time judgment and opinion are being used, the possibility of error exists. It is better to take a conservative point of view and make sure the system's predicted operation is no better than its actual operation will be.

5. *Accepted as Gospel.* Another problem that can occur over the course of a simulation study is the tendency of the users to accept any output as gospel. Always remember that simulation is a tool used by humans. Therefore, it is subject to any error that a person can make. Output reports should always be subject to rigorous analysis by the data user. Not only should statistical testing be employed but common sense should be used as a mechanism for acceptance. Many times problems can be detected by thinking through the process being simulated and the formulation of opinions on what should happen. If some data does not appear to be in line with expectations, it should be investigated more closely. In this way a problem may come to light.

3.8 To Sim or Not To Sim

"To sim or not to sim?" that is the question. In many companies, the decision to use simulation is one that requires careful thought and an up-front investment of thousands of dollars. For the company that has a simulation department in place, the question takes on a different meaning; it means "Should this particular problem or system be modeled?"

Having an in-house simulation department can be a great asset to a company but it can also spawn laziness in other departments. In many cases, it becomes easy for an engineer (for instance) to send a system concept to the simulation department for analysis without putting in the required design time. The system is modeled and conceptual errors are found that could have been eliminated before the simulation effort began. Time and resources are wasted, and the system needs to be redesigned.

Since simulation can be expensive and time-consuming, the importance of using it for analysis within the proper context is evident. The possibility of over-simulating exists. Do not use modeling to analyze every problem, especially when many of them can be solved on paper. Simulation should not be used until other methods of analysis have verified that the system being studied is viable. The following steps can help prevent the problem of over-simulation.

1. *Make sure that the conceptual designs are complete and viable.* An important step in system development is the forming of overall concepts. Simulation can be used to test a concept to see if it will work or to compare different concepts. Before simulating, make sure that the concepts are complete and can be used if they are found to be workable. Do not take the easy way out by saying the simulation will prove this concept. Think it through carefully before considering model development.

2. *Look for obvious bottlenecks.* Do not simulate a system that obviously cannot work. Many bottlenecks can be spotted before the modeling effort begins. These evident problems should be resolved prior to simulation so that extra effort and costly delays are avoided. For the same reason, when a system is being simulated, the analyst should continue to look for bottlenecks. The sooner a problem comes to light, the sooner it can be dealt with.

3. *Make sure that a simple mathematical solution does not exist.* Before the modeling process begins, try to use mathematics to answer questions. Not only does math often provide an exact answer, it seldom involves the time and cost that simulation requires.

By using these three steps, the cost of unnecessary simulation effort can be saved. Simulation should be used to analyze sound designs and concepts. It should not be used as an easy way out.

3.9 Estimation of Simulation Time

Many simulation projects in industries are completed within the context of a job contract. Consultants, materials handling vendors, and even in-house simulation departments are usually obligated to provide an accurate estimate detailing the amount of time a project will require. Since simulation is based on the analysis of processes that are unknown, potential problems requiring additional analysis time can easily arise. Therefore, an accurate estimate of time can be very difficult to decide.

When simulation projects overrun their allotted time, one of the following scenarios is usually to blame:

- *Unexpected problems in the system being modeled are found, and the solutions are sought using the model as a tool.*

A function of simulation is to detect unexpected problems and help test potential solutions. If a large number of problems or a single complex problem is found, the amount of simulation time needed can increase drastically. When completion time is being estimated for the simulation, the importance of recognizing potential problem areas of the system and the addition of time for these areas is essential.

A possible solution to the estimating dilemma is to set up an initial time frame for completing a model of the system as it has been designed. If problems are found requiring design changes and additional simulation time, a new end date needs to be set. In that way, the end date is extended on an "as required" basis.

- *The customer of the simulation wants "just one more 'what if' tested".*

A tendency exists to keep playing different "what if" games once a model has been created. This tendency can lead to creative and innovative enhancements to a system but can also extend simulation project time and cause deadlines to be missed.

When estimating time for a simulation project, areas that can be changed and "played with" should be identified as experimental variables. Extra time can be added into the up-front estimate that takes into account the desire to try several different ideas after the initial model is complete. Once the estimated time is used up, no more "what if" games should be allowed unless extra time is purchased or approved.

- *The system is more complex than expected.*

Sometimes an initial inspection of a system does not reveal all of its hidden complexities. What may appear to be a straightforward process may in fact be very complicated. For this reason, the estimator must be certain that he or she fully understands all aspects of the system to be simulated.

- *The simulation analyst lacks experience.*

Another reason for estimates exceeding their time frames is the lack of experience by the simulation analyst. On a first time project, extra time has to be included to allow the analyst to learn the simulation language, hardware, and experimentation methods. It is generally not possible to build a first time model without experiencing some delays due to the learning curve. Once the simulation team has a few projects under their belts, these delays will no longer be a factor.

- *Too much nonessential detail is included.*

The construction of a simulation requires that the analyst know what information is being sought. By having a question to answer, the system can be broken into essential and nonessential subsystems. The key subsystems can be modeled in detail and the other subsystems in less detail. By taking this approach, the model will remain realistic while conserving development time and effort. The following example illustrates breaking a system into essential and nonessential subsystems.

Robot Welding Station

The assembly department in a large manufacturing plant would like to speed up production by automating a welding operation with a robot. The system will consist of a forklift truck dropping the workpiece on a conveyor. The conveyor moves the piece to the welding robot. When the operation is complete, the workpiece moves on to a manual station for grinding and deburring. It is then removed with a crane and placed into a crate for shipping (Figure 3.5).

The goal of the simulation is to determine if the robot's workcycle time will be fast enough to process 12 workpieces per hour. The system to be simulated can be broken into these components.

1. Forklift truck
2. Conveyor to robot workstation
3. Robot weld operation
4. Conveyor away from robot workstation
5. Grinding and deburring operation
6. Crane move to shipping crate

The most essential subsystem to be modeled is the robot weld station. It needs to be modeled in explicit detail. The conveyor system to and from the robot may have a significant impact, so it should also be modeled in detail. The grinding operation is manual. Workers can be added if needed, so it does not require the same level of detail. The crane operation will not be modeled in detail since unmoved workpieces do not slow down the grinding operation (see Figure 3.6).

By breaking the system into subsystems and defining the necessary level of detail, the goals of the simulation can be met and time can be conserved.

In the business world or manufacturing sector, it is important to be able to predict the length of time to create a simulation model. Some factors to be considered are the level of detail desired, size of simulation, project objective, and simulation software language being used.

3.10 "Make It Work" versus "Does It Work?"

A simulation project will be conducted differently based on its overall objective. Two common objectives are termed *"does it work?"* and *"make it work"* (Figure 3.7).

Does It Work? This project objective is generally what a simulation analyst likes to hear. It implies that the model is to be used to evaluate a single concept and must supply information indicating if the system will work. The simulation results provide a "yes" or "no" answer to whatever problem is being modeled. The "does it work" objective is usually easier to estimate and involves very little "what if" game playing. Consider the following example.

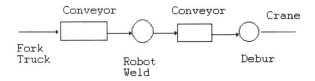

Figure 3.5 Components of the robot weld station.

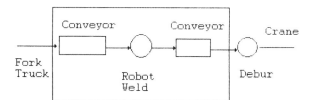

Figure 3.6 Scope of detailed model.

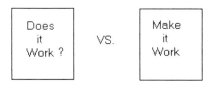

Figure 3.7 Simulation objectives.

X-Y-Z Company: Simulation #1

A stamping machine purchased several years earlier became a point of controversy at the X-Y-Z Company. Not enough workpieces were being processed each day to meet the requirements of a new contract. Management pointed its finger at the machine operators saying they were not doing their job fast enough. The operators in turn pointed their fingers at the machine saying it could not stamp the parts fast enough. A stalemate developed and as a means of resolution a simulation analyst was brought in to create a model of the process. The objective of the model was to determine if the machine was fast enough to perform the required work. In other words, the model had the "does it work?" objective.

Make It Work The "make it work" objective is used when a problem exists and the simulation analyst has the freedom to experiment with the system (within reason) until a solution is found. Estimating an accurate completion date for models with this objective can be very difficult. It is not known prior to the simulation process how many different scenarios must be tried before a usable one is discovered. The X-Y-Z example is continued.

X-Y-Z Company: Simulation #2

The initial simulation was completed at X-Y-Z Company and showed that management was right and the machine was fast enough to process enough workpieces to make the new quota. But the model revealed a problem that had not been noticed before. Although the stamping machine was fast enough to process the parts, the system delivering the workpieces to the operators was not fast enough to keep the machine busy 100% of the time. A decision was made at X-Y-Z Company to authorize a second simulation study. The model created would have the objective of "make it work." The simulation analyst together with a plant engineer were told to keep trying different delivery schemes until a workable solution was found.

3.11   Optimizing and Developing Solutions

A widespread misconception about simulation is the type of information it will normally provide. A common belief is that simulation will not only solve problems but will also produce an optimal solution. This is not necessarily true. Simulation can be used to optimize system performance but only in conjunction with the careful design of proper experiments.

In many simulation studies, especially in the context of a manufacturing environment, only a few feasible alternatives exist. These alternatives can be ranked subjectively in order of preference, cost, and performance. The most desired solution is simulated first. If the system does not perform at the required level, the next alternative on the list is tried and so forth until a workable solution is discovered. Use of this methodology is not very scientific and may not optimize performance, but it is very practical.

If the list of possible solutions is difficult to rank and an optimal solution is desired, some common methods of experimental design can be employed. The first step is to identify the model's factors. Factors are defined as input parameters and structural assumptions. These factors can be quantitative (consisting of numeric values) or qualitative (representing the structural assumptions of the model).

An example of a qualitative factor is an automatic guided vehicle (AGV) programming algorithm. Whether the AGV picks up the closest or oldest load is a structural assumption used in the model. Factors can also be identified as either controllable or uncontrollable. Controllable factors can be changed or managed to help improve system performance. The number of AGVs used in a warehouse simulation is a controllable factor. Uncontrollable factors cannot be changed within the context of the model. An example of an uncontrollable factor is the AGV's top speed.

The second step in optimizing a solution is to use viable combinations of the controllable factors as inputs in different simulation runs. The model can be run and the output performance measured. This output is termed the response. The varying responses can be screened based on meeting a *minimum acceptable performance* level. Experiments falling below this level will cause that particular potential solution to be dismissed.

The next step in optimizing the solution list is to employ some method of analysis to rank the list of acceptable factors and their responses. It may be possible to do this through inspection, by using methods of linear programming, or based on some other criterion. When the ranking process is complete, the model with the best combination of inputs and outputs will be chosen as optimal (Law and Kelton, 1982).

3.12 Other Pitfalls

The use of simulation can reduce the risk involved with implementing a new system or changing an existing one. However, unless simulation is used prudently, the possibility of developing an invalid model exists. In order to insure the success of a simulation project, care has to be taken to avoid modeling pitfalls (Smith, 1989). Some examples are:

1. *Failure to define goals for the simulation effort.* As mentioned earlier in this chapter, one of the first steps in the simulation process is to clearly define the project's goals. The purpose of the simulation and the questions it is intended to answer must be known early in model development. By knowing the goals for the study, the simulation analyst is able to structure the model appropriately. Failure to know these goals can result in improper levels of detail and ultimately an inability to answer the desired questions.

2. *Use of false assumptions in model construction.* A pitfall that is often hard to detect is the use of false assumptions in model construction. These assumptions become even more difficult to detect if they are of a qualitative nature. To prevent this problem, information needs to be gathered from sources having an interest in the model's output. The assumptions need to be well-documented and reviewed by all involved parties prior to model development.

3. *Selection of inappropriate level of detail.* The level of model detail is dependent on the goals of a simulation study. By knowing which questions need to be answered, certain parts of the model can be made more detailed and generalizations can be made for other less critical parts. By including too much detail, development time and the cost of a model will be greatly increased. Too

little detail can result in an invalid model that cannot provide accurate information responsibly.

4. *Poor selection of simulation software.* Selection of software is very important to the success of a simulation project. Concept simulation is often best done with a rapid-modeling tool. Detailed simulation may require a simulator or a general purpose language. Selection of the wrong tools may result in excessive model development time, inability to obtain certain statistics, and difficulty in debugging.

5. *Inexperienced simulation analyst.* The simulation analyst is critical to the successful implementation of a model. The analyst needs to be skilled in the techniques of simulation as well as possess knowledge about the system being modeled. A great deal can be learned from books, but practical firsthand simulation experience cannot be replaced as a learning tool. A new analyst should work closely with experienced simulation personnel at least until his or her skills are sufficient to tackle their own project.

6. *Inadequate participation by other "team" members.* Simulation is a team effort requiring the participation of not only the simulation analyst but also the system's engineers, designers, management, users, and experts. Without the input of all these individuals, it is unlikely that an accurate simulation will be developed. After the modeling effort is complete, the same people need to receive output information. If the information is not passed on or is ignored by its recipients, a high probability exists that the system will not operate as modeled.

3.13 A Failed Simulation Project

The pitfalls mentioned in Section 3.12 are real problems that happen more often than might be expected. Very few professional simulation analysts can honestly report that every model they have built has been flawless. The following example analyzes a real simulation project that became disastrous and the steps that were taken to revive the system.

Case Study: The Wrong Way

A young engineer, fresh out of college and ready to take on whatever challenges his new job had to offer, was assigned the task of simulating a proposed materials handling system. The system would be installed in a large engine plant to service 30 manual assembly stations. Engine blocks would enter the system and be moved from station to station via automatic guided vehicles (AGVs). At each assembly station, the AGV would drop off the engine block together with a part tray. The station operator would perform the required work and then press a button to signal that the engine was ready for removal. An available AGV would be called to the station, and the engine

---

would move to its next stop in the assembly operation. The concept seemed to be workable in theory, so a simulation study was commissioned.

Since this was one of the first simulations the young engineer had worked on, he was careful to use a textbook approach to the project. He was given an objective by the system engineer to "see if it works." The first step was to gather information about the system. He obtained workcycle times, a plant floor layout, information about the factory coffee breaks and lunch time, shift information, AGV speeds, AGV loading and unloading times, system priorities, and other operation data. Feeling confident that this data was adequate, the model's coding commenced.

The model development stage was more complicated than the young man had anticipated. By the time the simulation was written, its scheduled completion time had all but elasped. The initial run of the system demonstrated that the required number of engines could not be manufactured. Tempers flared under the tight time constraints and the analyst was given a new objective of "make it work."

Feeling pressured, he (with the help of a seasoned analyst) identifed 32 controllable factors in the simulation. These were altered and tried in different combinations but throughput still could not be met. Finally, a solution was found but it would require assembly workers to operate at inhumanly fast speeds at certain stations. Management at the engine plant felt no more time extensions could be granted and the system was installed as is.

A year went by with the system operating at half-capacity. No unexpected incidents occurred. But when the time for full-production to begin arrived, the system was unable to meet its required throughput. The workcycle times used at certain stations were unrealistic and could not be maintained. The simulation was brought back out for further review. The model was updated and different ideas were tried. Eventually, a costly solution was implemented by adding automation hardware and more assembly stations to the system.

What went wrong with the simulation effort in this example? It is easy to identify several pitfalls looking at the process in retrospect.

- The simulation analyst was inexperienced. He lacked practical knowledge of the system's operation and did not have the insight necessary to foresee potential problems.
- The simulation "team" members did not participate adequately. Although the simulation demonstrated that problems did exist, time was not taken to solve the problems in a preventative frame of mind. Rather, the system was installed and then the problems were tackled (at a much higher cost).
- Goals changed in mid-simulation effort. The original simulation was meant to discover if the system would work. When it was discovered that it would not, a new goal of "make it work" became the directive.

The problems pointed out by this case study could have been avoided if the initial simulation effort had been taken more seriously. Had the system's inadequacies been carefully documented and solved prior to installation, costly corrections and time delays could have been avoided.

No one likes to work on a project that is less than successful, but there is something to be said for the learning process that accompanies it. The young engineer in this example tempered his book learning with some practical experience. The simulation projects he worked on following that project were far better because of what he had learned. . . the hard way.

References and Reading

AutoSimulations, Inc. 1984. *AutoMod Users Manual*. Revision 4. AutoSimulations, Inc., Bountiful, Utah.

Bobillier, P. A, B. C. Kahn, and A. R. Probst. 1976. *Simulation with GPSS and GPSS/V*. Prentice-Hall. Englewood Cliffs, New Jersey.

Cox, S. W. 1987. "The Interactive Graphics and Animation of GPSS/PC." *Proc. 1987 Winter Simulation Conf*. (Atlanta, Dec. 14–16). SCS, San Diego, pp. 276–285.

Cox, W. 1989. "A Methodology for Manufacturing Simulation." *Materials Handling Engineering* (May): 74.

Crosby, P. 1985. *Quality Improvement Through Defect Prevention*. Phil Crosby Associates Inc., Winter Park, Florida.

Davis, D., and C. D. Pegden. 1988. "Introduction to SIMAN." *Proc. 1988 Winter Simulation Conf*. (San Diego, Dec. 12–14). SCS, San Diego, pp. 61–70.

Henriksen, J. O., and R. C. Crain. 1989. *GPSS/H Reference Manual*, Third Edition. Wolverine Software Corporation, Annandale, Virginia.

Law, A. M., and W. D. Kelton. 1982. *Simulation Modeling and Analysis*. McGraw-Hill, New York.

O'Reilly, J., and W. Lilegdon. 1988. "SLAM II Tutorial." *Proc. 1988 Winter Simulation Conf*. (San Diego, Dec. 12–14). SCS, San Diego, pp. 85–89.

Russell, E. C. 1988. "SIMSCRIPT II.5 and SIMGRAPHICS : A Tutorial." *Proc. 1988 Winter Simulation Conf*. (San Diego, Dec. 12–14). SCS, San Diego, pp. 115–124.

Smith, C. A. 1989. *Computer Simulation of Materials Handling Systems: An Introductory Workshop*. Mannesmann Demag Corporation, Grand Rapids, Michigan.

Suri, R., and M. Tomsicek. 1988. "Rapid Modeling Tools for Manufacturing Simulation and Analysis." *Proc. 1988 Winter Simulation Conf*. (San Diego, Dec. 12–14). SCS, San Diego, pp. 25–32.

Thesen, A., and L. Travis. 1988. "Introduction to Simulation." *Proc. 1988 Winter Simulation Conf*. (San Diego, Dec. 12–14). SCS, San Diego, pp. 7–14.

Trunk, C. 1989. "Simulation for Success in the Automated Factory." *Materials Handling Engineering* (May): 64–76.

Wild, W. G. and O. Port. 1987. "This 'Video Game' is Saving Manufacturers Millions." *Business Week* (Aug. 17): 82–84.

CHAPTER 4

Six Symptoms of a Sick Simulation

Computer simulations are no longer limited to a select group of specialists. They are readily available to the layperson and are becoming easier to use all the time. The benefits of this revolution are far-reaching and easily seen. An industrial engineer can simulate a conveyor system and verify that it can move the required number of loads per unit time. A bank manager can simulate arrivals at the bank's automatic teller machine (ATM) and determine if an additional terminal needs to be purchased to alleviate delays experienced by customers during peak usage times. The manager of a fleet of buses can apply simulation techniques and reorganize the routes the buses follow. Urban development analysts can use simulation to examine a city's road system and suggest traffic light sequence changes to improve the flow. The list goes on and on. Simulation can be applied to nearly any area of analysis and used to provide insight to many problems.

It is a common occurrence in business and industry today to receive a simulation report prepared by a potential vendor or outside supplier with little personal contact made. When information is received under these circumstances, the manager or person using the results must often ask, "How credible is this model?"

Since simulation work has become so widespread and many models are a first try effort by a layperson or part-time practitioner, the competency of the methodology used must be carefully examined. The manager, who is not a computer expert, must evaluate the results of a prepared simulation and needs to be able to distinguish between what is valid and what is less than valid. This can be difficult, especially if the only means of interpretation is through an examination of a report containing the results. The manager in this situation must often rely on intuition and personal judgment as a criterion for accepting or rejecting the findings.

To aid in the decision regarding credibility, there are six factors that can be pinpointed as symptoms of a sick simulation. If any of these symptoms are present, the credibility of the model should be questioned. The symptoms are as follows.

1. Inaccurate input data.
2. Improper run times.
3. Inconsistent output.
4. Vague references to assumptions.
5. Incomplete output.
6. No animation or detailed trace of events.

4.1 Sickness (1): Inaccurate Input Data

Input data can provide a good measure of a model's veracity. Simulation output is generally a function of the data that is input. Inputting vague data will produce vague results. Detailed input information can produce useful and detailed simulation output (Figure 4.1). Some examples of input data are:

- Speeds of automatic guided vehicles in a materials handling model.
- Distances between bus stops in a bus route simulation.
- Average time spent per transaction in an ATM simulation.

It can easily be understood how important input parameters are to a model. For instance, without knowing how long an average customer spends per transaction, an ATM simulation for the bank manager will have limited usefulness and very little credibility. A simulation can still be written and run and have its results reported, but these results will be flawed. To insure that this does not happen, it is essential that the input data be realistic, accurate, and relevant.

Realistic Input data must reflect what actually occurs in the system being modeled. Consider the case of a truck dock. When a truck arrives, a certain number of pallets will be unloaded. To be realistic, each pallet will require time to be removed from the truck. If this time is too short, the truck will be unloaded faster than possible in actual operation. This unrealistic time will allow a greater number of trucks into the dock area each shift and give flawed simulation results.

Accurate Supplied input data must be accurate. If a blueprint drawing of a factory floor is part of the input data for a manufacturing simulation, it is essential that the dimensions be correct. A common saying that can be applied to the simulation environment is GIGO (Garbage In—Garbage Out).

Relevant It is important that the data supplied for a simulation be relevant to what is being modeled. The less "excessive baggage" the better. A major task for the analyst is to sift through all the supplied information and try to decide what is necessary. By restricting data to what is needed in the model, a cleaner simulation will result.

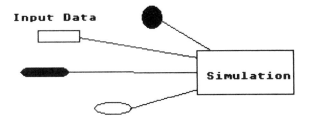

Figure 4.1 Accurate input data is needed.

4.2 Sickness (2): Improper Run Times

Another pitfall that can be identified as a symptom of a poor simulation is the use of improper run times (Law and Kelton, 1982).

Two types of simulation models can be developed with regard to run time: *terminating* and *steady state*. Terminating simulations run for a specific amount of time and are stopped by a natural event. An example would be a barber shop. It opens at 9:00 A.M. and closes at 5:00 P.M. each day. The model would be set up with a specific set of initial conditions to reflect the shop being vacant when opened in the morning. At 5:00 P.M., the closed sign would be posted and the customers already inside served. After completing their haircuts, the workday and model would terminate.

A steady-state simulation is a model of a system that runs indefinitely. An example is an ATM that is open for business all the time. There is no natural event that triggers the simulation's end.

In some cases, a situation that can be viewed as terminating might be modified and modeled as a steady-state system. An example might be an assembly line in a factory. Although the factory shuts down at 6:00 P.M. every evening, a steady-state simulation may be developed to estimate the characteristics of the line during peak production. In reality, the production line would run only eight hours. However, by analyzing a production as a steady-state operation over long periods of time, a maximum throughput figure independent of the initial conditions can be arrived at and studied. Depending on the information desired, an analyst may choose to use either terminating or steady-state simulation methodology.

When evaluating a simulation, it is important to identify the type of model that has been developed. The analyst must verify that steps have been taken to either set up proper initial conditions (in a terminating simulation) or to run the model long enough to override any effects the initial conditions might have on the results (in a steady-state simulation).[1] If this effort is not taken, the

---

[1]For a good discussion on how long to run a simulation see Chapter 8 of Law and Kelton (1982). In a simulation language such as GPSS/H, special provisions have been included that allow the modeler to reset all statistics being gathered after he/she is confident that a steady state has been reached.

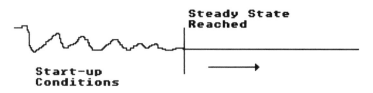

Figure 4.2 Model output.

simulation output will not contain a true representation of the system's operation (Figure 4.2).

4.3 Sickness (3): Inconsistent Output

Another symptom of a sick simulation is inconsistent output data. When reviewing a simulation report, challenge its findings. Use common sense to evaluate what is being presented. It is not unusual for computer-generated data to be accepted as gospel. Recognize that this output is not gospel but rather information created by a human using a tool. If the output does not agree with what is expected, look for reasons to explain the difference.

The process of making sure a model represents real system behavior closely enough to provide useful results is known as validation. Validation needs to be performed on all elements of a simulation. For instance, a person receiving a simulation report must examine the results for validity. Both magnitudes and statistical trends should be examined (Krepchin, 1988). Use some mathematical tools to calculate standard deviation. If the deviation is found to be quite high, or if one item seems to stick out like a statistical sore thumb, a validation problem could exist.

The inconsistent output might appear in a form such as this sample from an automatic guided vehicle simulation (Table 4.1).

The numbers for AGV #7 are a statistical sore thumb. By inspecting the chart, it can be seen that they are significantly different from the other statistics. A standard deviation calculated for the "Average Time per Load Move" category comes out to 492. This places the 2160 "Load Move Time" for AGV #7 more than two deviations from the mean.

What does a statistic such as this mean to the person analyzing the simulation output? It probably indicates that a flaw exists in the program. What may have happened in the model is an AGV picked up its final load and never arrived at its drop off position. AGV #7 is "wandering" through the simulation logic. The 90% figure in the "% Time Moving Loads" statistic indicates that the loads remained on the vehicle a high amount of time. This boosted the "Average Time per Load Move" statistic up to 2160 seconds.

Unless AGV #7 is performing a special function in the simulation (such as an isolated pick/drop) and is therefore not free to intermix with the other AGVs, this output would indicate a sick simulation. If the vehicle is performing a special

TABLE 4.1
Sample Output Statistics
from an Automatic Guided Vehicle Simulation

AGV #	# Loads Moved	% Time Moving Loads	Average Time per Load Move (sec)
1	21	55	754.28
2	19	54	818.53
3	24	64	768.00
4	19	49	742.74
5	19	56	848.84
6	20	58	835.20
7	12	90	2160.00
8	22	52	680.73
Average	19.5	59.8	951.04

function, it should be noted in the section of the report dealing with assumptions and facts.

4.4 Sickness (4): Vague References to Assumptions

An important part of any simulation report is the listing of the key assumptions that are made. The assumptions are constraints affecting the input data and processes used in the model (Figure 4.3).

A successful simulation requires a team approach (Higdon, 1988). A programmer will generally not have the expertise necessary to produce a model without relying on input from others. The data received by the modeler must be interpreted and reproduced in the form of code. For this reason it becomes very important to document the assumptions built into a model. The person using or evaluating the results of the simulation must insure that the ideas used are valid. If these assumptions are faulty or not clearly documented, confidence cannot be placed in the simulation.

Table 4.1 illustrates the important role that documentation can play in a simulation. Unless specifically stated, AGV #7 would be assumed to be performing the same tasks as the other vehicles. If it were performing a unique function that would cause its statistics to be different, a clearly stated assumption defining this function would need to be listed. Without this documentation, a person evaluating the simulation might consider the model to be invalid.

4.5 Sickness (5): Incomplete Output

One more symptom of a sick simulation is the dearth of complete output or conclusive results. If only selected portions of output data are made available, the possibility of overlooking some faulty logic is increased.

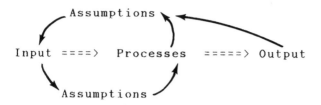

Figure 4.3 Assumptions affect modeling processes.

In order to provide useful information, a simulation must generate some output data. Output can take many forms as listed below.

1. *Statistics.* Simulation output can be interpreted through statistical analysis. Statistics can be used to measure the performance in one specific output category or to help decide which simulated system is best relative to some measure of performance (Law and Kelton, 1982).

2. *Answers to Questions.* Simulations are often written to address a specific question. Therefore the generated output may take the form of an answer. Some examples might be:

How Many?

(a) How many machines, conveyors, pallets, carts, AGVs, and stands are needed for the system to operate?
(b) How many employees are required for desired production?
(c) How many shifts should be operated?

Which?

(a) Which station is a bottleneck?
(b) Which process flow is best?
(c) Which schedule is best?
(d) Which product mix is best?

What?

(a) What is the maximum throughput possible in the system?
(b) What is the expected average throughput?

3. *Animation.* The graphic representation of a model as an animated image on a computer screen is a form of output that has recently been gaining in popularity.

4. *Data to be Further Processed.* A simulation can create data that is an intermediate step and will be processed further by another computer program. An example from the simulation of an automatic guided vehicle system might be the generation of a detailed trace of vehicle activity that can be read into a battery analysis program. This battery analysis program would "crunch" through the activities and recommend a vehicle battery type and size to optimize performance in the system.

A good format for simulation output statistics is as follows:

1. Construction of a report that summarizes the most pertinent facts in a concise, easy-to-read manner.
2. In the form of an appendix, generation of a detailed output document giving all supporting data in long form.

The ultimate goal of a simulation is not to create a model but to provide a step in the process of building or modifying a real world system. If the output is not properly documented, it will be impossible to insure that the simulated parameters can be incorporated into the real world system (McHaney, 1988).

4.6 Sickness (6): No Animation or Detailed Trace of Events

A growing part of the simulation environment is the use of animation tools to produce a dynamic representation of the system being modeled. Although animation is not a required part of simulation and many valid and useful simulations are developed without this feature, it does play a very helpful part in determining model veracity. Seeing is believing, and if a simulation can be watched, it can be understood much more easily.

Animation has several advantages (Grant and Weiner, 1986):

1. *It can provide a user friendly method for analyzing a simulation.* The system "comes to life" when animated. Processes that previously were only thought about can now be seen. No knowledge of computers is required to observe. System experts who are not computer literate can visually verify that the model works as it should.

2. *The ability to find and debug errors in the simulation is enhanced.* Subtle system problems can come to light in an animation. Quite often statistically insignificant deviations can be seen by the analyst and corrected before the results of a simulation are released.

3. *There is more of an impact watching the model operate as opposed to looking at printed statistics.* It can be very difficult to interpret the results of a simulation by only looking at printed statistics. An animation provides a method of presentation and can be used as a means of "selling" an idea.

Some dangers associated with the use of animation as a validation tool also exist. The glitter and excitement of watching a system perform on the screen might create some overconfidence. If it looks good, a manager might be led to think that only one short simulation run can provide all the answers (Wild and Port, 1987).

It is important to remember that a simulation is still a model, and all input data and assumptions need to be analyzed. It is very difficult to watch an animation and be aware of all the activity that is occurring, especially in the larger and more detailed systems.

If an animation is not available, it might be useful to try to obtain a detailed trace of several of the simulation entities taken as the model runs. This provides the same type of information yielded by an animation but not in a dynamic form. Data of this sort may be best taken at random intervals, since it may accumulate very quickly.

4.7 Summary

The best recommendation that can be given to a manager who needs to interpret simulation-generated data is to try to be involved from the start of the project. The best method to insure that the model being developed is accurate and valid is through constant communication and teamwork.

If it is not possible to participate in the development of a model, be aware of certain symptoms that signal what may be a sick simulation. These symptoms include:

1. Inaccurate input data.
2. Improper run times.
3. Inconsistent output.
4. Vague references to assumptions.
5. Incomplete output.
6. No animation or detailed trace of events.

It is important to remember that simulations are a tool and are subject to human error. Simulations are not an excuse to allow someone else to do the thinking. So do not accept the results without applying a little common sense to what is being presented. A better simulation will result and in turn a better system will be developed.

References and Reading

Grant, John W., and Steven A. Weiner. 1986. "Factors to Consider in Choosing a Graphically Animated Simulation System." *Industrial Engineering* (Aug.): 37–40, 65–68.

Henriksen, James O., and Robert C. Crain. 1989. *GPSS/H User's Reference Manual*, Third Edition. Wolverine Software Corporation, Annandale, Virginia.

Higdon, Jim. 1988. "Planning a Material Handling Simulation." *Industrial Engineering* (Nov.): 55–59.

Krepchin, Ira P. 1988. "Don't Simulate Without Validating." *Modern Materials Handling* (Jan.): 95–97.

Law, Averill M., and W. David Kelton. 1982. *Simulation Modeling and Analysis*. McGraw-Hill, New York.

McHaney, Roger. 1988. "Bridging the Gap : Tranferring Logic from a Simulation into an Actual System Controller." *Proc. 1988 Winter Simulation Conf.* (San Diego, Dec. 12–14). SCS, San Diego, pp. 583–590.

Wild, Jr., William G., and Otis Port. 1987. "This Video Game Is Saving Manufacturers Millions." *Business Week* (Aug. 17):82–84.

CHAPTER 5

The Professional Simulation Analyst

Growth in the simulation field has created a demand for personnel with qualifications and experience in the area of computer modeling. The opening of this relatively new career path has been attractive to a wide range of people. Scientists, mathematicians, statisticians, engineers, programmers, and a wide variety of other professionals have found challenging and rewarding work in the simulation field.

This chapter provides an overview of the simulation analyst's job, including what it involves, different issues that affect it, and other career-related factors deserving consideration.

5.1 Careers in the Simulation Field

Careers in the simulation field can be broken into two separate categories. The first category includes the simulation analyst and other people involved in the actual modeling process. The second category includes the people in the simulation software industry who write, sell, and support the tools that are used by the simulation analyst. The two groups are interdependent, so it is common to see individuals moving from one category to the other (see Figure 5.1).

5.1.1 The Simulation Analyst

The simulation analyst is defined as the individual responsible for all aspects of the modeling process. This person will be called on to perform a variety of different tasks that may include the following:

Detective Work Collecting simulation input data can be compared to detective work. The assumptions and data used in model creation must be gathered from a variety of disparate sources. Different individuals are usually experts

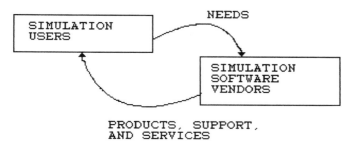

Figure 5.1 Simulation software industry and users share a close relationship.

on different parts of the system being modeled. It is up to the simulation analyst to create a "big picture" from all the smaller bits of data that are collected.

Computer Programming The process of writing and running a simulation is a form of computer programming. Models are designed, written, documented, and debugged just like any other computer program. This makes software and hardware knowledge a prerequisite for the simulation analyst. An equally important part of the analyst's job is being able to understand the thought process involved in creating a computer program.

Data Entry The simulation analyst will have to endure some drudgery from time to time. This may involve the entry of lengthy data bases or the process of typing in repetitive code. Although a task such as this requires little brain work, it can be a welcome respite from the intensive thinking required by other aspects of the analyst's job.

Experimentation When the model has been created, a series of runs that are designed to test different system parameters must be devised. The simulation analyst must be able to use judgment to determine the direction and method of carrying out this experimentation.

Statistical Analysis The simulation analyst must be able to don a statistician's cap occasionally. When model results are tabulated, they must be analyzed using the proper methods. To do this, simulations are often run for long periods of time and then estimates of the system's true behavior derived through the use of statistics.

Report Creation After a simulation has been completed, the analyst must be able to draw on technical writing skills to prepare a report detailing the results and methodology used during the process. It is essential that complete and detailed information be provided to the simulation users. Many times these reports will include computer-generated charts and graphs.

Communication One of the most important skills that a simulation analyst can possess is the ability to communicate effectively. Communication is required throughout the entire modeling process. The analyst must communicate with system experts while gathering model input data. Model assumptions and ideas must be generated and discussed with system users. Finally, the model results must be communicated. This is often done with a formal presentation.

The job of a simulation analyst is not cut and dried. It requires a dynamic person who is a jack-of-all-trades. This person must be able to apply common sense and experience to a wide variety of tasks and produce answers to very complex questions.

Modeling carries with it a tremendous responsibility. The information produced by a simulation often forms the basis for multimillion dollar decisions. The simulation field offers great challenges and provides great rewards. It is very satisfying to see an implemented system that has been heavily influenced by your simulation effort performing as modeled.

5.1.2 The Simulation Support Industry

An entire industry has sprung up from the demand for simulation software and services. Within this industry are programmers, engineers, and marketing personnel, as well as other positions common to every business. Many people move between simulation analyst jobs and the simulation support industry. They bring with them fresh perspectives on what software is needed and how it should be implemented.

5.2 Teamwork Approach to Simulation

One of the key aspects in conducting a successful simulation project is teamwork (Higdon, 1988). Due to the increasingly complex nature of many such projects, a variety of people need to become involved and act as a part of the team (Figure 5.2). A simulation team requires a free exchange of information throughout the life of a project and should at a minimum involve the following people:

Management In order to conduct a simulation study, management needs to provide the necessary resources and support. This includes the proper equipment,

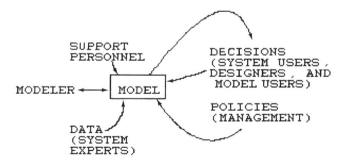

Figure 5.2 Modeling requires teamwork.

personnel, and budget, as well as advocating policies that promote the simulation process. In companies that lack a management commitment to the simulation effort, there is little chance that model development will be successful.

Simulation Analyst The simulation analyst needs to act as a team leader by coordinating the project and providing a framework that facilitates team communication. Data from all parts of the system and from different members of the team must be compiled into an overall picture by the analyst.

System Experts People who know how the modeled system (or parts of the modeled system) will operate are of essential importance to the simulation team. It is up to system experts to provide realistic input data and help validate the model. They can identify feasible alternatives that need to be tested and screen out unrealistic ideas. System experts might be engineers, system designers, potential users, or anyone else possessing knowledge pertaining to the system.

Model Users Model users play an important role on the simulation team. They will be using the simulation to aid in the decision-making process, and because of this they need to be involved from the very beginning of a project. The simulation analyst must be aware of the user's objectives and requirements prior to starting a simulation and should maintain close ties throughout the life of a project.

System Users Users of the system being modeled need to be active members of the simulation team. They will be able to provide input as to their preferences on system operation and therefore have a stake in the overall success of the project. In addition, they will receive an education on system operation. After the system has been installed, they may be able to provide feedback to the simulation team. This feedback can be a means of validating the existing model and will help make future models even better.

Support Personnel Other people playing roles on the simulation team might be draftsmen, data entry clerks, programmers, secretaries, or anyone else performing specific tasks for the project. It is important to make sure that even the small contributions to the process are recognized as important and treated

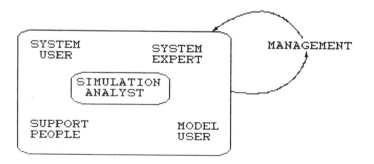

Figure 5.3 Simulation team.

with respect. Many projects are successful due to the efforts of the "small guy."

A simulation project must be a team effort to be successful (Figure 5.3). The simulation analyst is largely responsible for forming a team and promoting communication within the group. This analyst should not act as a lone ranger and attempt to develop simulation assumptions without the inputs and opinions of experts. A sure path to the failure of a simulation project is the isolated development of a model.

The following example of the Drak-Co company illustrates the team effort concept.

Drak-Co's Simulation Team

Drak-Co is an industrial materials handling equipment vendor. They work very closely with their clients to develop innovative solutions to complex problems. Much of this analysis work is done using computer simulation. In the ten years Drak-Co has been using modeling, an informal *simulation team* that contributes greatly to the success of their efforts has evolved. Although the team rarely meets as a single unit, all members work very closely. The following people are routinely involved on the simulation team.

Simulation Analyst The simulation analyst leads the team and coordinates the flow of information between different members. The analyst is ultimately responsible for model development.

Customer Drak-Co's customers usually provide at least two members on the simulation team. These members can be categorized as system users or system experts. The system users are the personnel who will eventually be maintaining and operating the materials handling equipment. It is important to get their ideas so that they will have a personal stake in the success of the project. In addition, information flow will start their education process. The system experts are manufacturing engineers or other individuals that can provide the simulation team with valuable data and a means of validating the model.

Sales The sales force at Drak-Co plays an important role on the simulation team. They gather data from customers and help them arrive at a preliminary system design. The salesperson will often have the best understanding of the objectives that are to be met by the system being modeled.

Estimating Drak-Co's estimators work closely with the rest of the simulation team. They take responsibility for insuring that the system designed is feasible in terms of cost, delivery date, and functionality. They often play the role of system experts as well.

In-House Engineers The internal engineering staff performs a consulting role. They provide the simulation team with data concerning the operation of Drak-Co's equipment. They also offer different ideas as to how the materials handling systems might be implemented.

Support Personnel Draftsmen, secretaries, and data entry clerks contribute their efforts to the simulation team.

Management Due to the ongoing success of Drak-Co's modeling efforts, management has made sure that the simulation team is provided with all necessary resources including equipment, education, and budget. In addition, certain members of the management team will take time to review problem systems and may provide some innovative solutions.

Because of the participation of many people and their spirit of cooperation and communication, Drak-Co has been able to produce many top-notch simulations.

5.3   Simulation Analyst versus System Expert

Originally, simulation was intended to be an engineer's tool. The idea was that an engineer could sit down and use a model to help design the system that was assigned. This approach to modeling is found in some applications, but more often an engineer works with a simulation analyst to produce a model. The reasons for this occurrence are:

1. The engineer does not have the time.
2. The engineer would use simulation so infrequently that it would not be worth spending the time to learn.
3. The engineer is not comfortable as a computer programmer.

Because of the separation between system expert and simulation analyst, some confusion may occasionally develop. First, the simulation analyst may make assumptions that are not really feasible. Second, the system expert may falsely assume that the analyst is aware of certain information.

All problems that arise because of this separation can be avoided by making proper use of the team approach to modeling and through careful communication.

5.4   Simulation and Quality

The 1980s may be remembered as the decade that Japan assaulted the shores of the United States with a flood of imports. Corporations in the United States ranging from members of the steel industry to high-tech computer firms were forced to examine what was making so many Japanese firms successful. It was discovered that Japan had streamlined their manufacturing and clerical operations with just-in-time inventory techniques, new manufacturing practices, and a strong emphasis on quality management. Computer simulation plays a role in all these areas.

5.4.1 What Is Quality Management?

Japan's most successful weapon in their economic resurgence probably has been their use of state-of-the-art quality management techniques. Present day Japanese quality management originated through an evolutionary process beginning with the birth of statistical quality control in the United States.

In 1924, W. A. Shewhart of Bell Laboratories, developed what is considered to be the beginning of statistical quality control. Later in the same decade, H. F. Dodge and H. G. Romig, both of Bell Laboratories, developed the area of acceptance sampling as a substitute for 100% inspection. Although these techniques were developed in the 1920s, it was not until World War II that quality control found widespread acceptance (Besterfield, 1979).

In the 1950s and 1960s, quality control developed into quality assurance. This involved auditing vendors, product reliability, quality cost analysis, and quality training. In the 1970s, total quality control (TQC) was the new catchphrase used to recognize the advancements made in the field of quality. Armand V. Feigenbaum is credited with developing this quality system in which all internal and external transactions must be identified and optimized (Feigenbaum, 1983). Statistical methods were used to spell out the role of marketing functions. The Japanese later applied this methodology to nonmanufacturing areas such as data processing and office work. This was called Japanese total quality control (JTQC).

In the 1970s and 1980s, total quality control was updated by the work of several quality theorists, including W. Edward Deming and Phil Crosby. Their newly developed techniques define an implementation of quality called quality management.

Quality management was quickly adopted by the Japanese and used successfully as a means of insuring that quality was built into their products. It took the United States longer to realize the potential benefits offered by quality management techniques, but by the mid-1980s most major corporations were involved in some type of quality program.

5.4.2 Simulation as a Quality Management Tool

Both Deming and Crosby stress that one of the keys to economic success is to *build in* quality. Finding and correcting mistakes after a product has been built is not good enough. Rework costs can be high, and valuable customer relations can be negatively impacted by the resulting schedule delays (Gitlow, 1987; Crosby, 1979).

A need exists for tools to insure, prior to construction and installation, that products will work properly. For the manufacturers and designers of automated factories, robotics, or other systems, a means of implementing quality management can be through the use of computer simulation. The construction of a model will provide the following benefits as recommended by most quality management programs:

1. Detection of unforeseen problems prior to the design being finalized.
2. Prevention of errors in system design and construction.
3. Providing additional knowledge about the system being designed.
4. Encouraging communication.
5. Helping to *build in* quality.

Computer simulation can play an important role in helping make quality management techniques work.

5.5   Ethics in Simulation

All designers, managers, programmers, and engineers must at some point in their careers face an issue that requires some amount of ethical or moral judgment. The simulation analyst also faces similar issues.

A great deal of trust is usually put into a simulation study. The analyst must produce the answers to questions that can involve large amounts of money, prestige, and whether or not jobs will be bought by prospective customers. Due to the nature of the job itself, the analyst will occasionally be faced with dilemmas similar to the following. (These scenarios are not based on specific instances; they are all hypothetical.)

Scenario #1

Your boss comes to you and says, "If this simulation proves that our new concept will work, the buyer will select us as the vendor for sure. This contract could mean millions in new revenue and a dozen new jobs. Plus, it could mean big raises for both you and I!"

After completion, simulation proves that the system falls just short of the desired performance. Your boss is informed and says, "Find a way to make the system work and do it by Friday." Friday comes around and the system still does not work (albeit marginally). Do you say it will work (and hope to find a way to make the system more efficient before installation) or do you stand your ground, say it does not work, and take a chance of losing the job for your company?

Scenario #2

The designer of a project would like the system to operate in a certain way. She asks you to "color" some of the simulation data to give her argument additional weight when the concept is presented to her manager. "It won't really change anything," she says, "it will just make it easier to justify my idea." What should you do?

Scenario #3

A salesman reported to the simulation department that all other vendors bidding on a hotly contested job were proposing that eight robotic workstations be used.

An in-house simulation study revealed that only five were required to produce the number of parts needed by the potential customer. The salesman suggests a simulation report be produced recommending the use of seven stations when only five are really necessary. Our company would still come in at a lower price than the competition. However, we would be quietly making some extra money by selling seven stations rather than five. Do you go along with this request and help generate the extra business for your company?

Scenario #4

A potential customer's rush order is waiting for a simulation study to be completed. After getting the base model running, but before validation and proper output analysis can take place, your boss comes in and tells you to publish a report. You voice your objections and say that model validation and the proper analysis of the output will require several more days of work. Your boss replies that she does not care and wants whatever you have completed now. What should you do?

To help deal with situations such as these, which are bound to arise, it is important for the simulation analyst to adopt a set of guiding ethics. The simulation analyst, as any scientific experimenter, must be able to have unbiased opinions. Simulations should be conducted as experiments and the results presented as they are observed. The simulation analyst is often put in the position of representing both in-house interests and the interests of a client. It is important to maintain a balance and try to remain impartial in the presentation of facts.

The following list contains advice concerning ethics in simulation. It is compiled from the opinions of several seasoned simulation analysts.

1. Simulation should never be used to misrepresent data.
2. Simulation should never be used to mislead or as a means of false justification.
3. The simulation analyst should always conduct experimentation objectively.
4. The simulation analyst should always be truthful in reporting.
5. Do not let your own optimism or pessimism color output reports.
6. If a mistake is made, the analyst should face up to it immediately; do not give in to the temptation of "covering it up."
7. If a system marginally does not make the required production rate, tell your customer the results and the margin of error and then help them decide if the results are close enough to warrant the risk of producing with this system.
8. When a model shows that a system will not work, agree to spend extra time verifying that the model is accurate.
9. Always work closely and openly with the users of your model.
10. Remember, it will be very hard to explain why a "supposedly valid" model meets production when the real world system is found not to work.

Fixing a system after installation is very expensive in terms of both money and your career.

By using a code of ethics, a simulation analyst is able to develop a set of guidelines that will help in making difficult decisions. Although the courses of action decided on may not always be popular, they will be consistent and defendable. You will gain respect for your professionalism.

5.6 Education in Simulation

Nearly all simulation analysts receive their formal education in fields such as industrial engineering, management science, computer science, mathematics, and statistics. Most did not train specifically for the simulation field. Rather, they were assigned simulation projects on the job and entered the field that way.

The five most common methods of receiving education in the simulation field are on-the-job training, professional seminars and conferences, university courses, special university curriculums, and self-study.

On-the-Job Training There is no substitute for on-the-job training in the simulation field. A formal education can help the analyst prepare for the technical portions of the job, but dealing with the people and politics involved in a simulation study requires firsthand experience. A simulation analyst often relies on judgment in deciding the level of necessary detail in a model, determining how many experiments to run, conceptualizing what type of model to use, and in making a number of other subjective decisions. The ability to use this judgment wisely comes through on-the-job training and experience.

Professional Seminars and Conferences Chapter 2 mentions the Winter Simulation Conference, which is sponsored by the Society for Computer Simulation (SCS). In addition to this conference, dozens of others are held each year. Many are dedicated to specific applications of simulation. Conferences such as these are an excellent means of education. Together with the conferences are many professional development seminars. These are offered by universities, consultants, or the vendors of software products. A listing of many seminars and conferences can be obtained from the SCS (address given in Chapter 2).

University Courses The business, industrial engineering, or computer science departments at many universities offer simulation courses. These courses will usually cover a specific simulation language and use it to provide an introduction to the simulation field.

Special University Curriculums Several universities have begun offering specific curriculums for the simulation field. Many of these curriculums can be classified as a concentration for a business or an industrial engineering major. However, some universities now offer a specific degree in simulation. An example of this is a Master of Science program offered at the University of Central Florida.[1]

Self-Study Another popular method of receiving education in the simulation field is to use the wide variety of published resources. Books, magazines, newsletters, textbooks, users manuals, and tutorial software packages are all readily available.

Education cannot be stressed enough in a young, growing, and changing field like computer simulation. It is very important to stay current by taking classes, attending seminars and conferences, and keeping up to date on literature. This will help insure professional success.

5.7 Summary

Professionals in the simulation field are very much in demand. They are typically employed to help make complex decisions and reduce the risks involved with installing expensive and complicated systems. Because of the responsibility assumed by these individuals, it is necessary that they recognize the important roles that teamwork, ethics, education, professionalism, and quality play in their job functions.

References and Reading

Besterfield, D. 1979. *Quality Control*. Prentice-Hall, Englewood Cliffs, New Jersey.

Crosby, P. 1979. *Quality is Free*. McGraw Hill, New York.

Feigenbaum, Armand V. 1983. *Total Quality Control*. McGraw-Hill, New York.

Gitlow, H. 1987. *Guide to Quality and Competitive Position*. Prentice-Hall, Englewood Cliffs, New Jersey.

Goodpastor, Kenneth. 1984. *Ethics in Management*. Harvard Business School, Boston.

Higdon, Jim. 1988. "Planning a New Materials Handling System." *Industrial Engineering* (Nov.): 55–59.

McLeod, John. 1982. *Computer Modeling and Simulation: Principles of Good Practice* **10**(2). Simulation Councils, Inc., La Jolla, California.

---

[1]Master of Science Program in Simulation Systems, Department of Industrial Engineering and Management Systems, University of Central Florida, P.O. Box 25000, Orlando, Florida 32816–0993.

CHAPTER 6

Building a Simulation the Right Way

This chapter is aimed at the person who will be working on a simulation project. This involvement should not be thought to start and end with the process of coding a model. Instead, much more is involved. System definition, model development, verification, experimentation, and insuring that the logic developed in the model can be used in actual system implementation are some examples of the many components present in the life cycle of a simulation project.

In order to insure that a simulation project is successful, several events need to occur before any other work begins.

- The customer of the modeling project needs to define objectives of the study. A simulation's customer may be someone external to the company, another person within the company, or the actual simulation analyst. The objectives describe what questions the simulation needs to answer.
- A means for gathering information needs to be established. Support from management and other individuals needs to be present to facilitate the simulation process. Simulation requires teamwork.

Table 6.1 breaks down the responsibilities of the simulation analyst and the consumer in a typical simulation project.

6.1 Defining the System

After the objective of a simulation study has been stated and the resources allocated, the system to be modeled must be defined. In Chapter 1, a system was defined as a set of components or elements that are related to each other to create a connected whole. The relationship between the elements comprising the system

TABLE 6.1
Division of Responsibility in a Typical Simulation Project

	Simulation Customer	Simulation Analyst
Objectives	X	
Communication	X	X
System Definition	X	X
Model Development		X
Report of Results		X
Use of Results	X	

are essential in predicting the behavior of the whole. If the system is reduced to a group of independent subsystems, each can be studied separately but the true characteristics of the system may be lost. The interaction between various system elements are often so complex that the system must be viewed as a whole.

An example of a system with complex interacting elements is an orchestra (Figure 6.1). Various subsystems consisting of groups of musicians playing similar instruments are related to each other to create a connected whole. The stringed instruments can be viewed as a subsystem. So can the musicians playing only the first violin part. Percussion, brass, clarinets, flutes, cellos, timpani, french horns, and oboes can all be defined as subsystems. The various groups of musicians are dependent on their musical score and the direction of a conductor to achieve an overall goal. Each subsystem can be removed from the system to be studied and analyzed. But it would become very difficult if not impossible to predict the overall behavior of the system in this way.

A system can be broken into its individual elements structurally. However, it cannot be broken into individual elements and still maintain its functionality. For example, a computer system can be studied only in terms of its components such as microchips, wires, capacitors, resistors, transistors, and electricity. If such a

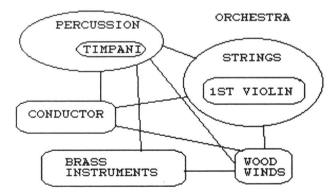

Figure 6.1 Example of a complex system.

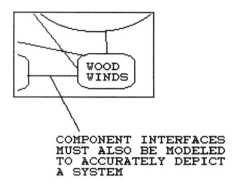

COMPONENT INTERFACES
MUST ALSO BE MODELED
TO ACCURATELY DEPICT
A SYSTEM

Figure 6.2 System interactions.

study were completed, the true characteristics of a computer would be lost. The crucial interaction between the individual components would not be present.

Within the context of a simulation project, the importance of viewing the system as a whole is quite evident. In order to maintain an accurate representation, all interactions between the various components must be included in the model (Figure 6.2). In addition, the components and their interrelationships and the system's environment and its boundary needs to be defined (Figure 6.3).

The environment lies outside the system, influencing its behavior but is not controlled by it in any way. A system's boundary is the line that separates the system from its environment. In the development of a simulation, influences of the environment must be taken into consideration (Neelamkavil, 1987).

The example of an assembly line in a United Auto Workers (UAW) unionized plant can be used to illustrate environment and boundary. The system to be modeled is an auto assembly line. The system boundary encloses the materials handling system, the assembly operation and operators, and the product moving through the system. The environment that exerts influence on the system would

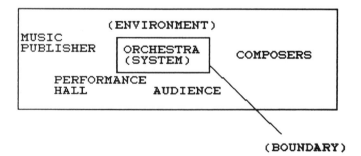

Figure 6.3 Boundary and environments of a system.

be the set of rules that the UAW operates under. The coffee break times, lunch breaks, shift changes, and holidays are all examples of environmental influences.

The division between system and environment is often a very delicate line to define. The aptitude for defining systems, subsystems, and environment is an acquired skill that might take an analyst years to refine. This skill falls more under the *art of simulation* side of the debate discussed in Section 3.4.

6.2 Model Scope and Scaling

Following definition of the system, the model's scope and its level of necessary detail need to be determined. Model scope is defined as that portion of the system that will be represented by the model. The necessary level of detail is a determination of how closely the model needs to emulate the real world system to still provide the required information.

Since a model is an approximation of the system being studied, it is not always best to develop a full-scale representation. If the system were modeled down to the finest detail, excessive amounts of time and energy would be expended with minimal gain in useful information. The law of diminishing returns can be applied to the level of detail versus gain in knowledge (Figure 6.4).

The best approach to model development is to incorporate the least amount of detail while still maintaining veracity of the simulation. This process, called scaling (Figure 6.5), is somewhat subjective in nature and is a skill that will develop as the simulation analyst becomes more experienced. Different analysts will build their models with varying levels of detail (again strengthening the *simulation is an art* argument).

Another common technique can be used as a means of keeping a model's size manageable. This is called partitioning (Smith, 1989). Partitioning is the study of the individual subsystems making up a system. Although this technique can work very well under certain circumstances (when little interaction occurs between the

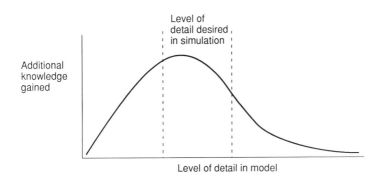

Figure 6.4 Level of detail versus knowledge gained (law of diminishing returns applies after a certain point).

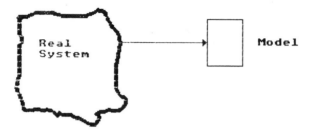

Figure 6.5 Scaling makes a simulation more manageable.

subsystems), caution should be exercised to avoid the pitfalls mentioned in Section 6.1.

Partitioning can be either serial or parallel. Serial partitioning will break a system into separate successive stages for modeling. The outputs from each stage will become the inputs for the next stage. If the interaction between the stages is unidirectional, serial partitioning will work quite well. If the interaction is bidirectional and complex with an interdependency between the systems, partitioning should not be used. Instead, the system should be modeled as a single unit.

As an example, consider the following case:

Computer Manufacturing Company: Serial Partitioning of a Model

A large manufacturer of microcomputers wants to develop a model of its manufacturing and shipping operations. The analyst assigned to the project decides that a single model would be too large and would require long periods of run time on their computer system. The analyst decides that as a method of simplification serial partitioning should be used. The first step in using this technique is to identify a natural break in the system's operation. After collecting data, the analyst finds that all manufactured computers are stored in a warehouse and when ordered by a customer, the computers are removed and proceed through the packaging and shipping operations. The point when the computers leave manufacturing and enter the warehouse is a natural break. The interaction is one-way and could be used as a place to break the model into two separate serial portions. The outputs from the manufacturing model can be used as inputs to the storage and shipping model.

Parallel partitioning can be used where a set of independent, identical processes are replicated a number of times. These processes can be modeled by a single entity having the capacity of simultaneously performing duties that in reality would be occurring in parallel.

Defining which parts of the system need to be modeled is very important to the success of a simulation project. Modeling in too much detail leads to excessive development time. Too little detail may result in a model that does not realistically predict actual world behavior. The analyst must use caution during this part of the simulation process to insure that the model accurately reflects system operation.

6.3 Modeling Views

Development of a discrete event simulation requires that a system be viewed in a manner that will facilitate the modeling process. Nearly all available simulation software products use one of three approaches: event orientation, process orientation, and activity orientation.

6.3.1 Event Orientation

Using this modeling approach requires the simulation analyst to identify all different events that can occur in the system and determine what effects these events will have. An event is defined as any instantaneous occurrence that may change the state of a system. The following example illustrates an event orientation approach used in defining a system.

The 21-Club

Mr. George, a local nightclub owner, likes to spend his free time dabbling with modeling on his home computer. He recently opened the 21-Club, a dance place aimed at attracting the young college-age crowd. He did not know whether one or two doormen should be used for checking identifications and stamping hands, so he decided to develop an event-oriented model to help make the determination. Mr. George identified the following key system events:

1. *Customer Arrival.* If the doorman is occupied, the person arriving will wait in queue. Otherwise, the person uses the services of the doorman.

2. *Customer Service Complete.* Following completion of service by the doorman, the customer is either free to enter the establishment or banned from entrance. The next person in queue can be serviced. If the queue is empty, the doorman becomes idle.

Mr. George knew that if either one of these events occur, the system's state would change. Having identified the key events, he was ready to begin coding the model using the event orientation approach.

6.3.2 Process Orientation

A process is a time-ordered sequence of interrelated events separated by passages of time. This sequence will describe the entire experience of a transaction as it moves through a system (Law and Larmey, 1984). When the process orientation approach is used, the modeler will define repeatable sequences of steps, each representing an event or a series of events. These sequences of steps can be represented by a network or flow diagram. Objects that may be required by a transaction during its movement through the sequence of steps are defined as resources. The following process orientation example takes another look at the 21-Club.

The 21-Club: A Second Look

After contemplating the use of the event orientation approach, Mr. George decided that maybe he would be better off to model the 21-Club's doorman using the process orientation approach. After some research and careful thought, he developed a diagram (Figure 6.6).

A customer entering the 21-Club is considered to be a transaction and the doorman a permanent resource. The process routine describes the experience of the customer from the time he or she attempts to enter the 21-Club until the time of being admitted or turned aside. Time passes while the doorman is checking identification and stamping the customer's hand. Time may also pass while the customer is waiting in queue for the doorman resource to become available.

6.3.3 Activity Orientation

The activity orientation approach is not commonly used in most U.S. simulation software products. It involves describing a system in terms of the conditions necessary to either start or stop an activity. The beginning or conclusion of an activity will have an effect on the system state. Activities may require specified amounts of time for completion or may be brought to completion by meeting certain logical conditions.

6.4 Scientific Method Approach to Modeling

Nearly every discipline that employs research as a tool looks to the scientific method as a means of organization. The simulation field is no exception. The following steps make up the scientific method:

1. Definition of the problem.
2. Formation of a hypothesis.

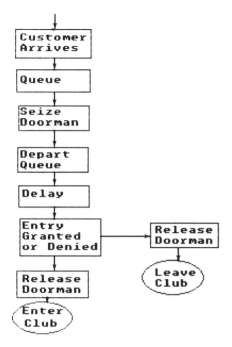

Figure 6.6 21-Club model logic.

3. Testing of hypothesis by experimentation.
4. Tabulation of results.
5. Drawing conclusions from results.

The scientific method can be used as a guideline for setting up simulation experiments. The correspondence between simulation methodology and the scientific method can be seen in Table 6.2.

TABLE 6.2
Scientific Methods in Simulation

Step in Scientific Method	Corresponding Simulation Activity
Problem Definition	Setting simulation objectives
Formulating Hypothesis	Defining model scope and detail Selecting modeling view Selection of language and coding model
Experimentation	Running model
Results	Obtain data from model
Conclusions	Using statistics and judgment to evaluate

6.5 Model Inputs

Valid input data forms the basis for an accurate simulation. Remember the old saying *"garbage in—garbage out"* (Figure 6.7). A simulation will be no better than the information and assumptions it contains. Many projects have no chance for success since the input data used is not reliable.

Input data can take many forms. It can be quantitative or qualitative. Quantitative input data takes the form of numeric values. Examples would be vehicle speeds, number of cars passing a particular point on a freeway, number of barbers in a barbershop, acceleration rate of a rocket, or the service time of the doorman at the 21-Club. Qualitative input data is a more difficult parameter to measure. It represents the algorithms used to perform certain logical operations. In the context of the 21-Club, a qualitative example would be the fact that customers unable to be immediately serviced enter a queue. If an improper assumption had been made and the majority of the customers left if unable to receive immediate service, then the model's current queuing assumption would be invalid.

Input data can be obtained in many ways (Figure 6.8). Examples of several methods are:

Observation A good method of obtaining input data is through observation. If a model were to be made of a busy intersection in a growing city's business district, the best method of obtaining input data would be through direct observation and measurement of the traffic flows. The data could be used as an input to the model or statistically analyzed and an appropriate input probability distribution chosen. (For a good discusssion on input probability distribution selection, see Chapter 5 of Law and Kelton (1982.)

Estimation If the system to be modeled does not exist, it may be necessary to estimate input data. Although somewhat less than scientific, estimation may still help provide valuable insight concerning a system's operation.

Interpolation If a similar system exists, its input data can be observed and interpolated for entry into a model sharing the same characteristics. An example of this situation may be found in a machine shop. Five years ago, a numeric controlled (NC) machine was purchased for use. It was able to keep up with required production rates until the present year when sales unexpectedly skyrocketed. In light of these changes, management was trying to decide if a different NC machine should be acquired. The manufacturer of the NC machine was contacted and recommended a new model that was able to process one-third more material than the existing machine. By using data based on the NC machine in current use, interpolated values were derived and the expected operation of the new machine modeled.

Expert Opinions Many times the only input data available will be based on the opinion of an expert. For example, an engineer who has been responsible for the operation of a warehouse over the last 20 years may be able to provide

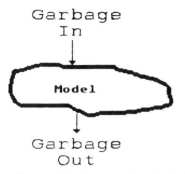

Figure 6.7 Input data is the basis for a valid simulation.

data to be used in simulating a shipping dock that will be added to the building. Although no real data can be collected, the engineer has an understanding of how the system will need to operate.

Projections Model input data is commonly derived from future projections. Recently, a Japanese auto plant has been enjoying great success in marketing its products. They have kept data depicting their growth rate over the last seven years. Next year they are forecasting a required increase in production of 21% to keep up with their expected sales. By using this projection, they are able to create input data to drive an assembly line simulation they maintain.

After input data has been collected, two approaches can be taken to use the information in the simulation. The first approach is to use the real data "as is." This technique is known as a trace simulation. The second approach is to fit a standard statistical distribution to the empirical data. The key to this procedure is to find a probability distribution with random samples that will be indistinguishable from the collected input data. Goodness-of-fit tests can be used in this process. Section 6.6 explores several common goodness-of-fit tests. After the probability curve has been chosen, a random number generator or a pseudorandom number generator can be used to draw samples from the distribution and drive the simulation.

Figure 6.8 Valid methods of collecting input data.

6.6 Statistical Methods and Input Data

Although empirical or "as is" data can be used for simulation input, the recommended approach (Law and Kelton, 1982) is to try to fit a theoretical distribution to the data. If observed data is used, the simulation will never be exercised beyond that which was collected. In other words, no extreme situations will occur in the model. By using a theoretical distribution, the rare large or small samples will occur a percentage of the time (Figure 6.9).

When an input variable is approximated with a probability distribution, the simulation analyst must be certain that the distribution does in fact represent the variable accurately. The first step in this process is to determine the specific form of the probability distribution to be used. Some examples of different probability curves are normal, gamma, exponential, and Weibull (Figure 6.10).

In order to choose the proper distribution, the statistical properties of the variable must be determined. Initially, this can be done with a visual inspection of the data in histogram form (Figure 6.11). To confirm the visual inspection, a goodness-of-fit test can be used. Two common methods of confirmation are the chi-square test and the Kolmogorov–Smirnov test.

6.6.1 Chi-Square Test

The chi-square test can be used to determine whether the frequencies of a collected set of data match a set of theoretical or expected frequencies. When the chi-square test is being used, degrees of freedom, or number of variables that can vary freely, must be calculated. The following formula can be used:

$$D = g - m$$

where D is the number of degrees of freedom; g the number of groups or frequencies in the collected data sample; and m the number of constant values used as constraints in finding the expected frequencies of the sample.

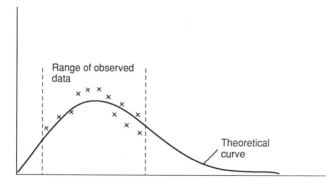

Figure 6.9 Use of theoretical curves exercises a model outside the range of observed data.

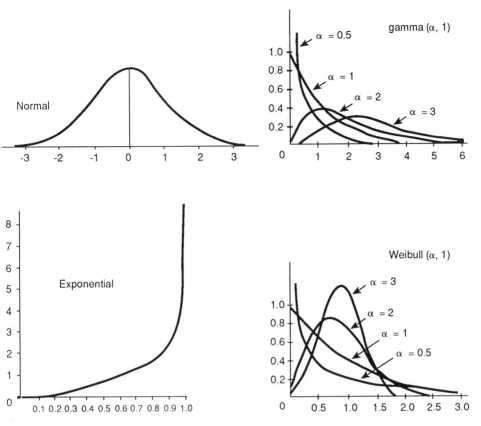

Figure 6.10 Examples of probability distributions.

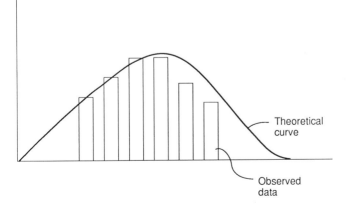

Figure 6.11 Theoretical curves can be determined through a "goodness-of-fit" test.

In applying the chi-square test, some important properties must be understood:

1. The mode of each distribution, where degrees of freedom are equal to or greater than 2, is equal to $D - 2$. For example, if D is equal to 7, then the mode will equal $(7 - 2)$ or 5.

2. The chi-square curve can be calculated using this formula:

$$Y = 1/(D/2 - 1)! * 2^{(-D/2)} * (\chi^2)^{((D/2) - 1)} * e^{(-\chi^2/2)}$$

where Y is the height of the chi-square curve; D the number of degrees of freedom; χ^2 the value input for chi-square; and e is equal to 2.71828 (base of natural logarithms).

3. As the degrees of freedom increase, the chi-square curve becomes more symmetrical.

4. As a safety factor in applying the chi-square test, the theoretical frequency in each class should be no smaller than five. If it is smaller, several classes should be combined to form a larger group.

21-Club Interarrival Time Distribution

Mr. George wanted to make sure his simulation used the proper probability distribution to model people arriving at the 21-Club. He traveled to a nearby city and observed arrivals at a club very similar to the one he envisioned opening soon. He collected the following data (Table 6.3).

Although Mr. George knew that interarrival times frequently occur as a Poisson distribution, his plot visually appeared to look more like a normal distribution (Figure 6.12). He decided to apply a chi-square test to verify his

TABLE 6.3
Customer Arrivals at a Club
Similar to the 21-Club

Classes of Customer Interarrival Times (minutes)	Frequency (f)
Under 0.5	0
0.5–3.5	2
3.5–6.5	6
6.5–9.5	18
9.5–12.5	14
12.5–15.5	4
15.5–18.5	6
18.5 and above	0

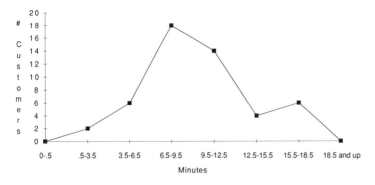

Figure 6.12 21-Club customer interarrival times.

hunch. Mr. George calculated the sample's mean (Table 6.4). The sample's standard deviation was calculated as shown in Table 6.5.

Mr. George set up a table to help him calculate expected or theoretical frequencies for each interarrival rate class (based on the normal curve) (Table 6.6). In Table 6.6 the columns represent the following:

- Column (1) gives each of the eight classes a reference number.
- Column (2) defines the upper and lower limits of each class.
- Column (3) shows the deviation of each class limit from the sample mean. (*Note:* The sample's mean is being used to estimate the population's mean for this example.)

TABLE 6.4
Sample Mean Calculation

Classes of Customer Interarrival Times (minutes)	Frequency (f)	Mid-Point of Class (X)	$f * X$
Under 0.5	0	—	—
0.5–3.5	2	2	4
3.5–6.5	6	5	30
6.5–9.5	18	8	144
9.5–12.5	14	11	154
12.5–15.5	4	14	56
15.5–18.5	6	17	102
18.5 and above	0	—	—
Total	50		490

$$\bar{X} = f * X/n = 490/50 = 9.8.$$

- Column (4) expresses deviation from the mean for each class limit in terms of standard deviation. (*Note:* The sample's standard deviation is being used as an estimate of the population's standard deviation.)
- Column (5) approximates the area under the normal curve from its maximum ordinate to the calculated ordinate z. See Table 6.7 for the area under the normal curve.
- Column (6) multiplies the value in column (5) by sample size of 50 to yield the theoretical frequency of occurrence expected in a normal population. This value is based on the area from the maximum ordinate to the calculated ordinate z.
- Column (7) expresses the expected frequency for each individual class.
- Column (8) expresses the observed frequency for each individual class.

Mr. George was now ready to test his hypothesis using the chi-square test. This hypothesis is written as:

Ho: *No significant difference exists between the distribution represented by the normal curve and the data that was collected at a club similar to the 21-Club.*

He noticed that expected frequency in several classes contained was less than five. He combined these in the manner shown in Table 6.8.

With the new class groupings, the chi-square statistic can be calculated using the following formula:

$$\chi^2 = \sum_{n=1}^{g} ((O - E)^2/E)$$

where O is the observed class frequency and E is the expected class frequency. Table 6.9 summarizes the calculations Mr. George completed.

He looked at a 0.05 level with one degree of freedom (Table 6.10), and found that the difference would be significant if the chi-square value were above 3.841. Since it was calculated to be 1.90, which is less than 3.841, it falls into the acceptance region. Mr. George's initial hunch was correct, and the data he collected can be estimated with a normal distribution.

6.6.2 Kolmogorov–Smirnov Test

The Kolmogorov–Smirnov test is another method of verifying goodness-of-fit between the distribution function of the collected data and a theoretical probability distribution function. It has some advantages over the chi-square test:

1. It does not require data to be grouped in any way. This keeps data from being lost.
2. No interval specification or class breakdown is necessary.

Kolmogorov–Smirnov also has some disadvantages:

1. The data being tested must be continuous. Discrete data cannot be used.

TABLE 6.5
Standard Deviation Calculation[a]

Classes of Customer Interarrival Times (minutes)	Frequency (f)	Mid-Point of Class (X)	$x = X - \bar{X}$	$f * x$	$f * x^2$
Under 0.5	0	—	—	—	—
0.5–3.5	2	2	−7.8	−15.6	121.68
3.5–6.5	6	5	−4.8	−28.8	138.24
6.5–9.5	18	8	−1.8	−32.4	58.32
9.5–12.5	14	11	1.2	16.8	20.16
12.5–15.5	4	14	4.2	16.8	70.56
15.5–18.5	6	17	7.2	43.2	310.04
18.5 and above	0	—	—		
Total	50				719.00

$$\text{Standard deviation } (s) = (\sum_{z=1}^{8} (fx^2)/n)^{0.5}$$
$$s = (719/50)^{0.5}$$
$$s = 3.792$$

[a] With $\bar{X} = 9.8$ from Table 6.4.

TABLE 6.6
Fitting a Normal Curve to Collected Data

Class # (1)	X Limits (2)		x $(X - \bar{X})$ (3)	z (x/s) (4)	Normal Curve Area Y_0 to z (5)	Theoretical Occurrences Y_0 to z (6)	Theoretical Class Frequency (7)	Actual Class Frequency (8)
	Low	−infinity	−infinity	−infinity	.500	25.00	0.38	0
1	Up	.5	−9.3	−2.45	.492	24.62		
	Low	.5	−9.3	−2.45	.492	24.62	2.05	2
2	Up	3.5	−6.3	−1.66	.452	22.57		
	Low	3.5	−6.3	−1.66	.452	22.57	7.18	6
3	Up	6.5	−3.3	−0.87	.308	15.39		
	Low	6.5	−3.3	−0.87	.308	15.39	13.79	18
4	Up	9.5	−0.3	−0.08	.032	1.59		
	Low	9.5	−0.3	−0.08	.032	1.59	14.65	14
5	Up	12.5	2.7	0.71	.261	13.06		
	Low	12.5	2.7	0.71	.261	13.06	8.61	4
6	Up	15.5	5.7	1.50	.433	21.66		
	Low	15.5	5.7	1.50	.433	21.66	2.79	6
7	Up	18.5	8.7	2.29	.489	24.45		
	Low	18.5	8.7	2.29	.489	24.45	0.55	0
8	Up	+infinity	+infinity	+infinity	.500	25.00		
						Total	50.00	50

TABLE 6.7

Area under the Normal Curve between Ordinate at Y_0 and Ordinate at z

z	.00	.01	.02	.03	.04	.05	.06	.07	.08	.09
0.0	.00000	.00399	.00798	.01197	.01595	.01994	.02392	.02790	.03188	.03586
0.1	.03983	.04380	.04776	.05172	.05567	.05962	.06356	.06749	.07142	.07535
0.2	.07926	.08317	.08706	.09095	.09483	.09871	.10257	.10642	.11026	.11409
0.3	.11791	.12172	.12552	.12930	.13307	.13683	.14058	.14431	.14803	.15173
0.4	.15542	.15910	.16276	.16640	.17003	.17364	.17724	.18082	.18439	.18793
0.5	.19146	.19497	.19847	.20194	.20540	.20884	.21226	.21566	.21904	.22240
0.6	.22575	.22907	.23237	.23565	.23891	.24215	.24537	.24857	.25175	.25490
0.7	.25804	.26115	.26424	.26730	.27035	.27337	.27637	.27935	.28230	.28524
0.8	.28814	.29103	.29389	.29673	.29955	.30234	.30511	.30785	.31057	.31327
0.9	.31594	.31859	.32121	.32381	.32639	.32894	.33147	.33398	.33646	.33891
1.0	.34134	.34375	.34614	.34850	.35083	.35314	.35543	.35769	.35993	.36214
1.1	.36433	.36650	.36864	.37076	.37286	.37493	.37698	.37900	.38100	.38298
1.2	.38493	.38686	.38877	.39065	.39251	.39435	.39617	.39796	.39973	.40147
1.3	.40320	.40490	.40658	.40824	.40988	.41149	.41309	.41466	.41621	.41774
1.4	.41924	.42073	.42220	.42364	.42507	.42647	.42786	.42922	.43056	.43189
1.5	.43319	.43448	.43574	.43699	.43822	.43943	.44062	.44179	.44295	.44408
1.6	.44520	.44630	.44738	.44845	.44950	.45053	.45154	.45254	.45352	.45449
1.7	.45543	.45637	.45728	.45818	.45907	.45994	.46080	.46164	.46246	.46327
1.8	.46407	.46485	.46562	.46638	.46712	.46784	.46856	.46926	.46995	.47062
1.9	.47128	.47193	.47257	.47320	.47381	.47441	.47500	.47558	.47615	.47670
2.0	.47725	.47778	.47831	.47882	.47932	.47982	.48030	.48077	.48124	.48169
2.1	.48214	.48257	.48300	.48341	.48382	.48422	.48461	.48500	.48537	.48574
2.2	.48610	.48645	.48679	.48713	.48745	.48778	.48809	.48840	.48870	.48899
2.3	.48928	.48956	.48983	.49010	.49036	.49061	.49086	.49111	.49134	.49158
2.4	.49180	.49202	.49224	.49245	.49266	.49286	.49305	.49324	.49343	.49361
2.5	.49379	.49396	.49413	.49430	.49446	.49461	.49477	.49492	.49506	.49520
2.6	.49534	.49547	.49560	.49573	.49585	.49598	.49609	.49621	.49632	.49643
2.7	.49653	.49664	.49674	.49683	.49693	.49702	.49711	.49720	.49728	.49736
2.8	.49744	.49752	.49760	.49767	.49774	.49781	.49788	.49795	.49801	.49807
2.9	.49813	.49819	.49825	.49831	.49386	.49841	.49846	.49851	.49856	.49861
3.0	.49865	.49869	.49874	.49878	.49882	.49886	.49889	.49893	.49897	.49900
3.1	.49903	.49906	.49910	.49913	.49916	.49918	.49921	.49924	.49926	.49929
3.2	.49931	.49934	.49936	.49938	.49940	.49942	.49944	.49946	.49948	.49950
3.3	.49952	.49953	.49955	.49957	.49958	.49960	.49961	.49962	.49964	.49965
3.4	.49966	.49968	.49969	.49970	.49971	.49972	.49973	.49974	.49975	.49976
3.5	.49977	.49978	.49978	.49979	.49980	.49981	.49981	.49982	.49983	.49983
3.6	.49984	.49985	.49985	.49986	.49986	.49987	.49987	.49988	.49988	.49989
3.7	.49989	.49990	.49990	.49990	.49991	.49991	.49992	.49992	.49992	.49992
3.8	.49993	.49993	.49993	.49994	.49994	.49994	.49994	.49995	.49995	.49995
3.9	.49995	.49995	.49996	.49996	.49996	.49996	.49996	.49996	.49997	.49997
4.0	.49997									

TABLE 6.8
Grouping Frequency Classes

Class Limits	Theoretical Class Frequency	Actual Class Frequency
−Infinity to 0.5	0.38 ⎫	0 ⎫
0.5 to 3.5	2.05 ⎬ = 9.61	2 ⎬ = 8
3.5 to 6.5	7.18 ⎭	6 ⎭
6.5 to 9.5	13.79	18
9.5 to 12.5	14.65	14
12.5 to 15.5	8.61 ⎫	4 ⎫
15.5 to 18.5	2.79 ⎬ = 11.95	6 ⎬ = 10
18.5 to infinity	0.55 ⎭	0 ⎭

TABLE 6.9
Chi-Square Calculations

Class Limits	Observed Class Frequency (O)	Expected Class Frequency (E)	$O - E$	$(O - E)^2$	$(O - E)^2/E$
−Infinity to 6.5	8	9.61	−1.61	2.59	0.27
6.5 to 9.5	18	13.79	4.21	17.72	1.28
9.5 to 12.5	14	14.65	−0.65	.42	0.03
12.5 to infinity	10	11.95	−1.95	3.80	0.32
Total	50	50.00	0		$\chi^2 = 1.90$

Mr. George calculated the degrees of freedom in this fashion:

$g = 4$ Expected frequency classes
$m = 3$ Number of constants used to estimate the population parameters and derive the expected frequencies. The constants used were sample size = 50, mean = 9.8, and standard deviation = 3.79.

$D = 4 - 3 = 1$

2. Parameters for the population cannot be estimated from the sample's characteristics as they are in the chi-square method.

6.7 Random and Pseudorandom Number Streams

A variable Z that can assume any value in the range (x, y) with equal probability is defined as being random (Figure 6.13). Random variables can be uniformly or

TABLE 6.10

Values of χ^2 for Various Probabilities

Degrees of Freedom	Probabilities (areas under χ^2 curve above given χ^2 values)								
	0.90	0.70	0.50	0.30	0.20	0.10	0.05	0.02	0.01
1	0.016	0.148	0.445	1.074	1.642	2.706	3.841	5.412	6.635
2	0.211	0.713	1.386	2.408	3.219	4.605	5.991	7.824	9.210
3	0.584	1.424	2.366	3.665	4.642	6.251	7.185	9.837	11.345
4	1.064	2.195	3.357	4.878	5.989	7.779	9.488	11.668	13.277
5	1.610	3.000	4.351	6.064	7.289	9.236	11.070	13.388	15.086
6	2.204	3.828	5.348	7.231	8.558	10.645	12.592	15.033	16.812
7	2.833	4.671	6.346	8.383	9.803	12.017	14.067	16.622	18.475
8	3.490	5.527	7.344	9.524	11.030	13.362	15.507	18.168	20.090
9	4.168	6.393	8.343	10.656	12.242	14.684	16.919	19.679	21.666
10	4.865	7.267	9.342	11.781	13.442	15.987	18.307	21.161	23.209
11	5.578	8.148	10.341	12.899	14.631	17.275	19.675	22.618	24.725
12	6.304	9.034	11.340	14.011	15.812	18.549	21.026	24.054	26.217
13	7.042	9.926	12.340	15.119	16.985	19.812	22.362	25.472	27.688
14	7.790	10.821	13.339	16.222	18.151	21.064	23.685	26.873	29.141
15	8.547	11.721	14.339	17.322	19.311	22.307	24.996	28.259	30.578
16	9.312	12.624	15.338	18.418	20.465	23.542	26.296	29.633	32.000
17	10.085	13.531	16.338	19.511	21.615	24.769	27.587	30.995	33.409
18	10.865	14.440	17.338	20.601	22.760	25.989	28.869	33.346	34.805
19	11.651	15.352	18.338	21.689	23.900	27.204	30.144	33.687	36.191
20	12.443	16.266	19.337	22.775	25.038	28.412	31.410	35.020	37.566
21	13.240	17.182	20.337	23.858	26.171	29.615	32.671	36.343	38.932
22	14.041	18.101	21.337	24.939	27.301	30.813	33.924	37.659	40.289
23	14.848	19.021	22.337	26.018	28.429	32.007	35.172	38.968	41.638
24	15.659	19.943	23.337	27.096	29.553	33.196	36.415	40.270	42.980
25	16.473	20.867	24.337	28.172	30.675	34.382	37.652	41.566	44.314
26	17.292	21.792	25.336	29.246	31.795	35.563	38.885	42.856	45.642
27	18.114	22.719	26.336	30.319	32.912	36.741	40.113	44.140	46.963
28	18.939	23.647	27.336	31.391	34.027	37.916	41.337	45.419	48.278
29	19.768	24.577	28.336	32.461	35.139	39.087	42.557	46.693	49.588
30	20.599	25.508	29.336	33.530	36.250	40.256	43.773	47.962	50.892

nonuniformly distributed and may be continuous or discrete. Random variables are selected by chance and are not influenced in any way by past values. Random numbers are widely used in experiments that are dependent upon chance. Examples of these are machine breakdowns, occurrences of rejected parts coming off an assembly line, and service times at an automatic teller machine.

Random numbers can be generated in many different ways. The flip of a coin, drawing numbers from a hat, roulette wheels, and playing cards are examples of physical generation methods. The most common method of obtaining random numbers for use in the computer simulation field is through algebra. A number

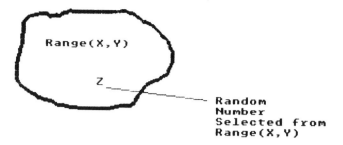

Figure 6.13 Random number.

called a seed is selected and used to produce a sequence of numbers in this manner:

$$Z_i = f(Z_i - 1)$$

where Z_i must be:

- Uniformly distributed (nonuniform distributions can be created from uniform ones)
- Statistically independent
- Nonrepeating (for a desired length known as the period of the generator)

Although the resulting number stream is not truly random, if created properly it will pass most tests for true randomness. Number streams generated through algebraic means are known as pseudorandom numbers.

The use of pseudorandom number streams has several advantages over the use of true random numbers (Henriksen and Crain, 1989) including:

1. The sequence of numbers is reproducible. This means different versions of a program can be tested using the same input data.
2. The streams can be generated quickly and efficiently for use in a simulation program.

Table 6.11 is a list of pseudorandom values generated with the Lehmer algorithm as implemented in the GPSS/H simulation language. The program shown in Figure 6.14 was used to create Table 6.11:

Although it is important to understand the concepts of random number generation and pseudorandom number streams, a simulation analyst will rarely have to create a random number generator. Most simulation software products already have a built-in means of creating pseudorandom numbers. As long as care is taken in selecting a seed value (this is usually done for the analyst as well), very few problems should occur.

TABLE 6.11

Pseudorandom Numbers Drawn between 0 and 1000

94	976	318	34	152	652	337	981	516	415
811	255	767	856	204	436	598	252	901	799
114	313	301	858	829	216	767	907	630	187
363	663	809	568	209	780	682	499	412	351
429	205	968	662	258	986	343	685	765	595
977	960	192	268	517	259	396	594	427	809
8	627	534	539	92	352	751	992	84	375
900	502	544	413	424	692	15	450	580	846
150	433	596	403	486	830	110	997	246	97
456	419	105	571	699	152	485	297	535	253
569	378	382	538	893	738	129	769	466	226
483	912	736	53	791	198	686	709	849	93
291	171	273	700	290	154	74	131	772	626
54	128	75	787	640	60	864	932	32	383
846	680	786	928	772	593	831	23	636	175
395	902	621	150	666	20	636	687	968	741
742	464	251	990	915	208	283	372	611	940
241	823	909	394	696	166	226	993	31	890
261	823	381	782	330	344	782	73	348	57
143	871	771	536	987	68	50	683	232	25
398	697	549	650	513	227	942	952	671	858
111	853	274	829	969	136	122	362	221	306
847	290	98	681	429	212	757	28	170	729
543	549	655	547	104	56	82	297	750	34
883	142	683	603	426	382	109	801	638	212
439	690	649	631	821	932	118	82	423	694
928	659	206	631	952	274	56	171	258	658
645	687	49	110	287	90	100	9	953	762
22	690	658	947	975	979	986	490	344	336
740	783	623	862	984	430	23	306	666	466
849	523	289	56	731	690	755	278	473	863
470	713	156	132	183	28	351	586	583	227
205	721	139	352	483	190	132	180	780	222
943	202	795	473	957	827	99	453	712	833
137	104	142	333	556	490	301	420	229	909
117	761	939	389	414	535	553	832	291	292
300	68	628	111	933	516	989	556	662	467
386	260	327	44	993	954	44	887	878	577
778	258	754	181	342	474	925	104	592	969
172	128	152	815	488	504	603	585	537	96
944	642	282	124	665	562	364	994	361	659
110	254	479	585	878	216	76	742	607	655
531	311	319	922	599	546	666	816	993	605
403	929	388	145	890	499	857	859	0	404
877	333	635	510	368	997	811	930	655	505
935	13	135	196	945	478	826	224	752	880
502	64	5	918	306	182	887	280	449	849
531	658	167	983	182	592	245	498	897	936
507	972	338	95	894	446	778	983	740	263
297	506	611	56	869	188	891	205	583	346

```
LINE# STMT# IF DO BLOCK# *LOC   OPERATION  A,B,C,D,E,F,G    COMMENTS
       1                            SIMULATE   15
       2                  *=========================================================*
       3                  *=========================================================*
       4                  *
       5                  *      CREATE TRANSACTION
       6         1        GENERATE   ,,,1,,11PF
       7                  *
       8                  * ASSIGN PF11 TO COMPLETE 50 ITERATIONS
       9         2        ASSIGN     11,50,PF
      10                  *
      11                  * ASSIGN TRANSACTION PARAMETERS DIFFERENT PSEUDO-RANDOM NUMBERS
      12         3  REDO  ADVANCE
      13         4        ASSIGN     1,RN4,PF
      14         5        ASSIGN     2,RN4,PF
      15         6        ASSIGN     3,RN4,PF
      16         7        ASSIGN     4,RN4,PF
      17         8        ASSIGN     5,RN4,PF
      18         9        ASSIGN     6,RN4,PF
      19        10        ASSIGN     7,RN4,PF
      20        11        ASSIGN     8,RN4,PF
      21        12        ASSIGN     9,RN4,PF
      22        13        ASSIGN     10,RN4,PF
      23        14        BPUTPIC    FILE=RESULTS,LINES=1,PF1,PF2,PF3,PF4,PF5,PF6,PF7,PF8,_
      24        14                   PF9,PF10
      25        14   *****  *****  *****  *****  *****  *****  *****  *****  *****  *****
      26        15        LOOP       11,REDO
      27        16        TERMINATE
      28                  *=========================================================*
      29                  *                        TIMING TRANSACTION               *
      30                  *=========================================================*
      31        17        GENERATE   1
      32        18        TERMINATE  1
      33                  START      1
      34                  END
```

Figure 6.14 GPSS/H program used to create a table of pseudorandom numbers.

6.8 Validation

Validation is the process of determining that the real world system being studied is accurately represented by the simulation model (Sargent, 1988). This process insures that the conceptual model is correct. It establishes an acceptable level of confidence that the conclusions drawn from running the simulation will give insight to the true operating characteristics of the system being modeled. This confidence, called *face validity* (Naylor and Finger, 1967), should radiate from both modeler and model user.

The validation process should begin during the initial stages of a simulation project and continue until the end. A simulation project can figuratively be illustrated as in Figure 6.15.

Validation techniques should be applied to the input and output segments of a simulation project to insure that the model developed is representative of the actual system.

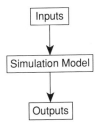

Figure 6.15 Main components of a simulation project.

6.8.1 Validation of Simulation Inputs

As mentioned in Section 6.5, simulation inputs are gathered in two formats: qualitative and quantitative.

Qualitative inputs are the underlying assumptions, rules, and other non-numeric data that will be used in the simulation. This information should be gathered and validated through one or several of the following methods:

1. *Observation.* If a model of an existing system is being developed, the analyst can observe different situations and insure that the assumptions to be used in the model are valid.

2. *Expert's Opinions.* A list of assumptions and rules can be evaluated by experts. A modeler should interact with both system experts and model users throughout the life of a simulation project, beginning with development of the input data.

3. *Intuition and Experience.* If a simulation analyst frequently models systems that share many common characteristics, an intuitive feeling will develop that will help give the model added validity.

In addition to these three methods, quantitative or numeric inputs to the simulation can also be tested for validity in the following ways:

1. *Statistical Testing.* If a theoretical input data distribution is being used to model empirical data, chi-square or Kolmogorov–Smirnov goodness-of-fit tests should be used to assess the theoretical data. If the fit is close, the theoretical data can be considered a valid representation.

2. *Sensitivity Analysis.* Sensitivity analysis involves altering the model's input by a small amount and checking the corresponding effect on the model's output. If the output varies widely for a small change in an input parameter, that input parameter may need to be reevaluated (Law and Kelton, 1982).

6.8.2 Validation of Simulation Outputs

Model validity can best be determined through analysis of the simulation's output data. If the model's output data closely represents the expected values for the system's real world data, it is considered to be valid.

When a model is developed for an existing system, a validity test becomes a statistical comparison. Data collected from actual system operation can be used as a guideline. When the system does not yet exist, validity becomes harder to prove. In many cases validity cannot be definitely proven until some time in the future when the system being modeled has been installed. Before that time, several methods can be used to increase the confidence level that a model is valid:

1. *Comparison with data from a similar system.* If a system exists that is similar in nature to the one that is being modeled, an interpolation of system output can be derived and compared to the simulation.

2. *Expert opinions.* An expert on the type of system being modeled can be consulted and shown the output data. An expert's opinion will help lend more confidence that the model is valid.

3. *Calculated expectations.* In some cases, expected output can be calculated and the model output compared to the result. If the model is too complex, it may be possible to analyze individual subsystems and perform calculations on each part to help establish validity.

6.8.3 Summary of Validation

Validity is a very important aspect of simulation. Without confidence that it is valid, a model may as well not be created. One key to validity is communication. With continual interaction between system designers, component vendors, experts, model users, and system analysts, the perceived and actual validity of a model will be greater.

6.9 Concept Model

Before the process of coding a simulation begins, a general concept model should be consulted. A concept or rough cut model was defined in Section 3.4.1 as a general modeling tool that can quickly produce an approximation of a system (Wallach, 1988). Concept modeling is used to provide answers in the initial stages of a simulation indicating whether time and resources should be invested in a more detailed model. These rough cut models can take the form of anything from a simple mathematical equation done by hand to a sophisticated network analysis done on a computer (Figure 6.16).

A great deal of work and effort can often be saved in a simulation project by taking a final look at system components from a quantitative viewpoint. If certain operations are found to be mathematically impossible, it may be desirable to postpone the detailed simulation and reevaluate the system's design. The following example illustrates the use of simple mathematics to avoid an unnecessary simulation.

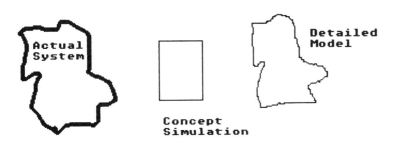

Figure 6.16 Concept models make more assumptions about the actual system than do detailed simulations.

Not-So-Fast Fast-Food Joint

Merlin decided to buy a small downtown cafe and turn it into Merlin's Magic Mushroom Burgers, a fast-food restaurant aimed at serving the nearby office complex and its luncheon crowds. Merlin hired a private restaurant consulting group, Lettuce Sim, to do an analysis. They came back in several weeks with estimated numbers of potential customers and the volume of business he could expect. It appeared that he could open a profitable business.

To help solidify the encouraging news, the consulting group recommended that Merlin not take any chances and further employ their services to create a simulation from the collected data. Merlin was on a tight budget but finally agreed to pay the extra money and have the restaurant modeled.

Input data, which included the number of burgers the grill could hold, cooking time, counter service time, and various other parameters, was estimated for the restaurant. After a few weeks and several thousands of dollars, a computer simulation had been created. The model provided Merlin with some additional data about the operation, including the fact that his grill could not produce enough burgers to satisfy all the hungry customers during the peak demand time at lunch hour.

Merlin priced a new grill and found it cost more than he could afford. It was approximately equivalent to the amount of money he had paid Lettuce Sim for the restaurant model.

This ruffled Merlin's feathers a little, and he decided to take a closer look at the simulation. He spent some time mulling over the data and was shocked to be able to quickly perform this calculation:

$$MB = \text{Maximum burgers on the grill at any one time: 10}$$
$$ACT = \text{Average cooking time per burger: 10 minutes}$$
$$EC = \text{Expected customers per hour during lunch hour: 120}$$
$$TBH = \text{Total burgers per hour} = (60 \text{ min}/ACT) * MB$$
$$= 60 \text{ min}/10 \text{ min} * 10 \text{ burgers}$$
$$= 60 \text{ burgers}$$

"In one hour, six batches of ten burgers can be cooked for a total of 60 burgers. To serve 120 customers, common sense dicates that my grill needs double its current capacity," Merlin reasoned.

Had Merlin taken the time to analyze the data quickly by hand before having the restaurant modeled, it is possible that he would have decided not to proceed with the simulation. An obvious bottleneck existed that could have been given attention prior to development of a simulation model.

Using a rough cut or concept model prior to building a detailed simulation can provide the analyst with several benefits:

1. Helps to identify problem areas early in the project.
2. Reduces the time and cost associated with unnecessary detailed simulation.
3. Allows rapid "what if" testing.
4. Easy to use, inexpensive, and widely available spreadsheet software can be used for many cases (Pope, 1989).

Concept modeling can be performed, as demonstrated in the *Not-So-Fast Fast-Food Joint* example, by manually performing some key calculations. It can also be done by using a sophisticated commercially available tool such as *Manuplan*[1] or *Operations Planner.*[2] Another tool commonly used for concept modeling is spreadsheet software such as Lotus 1-2-3. The following example uses Lotus 1-2-3 to develop a simple concept model of a series of delivery van routes.

Fastway Delivery

Fastway Delivery Company decided to open a new branch office that would deliver bread and bakery items to grocery stores and service stations in its immediate area. Ten different routes were mapped out, each one consisting of varying distances and numbers of stops. An average speed in miles per hour was calculated for each route based on expected traffic congestion and legal speed limits. Fastway wanted an approximation of the number of delivery vans their new operation would require. They developed a concept model using Lotus 1-2-3 and these assumptions:

1. A route is a round-trip leaving the bakery, servicing all stops, and returning to the point of origin.
2. A route can be taken at any time during the eight-hour workday.
3. If a delivery van finishes its route before the workday is over, it will start the next route.

The spreadsheet that was developed is shown in Table 6.12. Fastway was able to calculate a preliminary van count of 2.83 by using the concept model that had been developed. Besides providing the desired data, the model enabled management at Fastway to quickly alter certain parameters to experiment with the van count.

For instance, in Table 6.13 the stop times were changed from 10 to 12 minutes. This increase in time indicated that a 12 minute service time would cause the van count to rise above 3 to 3.10.

---

[1]Manuplan is a trademark of Network Dynamics, Inc., 128 Wheeler Road, Burlington, MA 01803.

[2]Operations Planner is a trademark of Palladian Software, Inc., One Kendall Square, Building 200, Cambridge, MA 02139–9836.

TABLE 6.12
Concept Model: Number of Required Delivery Vans

Route	Distance (miles)	Average Speed (mph)	# Stops	Stop Time (min)	Total Time (min)
1	15	17	4	10	92.94
2	12	15	4	10	88.00
3	13	15	4	10	92.00
4	18	20	6	10	114.00
5	24	25	8	10	137.60
6	52	25	8	10	204.80
7	28	20	6	10	144.00
8	29	30	6	10	118.00
9	58	40	10	10	187.00
10	61	40	9	10	181.50
Totals	310	24.7	65	100	1359.84

Total Delivery Time   1359.84 Minutes
Over Eight Hours (8 × 60)   480 Minutes

1359.84/480 = 2.83 Delivery Vans Required

TABLE 6.13
Using Concept Model for "What if" Questions

Route	Distance (miles)	Average Speed (mph)	# Stops	Stop Time (min)	Total Time (min)
1	15	17	4	12	100.94
2	12	15	4	12	96.00
3	13	15	4	12	100.00
4	18	20	6	12	126.00
5	24	25	8	12	153.60
6	52	25	8	12	220.80
7	28	20	6	12	156.00
8	29	30	6	12	130.00
9	58	40	10	12	207.00
10	61	40	9	12	199.50
Totals	310	24.7	65	120	1489.84

Total Delivery Time   1489.84 Minutes
Over Eight Hours (8 × 60)   480 Minutes

1489.84/480 = 3.10 Delivery Vans Required

Since the calculated van count is close to 3 in both scenarios, Fastway may wish to explore the option of developing a detailed simulation incorporating randomness in the delivery times, van speeds, breakdowns, and stop times. The detailed simulation would provide a firmer van count and help them decide whether three or four vans should be acquired.

Fastway has another option. They may decide to purchase four vans knowing that only three are required for the route work. The fourth van can be used as a spare, only working when one of the other three is in the repair shop or when extra deliveries are required. In this case, a detailed simulation would not provide any additional information that would impact the purchase decision. Therefore, the concept model may be the final step in the simulation process.

Concept modeling can be either an intermediate step in a simulation process or an end in itself, depending on the goals of the study. It can be used to provide quick, rough cut information for preliminary decision making and should always be used as part of a complete simulation study.

6.10 Selection of a Language or Tool

Following the completion of the concept model stage in a simulation project, a decision must be made to either redesign the system, stop and be content with currently available information, or proceed with development of a detailed simulation. If the development of a detailed simulation is the chosen course of action, a determination of the appropriate simulation language or tool must be made (Armstrong and Sumner, 1988).

Simulation software products can be broken into two major categories: simulators and simulation languages. Simulators are application specific, prewritten modeling tools. Simulation languages are general purpose programming languages that are specially adapted for use in modeling applications. Chapter 2 contains further discussion on simulation languages and simulators.

Choosing a software product is always a difficult procedure. Software is an intangible entity with numerous parameters and features to compare. Many vendors, based on their own testing criteria and definition, claim to have the fastest, most user friendly, or best package available. While it may not be possible to select an "absolute best" simulation package, it is very possible to select a simulation package that will meet the requirement of a particular project (Baer, 1988).

The software evaluation process is comprised of four steps:

(1) define needs, (2) research market, (3) compare available options, and (4) make selection.

6.10.1 Step 1: Define Needs

This is an information-gathering step during which the prospective software purchaser needs to answer several questions.

1. *Determine the frequency of future simulation work. Will this be a one time project or will simulation be used regularly from now on?* If a simulation is to be done only once for this project, the amount of time spent on the learning curve time should be minimized. This can be accomplished by purchasing a user friendly simulator or by hiring a simulation consultant. If simulation work is to be done on a regular basis in the future, serious development of an in-house simulation capability is desirable. This development would involve the training of appropriate personnel and the selection of either a general purpose simulation language or appropriate simulator.

2. *What type of system will be modeled? Is it unique in function?* If the system to be simulated is unique, it will be hard to find a simulator package that can be used without trouble. In this case a general purpose simulation language should be used. If the system being modeled is standard materials handling equipment purchased for in-house use, the probability that a simulator is available is quite high.

3. *Who will be doing the simulation work?* If an engineer who is not a programmer and not a computer expert will be doing the work, a simulator package may be desirable. On the other hand, a simulation analyst might feel constrained by a simulator package and may desire the full-range of capabilities that a language has to offer.

4. *What budgetary constraints exist?* The purchase of all tools and equipment is dependent upon a budget. Simulation software products exist in nearly all price ranges. The amount of money available will have an impact on what can be bought.

5. *Who will be using the results?* Will this simulation study be used to "sell" an idea to management? How impressive does the output need to be? If it is going to be used as a research tool, good statistical output is desirable. If it will be used to impress a potential customer or upper management, a top-notch animation may be desirable.

Answers to the preceding five questions will help start the software evaluation process by giving definition to the general needs of the prospective buyer.

6.10.2 Step 2: Research Market

A large and varied simulation software market exists at the present time. Based on the needs analysis conducted in Step 1, a list of important software features can be generated. Products exhibiting some or all of these features can then be researched further.

Most simulation software vendors advertise their products in trade magazines that are popular in a particular target market. For instance, magazines such as

Managing Automation, Materials Handling Engineering, and *Industrial Engineering* are all good sources of advertisements aimed at manufacturing applications of simulation products.

Another source of information about simulation software is the Society for Computer Simulation (SCS). The SCS is an organization dedicated to the advancement of computer simulation. Its primary purpose is to increase communication among simulation practitioners. It does this through the monthly technical journal *Simulation,* through national and regional simulation conferences, and through other publications. The SCS can be contacted at:

The Society for Computer Simulation
P. O. Box 1900
San Diego, CA 92117-9990
Phone (619)277-3888

6.10.3 Step 3: Compare Available Options

The process of selecting simulation software is similar to shopping for any other commodity. Certain features are more important than others. No one product will be able to provide the best of each desired attribute, so a somewhat subjective decision will have to be made.

In order to facilitate the process of comparing different software packages, a list of important attributes needs to be generated and each should be given a weighting factor. In this way an evaluation template is created. Each product can be compared by using a common template and weighting factors. An example evaluation template follows:

T–Co's Search for Simulation Software

T–Co is a manufacturer of t-brackets, hinges, and other small hardware items. They plan to install a new series of CNC machines to increase their capacity. Before making a major investment, management at T–Co decided to simulate the proposed system. They identified the following attributes as being important in the simulation software selection process.

1. This will be a one time simulation project.
2. The system being modeled is not unusual or unique.
3. An in-house engineer will be doing the simulation work.
4. An inexpensive package should be used.
5. Results will be for in-house analysis. Animation is not important but it would be nice.

The engineer assigned to the simulation project at T–Co developed the evaluation template in Table 6.14 to help in the software selection process. The weighting factors (1 to 10) were subjectively developed from the at-

TABLE 6.14
Simulation Software Evaluation Template

	Weighting Factor		Product Score		Total
Graphics	3	×	____	=	____
Hardware (IBM PC)	10	×	____	=	____
User-Friendliness	8	×	____	=	____
Software Capability	5	×	____	=	____
Ease of Use	9	×	____	=	____
Power	4	×	____	=	____
Cost	10	×	____	=	____
Output Reports	6	×	____	=	____
Ease of Debugging	8	×	____	=	____
Statistics	7	×	____	=	____
Customer Support	8	×	____	=	____
Training	8	×	____	=	____
Documentation	8	×	____	=	____
Vendor Stability	2	×	____	=	____
Application Specific Modules	9	×	____	=	____
			Total Product Score	=	____

tributes identified by management. The weighting factor is multiplied by the product score to produce a column of totals. These totals are added to give an overall numeric product score. The weighting factors range from 1 to 10, with 10 being the most desirable.

Before the engineer was able to get started on the evaluation process, the management at T–Co decided that simulation could be used for other future in-house projects. They went through the requirement list and altered it to read as follows:

1. Simulation will be used on a regular basis at T–Co.
2. The systems being modeled are not unusual or unique.
3. An in-house engineer will be doing the simulation work.
4. The best package, without regard to cost, should be used.
5. Results will be used both for in-house analysis and as a tool to sell our ideas to our parent company. Animation can be used to help perform this function.

The project's engineer received the new requirement list and modified the template as shown in Table 6.15.

6.10.4 Step 4: Make Selection

When all the options have been carefully researched and a template has been used to develop a product score, it is time to make a final selection. Most

TABLE 6.15
Modified Simulation Software Evaluation Template

	Weighting Factor		Product Score		Total
Graphics	10	×	____	=	____
Hardware (IBM PC)	2	×	____	=	____
User-Friendliness	6	×	____	=	____
Software Capability	10	×	____	=	____
Ease of Use	5	×	____	=	____
Power	9	×	____	=	____
Cost	2	×	____	=	____
Output Reports	8	×	____	=	____
Ease of Debugging	8	×	____	=	____
Statistics	8	×	____	=	____
Customer Support	10	×	____	=	____
Training	10	×	____	=	____
Documentation	9	×	____	=	____
Vendor Stability	10	×	____	=	____
Application Specific Modules	8	×	____	=	____
		Total Product Score	=	____	

software vendors offer either training seminars or trial use periods. Rather than rushing out and purchasing the software package with the highest product score, several top contenders should be investigated more closely through a trial usage period or at a training seminar. In this way intangible features of the software can be subjectively judged firsthand. Then the package best suiting the goals of the simulation project can be selected for usage.

6.11   Construction of a Model

The construction stage of a simulation involves writing computer code to accurately represent the system being modeled. Prior to coding, a flowchart or block diagram (Figure 6.17) should be developed as a means of thinking through the model. In addition to being a design tool, flowcharts and block diagrams provide formal documentation illustrating a model's logic.

The process of writing the model's code will be somewhat dependent on the simulator or simulation language chosen. However, by this time in a simulation project the system has a preliminary design, the model has been thought out and conceptually designed, and input data has been analyzed. This reduces the actual construction of a model to an almost clerical function. Some creativity must be used to find an appropriate means of representing an entity or process in terms of the constraints imposed by the software being used. Otherwise, model construction is a relatively routine procedure.

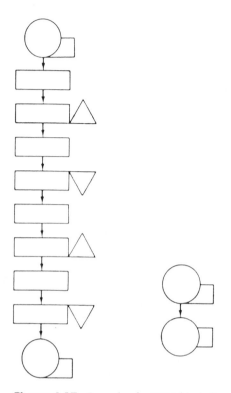

Figure 6.17 Example of a GPSS block diagram. Many simulation analysts use these diagrams to help design a model.

6.12 Verification

In order to insure that a model will be representative of the system it has been structured to emulate, a verification process must be followed. This process extends throughout most of a simulation development project and normally calls for program debugging and manually checking calculations used in the model. It insures that the computer implementation of the conceptual model is correct.

A number of measures can ease the verification task. These can be grouped in two broad categories: *preventative verification* and *appraisal verification*.

Preventative verification strives to insure that the simulation has been created in a way that will minimize errors. Two methods of preventative verification are:

Careful Documentation One of the best forms of verification is the careful documentation of a simulation model. This includes both documenting the programmed code and all the assumptions that have gone into building the model. The documentation process forces the programmer to think through the logic one more time and put this thought process down in writing.

Structured Programming Approach A structured approach to programming involves breaking the model into logical program modules that can be individually tested, debugged, and insured to work properly. It is much easier to debug 20 modules, each consisting of fifty lines of code, than it is to debug a single thousand-line program. If the program were run as one large unit, locating errors would be difficult and time consuming.

Appraisal verification is done to check or appraise the programming after it has been coded. Several appraisal methods are:

Trace Most major simulation languages have incorporated a tool called a trace. A trace enables each programming path to be checked by printing out the values of key variables, counters, and statistics after the occurrence of each event in the simulation. This feature enables the programmer to insure that proper statistical updates and logical decision making are taking place correctly.

Animation A very popular method of checking program veracity is through the use of animation. When a graphic animation is available, it becomes possible for a programmer to visually verify system operation by watching the computer screen. Although verification in this fashion is easy, it will not guarantee that subtle problems do not exist. It is best to use animation in conjunction with other methods of verification.

Run under Simplified Conditions A good method of verification is to run the simulation using simplified conditions. Hand calculations can be performed to prove that the model operates as expected.

Apply Common Sense to Output Reports An often overlooked method of verification is the use of common sense. If something in an output report looks unusual or out of place, it probably is. The more experience a simulation analyst has, the better he or she becomes at finding errors in this way.

6.13 Experimentation

After the model has been conceptualized, coded, verified, and validated, it is ready to provide information through experimentation. Experimentation is the process of initializing key parameters in the model and setting up production runs to make inferences about the behavior of the system under study. The experimentation process consists of three steps:

1. Experimental design
2. Production runs
3. Output analysis

6.13.1 Step 1: Experimental Design

The first step in the experimentation process is experimental design. The term *experimental design* implies that an experiment is being designed or set up. This is done by identifying key parameters and initializing these parameters to values of interest. An example of an input parameter that could be the focus of an experiment is the number of doormen needed at the 21-Club (see Section 6.3). The simulation could be initialized with either one or two doormen. Other issues that need to be resolved during the experimental design stage are:

Length of simulated run time Simulation run time must be determined during the experimental design stage. Simulations can be either terminating or steady-state. Terminating simulations end at a predetermined time. For example, if a barber shop opens at 9:00 A.M. and closes at 5:00 P.M. each day, a terminating model could be set up with run times that end specifically after eight hours of operation. A steady-state simulation, on the other hand, is set up to measure the long-run performance of a system. A model running in the steady-state mode is normally run for a period of time and then statistically "reset" to remove any bias caused by any unusual start-up conditions. The run is then continued and steady-state results are tabulated.

Replications Since simulation is an approximation, it is important to treat it as such. This means that one run of the model will seldom provide an absolute answer. The random inputs to a simulation will produce outputs exhibiting variability. The model should be run enough times to produce a sample size from which a mean and standard deviation with a satisfactory confidence level can be calculated.

Reseeding random number streams Each replication should either reseed the random number streams being used or start in the stream where the last run left off. If pseudorandom numbers are being used and each run starts with the same seed value, no variability will occur between runs. Each run would be using the same number stream.

Initial conditions In some models, it is possible to force the system to a particular state upon start-up. This action may be desirable in the case of a manufacturing system that will never cycle naturally to an unusual condition or that may cycle to that condition but only after hours of run time. By setting the initial conditions of a model to certain values, experimentation can be facilitated.

6.13.2 Step 2: Production Runs

After the desired experiments have been identified and the input parameters properly set, production runs can be made. Production runs are no more than executing the simulation code and creating output reports for each desired scenario.

6.13.3 Step 3: Output Analysis

The final phase of experimentation is the analysis of model outputs. If the output produced is sufficient to satisfy the simulation project's objective, the experimentation stage is over. If problems or new questions are raised, the model is returned to Step 1 for the production of additional runs. Sections 6.14 and 6.15 provide a detailed look at output reports and output analysis.

6.14 Output Analysis with Statistics

When a simulation has any type of stochastic behavior incorporated into its structure, it becomes necessary to view the results of a production run as an experimental sample. Enough samples must be taken to insure that the variability in the output can be accounted for in terms of a mean and standard deviation. Confidence intervals should be created to give the model users a range within which a parameter's true value is likely to fall (Emory, 1985).

Output Analysis: 21-Club

Mr. George had finally completed the simulation of the doorman at his future 21-Club. One particular experiment he ran produced the information shown in Table 6.16 and Figure 6.18.

Realizing he could get a better estimate of the true value of the doorman's utilization, Mr. George decided to calculate the mean and standard deviation of the sample set. He calculated the following values:

Mean = 0.967
Standard deviation = 0.03

TABLE 6.16
21-Club Simulation Output Data

Replication #	Average Doorman Utilization
1	0.998
2	0.975
3	0.945
4	0.978
5	0.985
6	0.943
7	0.996
8	0.995
9	0.995
10	0.906
11	0.942
12	0.920
13	0.978
14	0.993
15	0.956

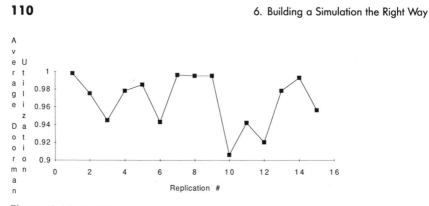

Figure 6.18   21-Club simulation output data.

If only one replication had been made in this experiment, the results could
have varied considerably. In the 15 replications of this sample set, doorman
utilization ranges from 0.906 to 0.998. Although the calculated mean is not
the true value of "doorman utilization," it is a closer estimate than one replication can provide. By using additional statistical methods, confidence intervals
can be constructed to provide an expected range for the true value of the
doorman's utilization.

6.15   Output Reporting

Knowing what statistics to gather from a simulation is a very important part of
the simulation process. Most models have the capability of providing much more
information than is required. The simulation analyst must be able to discern
between the summary data that will be useful to the model's customers and the
detailed supporting data which verifies that the model is performing as desired.

6.15.1 Simulation Report

A simulation report is a document intended to communicate the results of a
simulation study (Emory, 1985; McLeod, 1982). A typical simulation report
should contain the following elements:

   1. *Title page*. The title page should contain the name of the system being
simulated, the date of the report, a revision number or letter, the party for whom
the report is being generated and the name and/or company of the simulation
analyst.

   2. *Table of contents*. If the report is more than a few pages long, a table of
contents should be included.

   3. *Statement of objectives*. The goals and objectives for the simulation study,
including any specific questions that were to be answered, should be summarized
in this section of the report.

4. *Methodology.* This section should include simulation input assumptions and a brief statement describing the general methods used to develop the model. It should be kept in nontechnical terminology. The limitations of the model should also be discussed in this section.

5. *Conclusions and recommendations.* A summary of the major findings and any recommendations are included in this part of the output report document.

6. *Findings.* This section of the report should provide data that backs up the conclusions and recommendations. Graphs, tables, and charts that make the data easier to understand and more readable should be used. All data needs to be fully explained.

7. *Appendix.* The appendix can contain the actual simulation code, all input data, raw output data, reference materials, and calculations.

6.15.2 Quick Reports

Many simulation languages provide special output report generation facilities. These tools can be used to produce graphs and tables as well as to perform statistical analysis. A standard format can be developed for routine simulation runs that are used by the same customer time after time. The simulation can then produce a report automatically after each production run. An example demonstrating the usefulness of this "quick report generation" can be found in a job shop environment. Each time a new order is received, a simulation is performed to determine how long certain production machines will be in use. The same model is used for each new order with its input parameters set to reflect the quantities and types of parts being built. A standard report is generated by the simulation and copies sent to the appropriate shop personnel.

6.16   Logic Transfer

In some applications, more than an output report is needed to effectively communicate the results of a simulation study. In order to insure that all subtle aspects of a complex system's model are implemented in the real world, a logic transfer should be performed. Logic transfer involves moving information, data, or code from a computer simulation into the real world computer that will be controlling the actual system. Chapter 9 contains an in-depth look at logic transfer methodology.

6.17   Summary of Steps Used in Creating a Simulation

A computer simulation project is more than the act of writing code. It includes a wide array of activities ranging from the stating of objectives to model development to logic transfer. The following is a summary of the different phases in the life cycle of a simulation project:

- Phase (1): Model Users Define Study Objectives
- Phase (2): Resources Supporting Study Effort Made Available (computer, budget, means of gathering data)
- Phase (3): System Definition
- Phase (4): Model Scope and Level of Detail Determined
- Phase (5): Preferred Model View Chosen (may be postponed until software selection)
- Phase (6): Model Inputs Collected
- Phase (7): Model Validation
- Phase (8): Concept Model Developed (project may return to Phase (3) if problems are encountered)
- Phase (9): Selection of a Language or Tool
- Phase (10): Construction of Model
- Phase (11): Model Verification
- Phase (12): Experimentation
- Phase (13): Output Analysis
- Phase (14): Generation of Output Report
- Phase (15): Logic Transfer (optional depending on application)

References and Reading

Armstrong, F. Bradley, and Scott Sumner. 1988. "The Project Approach to Simulation Language Comparison." *Proc. 1988 Winter Simulation Conf.* (San Diego, Dec. 12–14). SCS, San Diego, pp. 636–645.

Baer, Tony. 1988. "The Simulation Market." *Managing Automation* (Aug.): 36–37.

Bhattacharyya, Gouri K., and Richard A. Johnson. 1977. *Statistical Concepts and Methods*. Wiley, New York.

Blank, L. 1980. *Statistical Procedures for Engineering, Management, and Science*. McGraw-Hill, New York.

Carson, John S. 1986. "Convincing Users of a Model's Validity Is Challenging Aspect of Modeler's Job." *Industrial Engineering* (June): 74–85.

Emory, C. William. 1985. *Business Research Methods,* Third Edition. Richard D. Irwin, Inc., Homewood, Illinois.

Henriksen, James O., and Robert C. Crain. 1989. *GPSS/H User's Manual*, Third Edition. Wolverine Software Corporation, Annandale, Virginia.

Kelton, David W. 1986. "Statistical Analysis Methods Enhance Usefulness, Reliability of Simulation Model." *Industrial Engineering* (Sept.): 74–84.

Krepchin, Ira. 1988. "Don't Simulate Without Validating." *Modern Materials Handling* (Jan.): 95–97.

Law, Averill M., and W. David Kelton. 1982. *Simulation Modeling and Analysis*. McGraw-Hill, New York.

Law, Averill M., and Christopher S. Larmey. 1984. *An Introduction to Simulation Using SIMSCRIPT II.5*. CACI, Los Angeles.

McHaney, Roger. 1988. "Bridging the Gap : Tranferring Logic from a Simulation into an Actual System Controller." *Proc. 1988 Winter Simulation Conf.* (San Diego, Dec. 12–14). SCS, San Diego, pp. 583–590.

McLeod, John. 1982. *Computer Modeling and Simulation: Principles of Good Practice* **10**(2). Simulation Councils, Inc., La Jolla, California.

Mihram, G. A. 1972. *Simulation Statistical Foundations and Methodology,* Volume 92 of the series *Mathematics in Science and Engineering.* Academic Press, New York.

Naylor, T. H., and J. Finger. 1967. "Verification of Computer Simulation Models." *Management Science* **14**: 92–101.

Neelamkavil, Francis. 1987. *Computer Simulation and Modelling.* Wiley, New York.

Pope, Don N. 1989. "The Uses of Spreadsheets in Simulation Practice." *Newsletter of the Society for Computer Simulation* (Winter): 24–25.

Sargent, Robert G. 1988. "A Tutorial on Validation and Verification of Simulation Models." *Proc. 1988 Winter Simulation Conf.* (San Diego, Dec. 12–14). SCS, San Diego, pp. 33–39.

Shoa, Stephan. 1976. *Statistics for Business and Economics,* Third Edition. Charles E. Merrill, Columbus, Ohio.

Smith, Charles A. 1989. *Computer Simulation of Material Handling Systems: An Introductory Workshop.* Mannesmann Demag, Grand Rapids, Michigan.

Wallach, Susan L. 1988. "Getting Started with Rough-Cut Modeling." *Managing Automation* (Aug.): 32–35.

Young, Robert, and Donald J. Veldman. 1977. *Introductory Statistics for the Behavioral Sciences,* Third Edition. Holt, Rinehart, and Winston, New York.

CHAPTER 7

Learning a Simulation Language

The remaining chapters in this book are built around in-depth examples of simulation programs and code. In order to insure that the value of these examples is not lost to miscommunication, this chapter presents a brief overview of a popular simulation language, GPSS/H.

This overview is intended for readers who are either completely unversed in any simulation language or who may be familiar with a simulation language or tool other than GPSS/H.

GPSS/H has been chosen as the language for the example programs for three major reasons:

1. *Completeness.* GPSS/H is a very rich language. It contains provisions for the gathering of many statistics and can be used to model a wide variety of situations.

2. *Ease of Use and Power.* GPSS/H is easy to learn and use; at the same time it retains full power as a complete simulation language. While basic simulation models can be developed with minimal time spent on the learning curve, the facilities to develop very intense, complicated models also exist.

3. *Time Tested.* The GPSS language was one of the first simulation languages developed (see Chapter 2). GPSS/H is a "state-of-the-art" implementation of that time tested and widely used language.

This chapter is not intended to be a complete GPSS/H tutorial. It provides a general overview of the language and its use. If a more in-depth study of GPSS or GPSS/H is desired, books by Schriber (1990), Bobillier et al. (1976), or Banks et al. (1989) should be consulted.

7.1   GPSS/H Overview

GPSS/H is a "state-of-the-art" implementation of Gordon's (1962) GPSS language. It was developed by James O. Henriksen and first released by his company, Wolverine Software, in 1977 (see Chapter 1 for mailing address).

GPSS/H is a superset of the original GPSS language. It runs on a variety of different computers including IBM and compatible mainframes, VAX machines, and MS/DOS microcomputers (Schriber, 1988).

The GPSS/H language uses the process orientation approach to discrete event simulation. It is structured as a block language. Temporary entities called transactions are created and allowed to move through a network of blocks that have been organized in a manner that is representative of the system being simulated. Statistics tabulating the use of various entities are maintained and made available for analysis at the end of a production run.

In addition to the blocks, GPSS/H employs a control language that uses a series of programming statements to initialize the model, set up experiments, produce output reports, and perform other maintenance functions. The control statements are typically executed first. They are used to start the actual block portion of the model. This chapter will refer to control language elements as "statements" and the block network elements as "blocks" (see Figure 7.1).

Using GPSS/H facilitates the gathering of model statistics, error checking, and logical representation of the system. Most of the information in this chapter has been derived from the *GPSS/H Reference Manual* (Henriksen and Crain, 1989).

7.2   Understanding the Basic Concepts

GPSS/H models a system by updating the simulation clock to the time that the next event is scheduled to occur. Events and their scheduled times of occurrence are maintained automatically on one of two ordered lists: the current events chain or the future events chain. The current events chain keeps a list of all events that will (or may) occur at the present clock time. The future events chain is a record of all events that can occur at some point in the future. The GPSS/H simulation clock is represented in the form of a real number. The system state of the model at any given time is defined by the status and attributes of both permanent and temporary entities in the model.

7.3   Entity Classes

In addition to the temporary entities called transactions (see Section 7.1), GPSS/H employs four other entity classes: equipment entities, computational entities, statistical entities, and data storage entities (Figure 7.2).

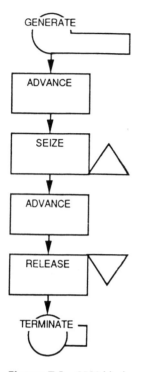

Figure 7.1 GPSS blocks can be represented in terms of pictorial diagrams such as this one. [For more information on block diagrams, see Schriber (1990).]

7.3.1 Transactions

Transactions are dynamic entities that traverse through the networks of blocks in a simulation. Their meaning is defined by the simulation analyst while building the model. They are often created to represent an active object such as an automobile in a traffic simulation, an AGV in a manufacturing simulation, or a customer in a barber shop simulation.

Multiple transactions can exist in a GPSS/H model at any given time. They move through the block network as far as the current system state allows and stop either for a predetermined delay (ADVANCE block), a logical delay, or because a desired resource is currently unavailable. Since multiple transactions can be present in a model, parallel processes can be simulated.

Each transaction has associated with it a list of attributes called parameters that can be altered according to logic contained in the model. These parameters can be used to define unique characteristics of a particular transaction, thereby affecting its movement through the block networks.

Transactions have another attribute known as a priority level. The priority level can be set with a PRIORITY block or upon transaction creation with a

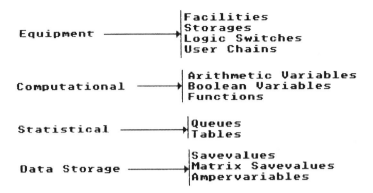

Figure 7.2 GPSS/H major entity classes.

GENERATE block. Priority level can range from 0 to 127. The higher the value, the closer to the front of the current events chain the transaction will be placed. A transaction at the head of the current events chain will be given the first opportunity to move through the network of blocks in each GPSS/H scan cycle.

Transactions are created by using either the GENERATE or SPLIT blocks. They are removed from the model with the TERMINATE or ASSEMBLE blocks.

7.3.2 Equipment Entities

Equipment entities are used to model constrained resources. This entity class includes facilities, storages, logic switches, and user chains.

Facilities Facilities are used to model single servers. One transaction is allowed
    access to a facility at any given time. If a transaction desires service from a
    facility that is currently in use, it is denied entry to the block and must wait for
    it to become available. An example of a system element modeled as a facility
    is the barber in a barbershop simulation. A SEIZE block is used to obtain
    possession of a facility, and the RELEASE block is used to return the server to
    an idle state. The PREMPT, RETURN, FUNAVAIL, FAVAIL, and GATE
    blocks are also used in conjuction with facilities.
Storages Storages are used to model multiple servers. Storage sizes or capacities
    are defined by the simulation analyst. As an example, a storage can be used to
    model a room that can only fit seven people. This storage could be named
    "room" and given a capacity of seven. An ENTER block is used by a transac-
    tion to acquire a number of units of the storage. If the storage is completely
    occupied, the transaction cannot move into the ENTER block and must wait
    for space to become available. A transaction relinquishes units of storage
    upon moving through a LEAVE block. Four other blocks are used with stor-
    ages: the GATE, SUNAVAIL, SAVAIL, and BSTORAGE blocks.

Logic Switches Logic switches are entities that have either an "ON" or "OFF" status. The LOGIC block is used to set, reset, or invert the switch. Logic switches can be used to represent any type of digital or logical device having an on or off state. An example would be whether an exit is opened or closed. The GATE block is also used in conjunction with logic switches.

User Chains User chains can be used to model constrained resources that have unusual queuing disciplines. User chains are similar to the current events and future events chains in that transactions are temporarily pulled from the model to wait for a predetermined condition (a clock time or logical condition). The user chains are controlled by the simulation analyst through the LINK and UNLINK blocks. User chains can significantly increase the execution efficiency of a model during times of heavy transaction queuing (Crain and Brunner, 1990).

7.3.3 Computational Entities

Computational entities are the class of entities that aid in calculation and computation. Included in this class are arithmetic variables, Boolean variables, and functions.

Arithmetic Variables

Arithmetic variables are entities with values that are calculated at the time they are referenced by a transaction. Under normal conditions, data reflecting the current system state will be used to perform a calculation. Two forms of arithmetic variables exist. They are defined with the VARIABLE (integer) and FVARIABLE (floating point) statements.

The following format is used for the VARIABLE and FVARIABLE:

```
Label  VARIABLE  Expression
Label  FVARIABLE Expression
```

Where: . . .

Labels can be either positive numbers or one to eight alphanumeric characters with the first character being alphabetic. A further restriction is that the leading characters may not form the names of standard numeric attributes (SNAs), standard character attributes (SCAs), or standard logical attributes (SLAs). See Section 7.6 for a complete list of all SNAs, SCAs, and SLAs.

Expressions can include SNAs, SCAs, SLAs, constants, symbols, or other variables. They use these operators:

```
+    Addition
−    Subtraction
*    Multiplication
/    Division
@    Modulo division
```

Some examples are as follows.

    14   FVARIABLE S2/2 + 5

This expression will compute the value of variable 14 (V14) as the contents of storage 2 divided in half and added to 5.

    HRS   VARIABLE   AC1/3600

HRS is evaluated as the value of the absolute clock (AC1) divided by 3600.

Boolean Variables

The Boolean variable is a statement of logic that is evaluated to produce a true or false answer. Like the arithmetic variable, the value of a Boolean variable is determined when referenced by a transaction. The information in the statement can then be used by the transaction to make a decision.

The following format is used for the BVARIABLE statement:

    Label BVARIABLE Expression

Where: . . .

Boolean variable labels follow the same convention as do the labels for the VARIABLE statement.

Expressions may be SLAs, comparisons, constants, arithmetic expressions, or some combination using all of them. A complete list of valid SLAs is given in Section 7.6. Comparisons consist of numeric expressions connected with the following operators:

    'G' or >   Greater than
    'GE' or >=   Greater than or equal to
    'L' or <   Less than
    'LE' or <=   Less than or equal to
    'E' or =   Equal to
    'NE' or !=   Not equal to

Arithmetic expressions (variables and fvariables) in Boolean variables are evaluated as true when nonzero or as false if zero in value. SLAs, arithmetic expressions, constants, and comparisons may be connected with the AND and OR operators:

    OR   logical or
    AND   logical and
    +   logical or
    *   logical and

Since the '+', means 'or', and the '*' means 'and', arithmetic expressions in Boolean variables cannot operate with the addition (+) or multiplication (*)

operators. Variables or fvariables must be developed outside the Boolean variable and their values used. Some examples are as follows.

```
20        BVARIABLE   Q4'GE'6*Q4'LE'12
```

Boolean variable 20 will be true if the current contents of queue 4 falls in the range from 6 to 12.

```
ZTEST  BVARIABLE   PF$DESTIN'E'4+PF$BATTERY'E'LOW
```

Boolean variable ZTEST will be true if the entering transaction's parameter called DESTIN is equal to 4 or if its parameter called BATTERY is equal to a constant called LOW.

Functions

Functions are either discrete or continuous data arrangements that describe a relationship between an independent variable and a set of dependent variables. Functions can be used to describe different probability distributions or to return specific values from a list based on a pointer value. Functions can be set up to reference other pointers.

The following format is used for the FUNCTION statement:

```
Label FUNCTION  Input_variable,type#pairs
pair1_independent,pair1_dependent
pair2_independent,pair2_dependent etc. . . .
```

Where: . . .

Label follows the same naming convention followed by the labels of other computational entities.

Input_variable is the argument containing the independent variable that will determine the value the function will return. This parameter cannot reference the function for which it is the argument. It can, however, be a random number stream, a transaction parameter, variable, Boolean variable, ampervariable, or nearly any other GPSS/H entity.

Type#pairs contains two elements of information. The first character specifies the type of function being used. It can be any of the following.

```
C    Continuous Numeric Function
D    Discrete Numeric Function
L    List Type Numeric Function
E    Discrete Attribute Function
M    List Type Attribute Function
S    Entity Selector Function
```

The second bit of information contained by type#pairs is the number of data pairs contained in the function.

The next elements of the function are called the follower statements. In the format example, these are written as "pair1_independent,pair1_dependent". The first number in each pair can be thought of as an index or selection criterion. The indexes must be in ascending order. The second number is a value to be returned by the function. Examples of each type of function are as follows:

1. Continuous Example

> ZORRO FUNCTION V$SPAIN,C2
> 0,0/1.0,10

Based on the value of the variable SPAIN, the function ZORRO will return a number from the range 0 to 10.

2. Discrete Example

> MASTER FUNCTION RN2,D4
> .25,3/.50,7/.75,10/1.0,20

The function MASTER will draw a number from random number stream 2 and based on this value return either a 3,7,10, or 20. Each number will be selected approximately 25% of the time. If random number stream 2 has a value between 0 and .25, 3 will be returned. If RN2 is between .26 and .50, 7 will be chosen and so forth. Note that the index values in this example are cumulative probabilities.

3. List Type Numeric Function Example

> WORKER FUNCTION PF$STATION,L5
> 1,300/2,400/3,200/4,350/5,500

In this example, the transaction parameter STATION is passed to the function WORKER. Based on this number, a value is returned. If the value of PF$STATION is 4, the value returned will be 350. In the context of manufacturing simulation, a transaction representing a worker moving between workstations could use this function to return operation cycle times. This list type function could be rewritten as:

> WORKER FUNCTION PF$STATION,L5
> ,300/,400/,200/,350/,500

The first member of the follower statement pairs can be omitted since it is known that they will be an ascending integer stream starting with one.

4. Discrete Attribute Example

> 30 FUNCTION RN3,E3
> .5,(PF$DESTIN+9)/.9,X1/1.0,4

The function 30 will draw from random number stream 3 and approximately 50% of the time return a value equal to the calling transaction's DESTIN parameter added to 9. Another 40% of the time, the stored value of savevalue 1 will be returned. The remaining 10% of the time, the number 4 will be returned.

5. List Type Attribute Function Example

```
ROGER    FUNCTION   PH5,M3
,V$PARK/,PF$DOG+V$REGGIE/,FN$YAK
```

Like the list type numeric function, the list type attribute function does not need the first entry in its ordered follower pairs. They are assumed to be counting integers ascending from one. This particular example returns the value of a variable named PARK, the sum of a transaction parameter called DOG and a variable named REGGIE, or the value of another function called YAK, all based on the contents of transaction halfword parameter five.

6. Entity Selector Example

```
PICKIT FUNCTION   RN4,S3,B,F,S
.25,CORE/.50,HALF/1.0,EMPTY
```

The entity selector function works in the same way a D-type function does except that the second number of the ordered follower pairs must be a symbol. The symbol type is defined by values that follow type#pairs parameter. In this example, the first symbol represents a Boolean variable, the second symbol a facility, and the third symbol a storage. The symbol type can be any of the categories as shown in Table 7.1.

7.3.4 Statistical Entities

Statistical entities are used solely for the purpose of deriving information from a model. Included in this category are queues and tables. Other entities and SNAs can be used for statistical purposes but they are not limited to this use.

Queues Queue statistics are typically used to gather information on delays experienced by a transaction while it moves through the model's block network. The QUEUE block is used by a transaction to enter a queue and the DEPART block to leave it. Queue statistics provide the information given in Table 7.2.

Tables Tables allow for the gathering of more specific statistics concerning model operation. The table statistic breaks observed values into user-specified categories. This enables the simulation analyst to obtain a more complete picture of how the model is running. The TABULATE block is used to record observations. The TABLE definition statement is used to specify how a table is to be constructed. Another table statistic in GPSS/H is associated with queues. It is activated with a QTABLE definition statement. Each time a transaction moves through a DEPART block (out of a queue), and if a QTABLE definition statement has been coded for that queue, an observation is recorded in the corresponding table. An example is shown in Table 7.3.

TABLE 7.1
Entity Selection Function Symbol Categories

Symbol Type Code	Symbol Represents
B	Boolean Variable
C	User Chain
F	Facility
G	Group
H,XH	Halfword Savevalue
L	Logic Switch
M,MX	Fullword Matrix Savevalue
MB	Byte Matrix Savevalue
ML	Floating Point
P	Parameter
PB	Byte Parameter
PF	Fullword Parameter
PH	Halfword Parameter
PL	Floating Point Parameter
Q	Queue
RN	Random Number Stream
S	Storage
T	Table
V	Variable or Fvariable
X,XF	Fullword Savevalue
XB	Byte Savevalue
BL	Floating Point Savevalue
Y,MH	Halfword Matrix Savevalue
Z	Function

7.3.5 Data Storage Entities

The final class of entity is known as the data storage entity. As the name implies, these entities are used to store state variables and other information generated or used by the model. This entity class includes savevalues, matrix savevalues, ampervariables, and synonyms.

Savevalues

The savevalue entity is a scalar variable used for global storage in GPSS/H. It is a permanent memory location set up by the simulation analyst. Its contents can be initialized with the INITIAL statement. Thereafter, it can be changed when a

TABLE 7.2

Information from Queue Statistics[a]

Queue	Maximum Contents	Average Contents	Total Entries	Zero Entries	Percent Zeros	Average Time/Unit	$Average Time/Unit	Qtable Number	Current Contents
1302	1	.035	1	0	0.0	125.000	125.000		0
1304	3	.200	6	0	0.0	120.016	125.016		0
1305	1	.968	3	0	0.0	1161.434	1161.434		1
1306	2	.905	7	0	0.0	465.589	465.589		1
1322	1	.055	6	0	0.0	32.984	32.384		0
1346	1	.018	2	0	0.0	33.112	33.112		0

[a] Column heading clarification:
Queue: Name or number of the queue for which statistics have been gathered.
Maximum Contents: Maximum number of transactions in queue at any time.
Average Contents: Average number of transactions in queue.
Total Entries: Total number of transactions to move into the queue.
Zero Entries: Number of transactions passing through the queue in zero time.
Percent Zeros: Percent of transactions spending zero time in queue.
Average Time/Unit: Average time each transaction spends in queue.
$Average Time/Unit: Average time each transaction spends in queue excluding the ones spending zero time.
Qtable Number: If a table is created in conjunction with a queue, its number will appear here.
Current Contents: The current number of transactions occupying the queue.

transaction passes through the SAVEVALUE block. Savevalues can be of four data types: (1) fullword, (2) halfword, (3) byte, and (4) single-precision floating point.

Matrix Savevalues

The matrix savevalue entity is the same as the regular savevalue with the exception that it is two-dimensional instead of scalar. The matrix savevalue, like the savevalue, can be initialized using the INITIAL statement. The MSAVEVALUE block is used to change its contents during model execution.

Ampervariable

The ampervariable is a variable type used by GPSS/H. It is distinguished by the use of the ampersand (&) character that must precede this program variable. The ampervariable may be of five different types and may be either scalar or in an array:

1. *Integer.* Positive and negative counting numbers.
2. *Real.* Real number.
3. *CHAR*N.* Character string with 'N' (user specified) length.
4. *VCHAR*N.* Character string of variable length. N is the maximum length.
5. *External.* GPSS/H can access external subroutines as ampervariables.

Ampervariables can be initialized using the LET statement or changed during model execution with the BLET block. Ampervariables may be declared as single element arrays. Examples of ampervariables are as follows.

TABLE 7.3

Example of a Table Created through Activation with a QTABLE Definition Statement[a]

Table WAITT

Entries in Table	Mean Argument	Standard Deviation	Sum of Arguments
197.0000	813.8274	1400.4980	1.6032E + O5

Upper Limit	Observed Frequency	Percent of Total	Cumulative Percentage	Cumulative Remainder	Multiple of Mean	Nonweighted Deviation from Mean
0.	67.0000	34.01	34.01	65.99	0.	−0.5811
. . .						
240.0000	5.0000	2.54	36.55	63.45	0.2949	−0.4097
300.0000	17.0000	8.63	45.18	54.82	0.3686	−0.3669
360.0000	8.0000	4.06	49.24	50.76	0.4424	−0.3240
420.0000	6.0000	3.05	52.28	47.72	0.5161	−0.2812
480.0000	12.0000	6.09	58.38	41.62	0.5898	−0.2384
540.0000	12.0000	6.09	64.47	35.53	0.6635	−0.1955
600.0000	14.0000	7.11	71.57	28.43	0.7373	−0.1527
660.0000	3.0000	1.52	73.10	26.90	0.8110	−0.1098
720.0000	3.0000	1.52	74.62	25.38	0.8847	−0.0670
780.0000	1.0000	0.51	75.13	24.87	0.9584	−0.0242
840.0000	2.0000	1.02	76.14	23.86	1.0322	0.0187
900.0000	2.0000	1.02	77.16	22.84	1.1059	0.0615
. . .						
1080.0000	1.0000	0.51	77.66	22.34	1.3271	0.1901
1140.0000	3.0000	1.52	79.19	20.81	1.4008	0.2329
1200.0000	2.0000	1.02	80.20	19.80	1.4745	0.2757
1260.0000	1.0000	0.51	80.71	19.29	1.5482	0.3186
1320.0000	4.0000	2.03	82.74	17.26	1.6220	0.3614
1380.0000	1.0000	0.51	83.25	16.75	1.6957	0.4043
1440.0000	1.0000	0.51	83.76	16.24	1.7694	0.4471
1500.0000	1.0000	0.51	84.26	15.74	1.8431	0.4899
. . .						
1680.0000	2..0000	1.02	85.28	14.72	2.0643	0.6185
Overflow	29.0000	14.72	100.00	0.00		

Average Value of Overflow   3507.3448

[a]Explanation of terms:
Table: Name or number of table; WAITT in this case.
Entries in Table: Number of observations recorded in the table.
Mean Argument: Average value of entries in the table.
Standard Deviation: Deviation from mean of values in the table.
Sum of Arguments: Cumulative sum of all entries in a table.
Upper Limit: Maximum value of entry for each frequency class.
Observed Frequency: Number of entries in this category.
Percent of Total: Percentage of entries falling into this category.
Cumulative Percentage: Contains the total sum of entries' percentages through this category.
Cumulative Remainder: Contains the total percentage remaining above the current category.
Multiple of Mean: Contains the upper limit of the current frequency class divided by the table mean.
Deviation from Mean: Contains the deviation of the current frequency class' upper limit from the table mean.
Weighted or Nonweighted: A table can be defined as being weighted. In other words, each observation is tabulated
    as a predefined weighted value rather than as one entry. The statistics in weighted tables will appropriately reflect
    the number of observations multiplied by the weighting factor.
Average Value of Overflow: The average value of the observations falling outside of the highest upper limit.

```
BLET     &TUGGER=V$WEIGHT+2000
```

The ampervariable &TUGGER is set to equal a variable named V$WEIGHT added to 2000. This is a block and would be executed each time a transaction moves through it.

```
LET      &CASE(3)=999
```

The third element in ampervariable array &CASE is set to a value of 999. This statement is not a block and would be executed either prior to running the model or between GPSS/H experiments as defined in the control statements set up by the simulation analyst.

Synonym

The synonym is a constant and can only be set by using a SYN compiler directive. Although it is not a member of the data storage entity class, the synonym is included in this section because of how it can function. Examples of the synonym are as follows.

```
TRUE    SYN    1
FALSE   SYN    0
EAST    SYN    1
WEST    SYN    2
NORTH   SYN    3
SOUTH   SYN    4
```

Each of these words have been given a constant value to be used during the running of the simulation.

7.3.6 Groups

Another entity used by GPSS/H is the group. It does not fit into the context of any other entity categories so it is being presented separately.

Groups are used for constructing sets of transactions or of numeric values. When operating in the transaction mode like a storage, the group counts transactions. Unlike a storage, it keeps track of each transaction that belongs to the set. A storage is a counter keeping track of the number of transactions in its set but does not track any type of individual transaction identity.

The JOIN block is used to place a transaction or numeric value into a group. The REMOVE block is used to selectively take a transaction or numeric value out of a group. The EXAMINE block is used to determine if a transaction or numeric value belongs to a group. The SCAN block is used to determine if a group operating in the transaction mode currently has a member transaction whose parameters are of a particular value. Transaction parameters can also be retrieved with the SCAN block. The ALTER block allows the attributes of member transactions to be changed.

7.4 Block Statements

A variety of blocks exist in the GPSS/H simulation language. These blocks can be pieced together to create models of virtually any system that can be logically broken down into a series of discrete events and processes. A partial list of the blocks found in GPSS/H and several of their most common functions and operands are found in Table 7.4.

Table 7.4 uses these categories for describing GPSS/H blocks:

Block Name of block statement
Primary Purpose Function of block
Operand(s) Parameters read in by the block
Auxiliary Operator Additional parameter located directly following the block name. This parameter usually specifies that the block is to perform in a certain mode of operation.

7.5 GPSS/H Control Language

The GPSS/H simulation language can be thought to contain two separate sets of syntax. One set is comprised of the block statements described in Section 7.4. The second set of syntax is used to set up experiments, to perform housekeeping chores such as defining memory allocation and setting initial conditions, and to provide output data reporting. Compiler directives and control statements make up the two divisions in this second category of syntax.

Compiler directives are statements that result in no specific run-time action. They are used to allocate memory, set data types, and define macros. Control statements, on the other hand, are used to start and stop the block portion of the simulation. Other uses of control statements include clearing statistics, printing output reports, and controlling experiments.

Table 7.5 lists some of the most common compiler directives and control statements and briefly describes their uses.

7.6 SCAs, SNAs, and SLAs

Standard character attributes (SCAs), standard numerical attributes (SNAs), and standard logical attributes (SLAs) are statistics that provide the simulation analyst with the current state of the system being modeled. Some of these attributes are associated with the various entity classes, the system status, and transactions. Other SNAs and SLAs provide independent statistical and mathematical functions. The SCAs allow operations to be performed on GPSS/H character strings.

Most SCAs, SNAs, and SLAs are automatically maintained by GPSS/H. Table 7.6 provides a list of the most commonly used SCAs, SNAs, and SLAs and their functions.

TABLE 7.4

Partial List of GPSS/H Blocks and Their Common Uses

Block	Primary Purposes	Operand(s)
ADVANCE	Delay transaction	A = Mean delay time B = Spread about mean (A + or − B delay) or Function to be multiplied by 'A' to yield delay time

Examples:

    ADVANCE   10,3

Entering transaction will be delayed from 7 to 13 time units.

    ADVANCE   10,FN$NORM

Entering transaction will be delayed for 10 multiplied by the value returned by FN$NORM.

Block	Primary Purposes	Operand(s)
ALTER	Changes attributes of a transaction belonging to a group. In this use for the ALTER Block, changes to an attribute on all members of the group will take place.	A = Name or number of group B = The word 'ALL' is specified. C = If PR is specified, Transaction priority will be changed. If the name or number of a parameter is specified, that parameter will be changed. D = Value to replace the priority or parameter specified by 'C' E = Leave empty F = Leave empty G = If no transaction can be altered, transfer to this block.

Example:

ALTER   LDALL,ALL,PR,15,,,ZTRT1

The entering transaction will cause the priority for all members of the group LDALL to be changed to 15. If no group members can be altered, the transaction will be routed to the block ZTRT1.

Block		Primary Purposes	Operand(s)
ALTER	G GE L LE E NE	Change attributes of a transaction belonging to a group if it meets the condition specified by the auxiliary operator. This condition can be greater than (G), greater than or equal (GE), less than (L), less than or equal (LE), equal (E), or not equal (NE). If no auxiliary operator is specified, equal is assumed.	A = Name or number of group B = Number of transactions to be altered C = If PR is specified, Transaction priority will be changed. If the name or number of a parameter is specified, this parameter will be changed. D = Value to replace the priority or parameter specified by 'C' E = If stated as 'PR' then the priority of the transaction group members is compared to the condition specified by the 'F' operand. If specified as a transaction parameter, then this parameter value is compared with the condition specified by the 'F' operand. F = Value to be compared to 'E' operand.

TABLE 7.4

(Continued)

Block	Primary Purposes	Operand(s)
		G = If no transaction can be altered, transfer to this block.

Example:

ALTER GE   LDALL,5,1PF,25,PR,5,ZTRT1

The entering transaction will cause parameter number one for up to 5 members of the group LDALL to be changed to 25. This will only happen if the transactions in the group have a priority level greater than or equal to 5. If no group members can be altered, the entering transaction will be routed to the block ZTRT1.

Block	Primary Purposes	Operand(s)
ALTER MIN MAX	Change parameters of the transaction belonging to a group that meets the condition specified by the auxiliary operator. This can be either the minimum (MIN) or maximum (MAX) priority or parameter value.	A = Name or number of group B = Leave empty C = If PR is specified, Transaction priority will be changed. If the name or number of parameter is specified, this parameter will be changed. D = Value to replace the priority or parameter specified by 'C' E = If stated as 'PR' then the priorities of the transaction group members are compared to find the maximum or minimum value. The attribute specified by the 'C' operand is then changed to the value of the 'D' operand for the proper transaction. If 'E' is stated as a transaction parameter, then these parameters of the transaction group members are compared to find the maximum or minimum value. The attribute specified by the 'C' operand is changed to the value of the 'D' operand for that transaction. F = Leave empty G = If no transaction can be altered, transfer to this block.

Example:

ALTER MIN   LDALL,,1PF,25,PR,,ZTRT1

The entering transaction will cause parameter number one for the member of the group LDALL with the lowest priority to be changed to 25. If no group members can be altered, the entering transaction will be routed to the block ZTRT1.

Block	Primary Purposes	Operand(s)
ASSEMBLE	Causes a number of transactions to be combined into one. The first transaction to enter the ASSEMBLE block initiates	A = Number of transactions to be combined. Transactions are combined only if they belong to a common assembly set. This means they were created from a parent transaction

(continues)

TABLE 7.4
(*Continued*)

Block	Primary Purposes	Operand(s)
	the operation. Other transactions completing the operation are destroyed.	using a SPLIT Block. Multiple assembly operations can be occurring at the same ASSEMBLE Block at any given time.

Example:

ASSEMBLE   5

One transaction will wait at this block until four other transactions from the same assembly set have been destroyed here.

Block	Primary Purposes	Operand(s)
ASSIGN	Changes the value of a parameter on a transaction moving through this block.	A = Name or number of parameter to be assigned a new value. If the last character in this operand is a '−' or '+' then the parameter will be incremented or decremented by the amount specified in operand 'B'. B = The value to be added to, subtracted from, or placed in the parameter specified by 'A'. C = A function to be multiplied by the value in operand 'B'. This product is then placed in the parameter specified by 'A'. D = The type of parameter specified by 'A'. It can be PF for fullword parameter, PH for halfword parameter, as well as others. If no function is specified in 'C', this operand can be moved one space to the left and used as the 'C' operand.

Examples:

ASSIGN   LOAD,FN$STATION,PF

Entering transaction will have its fullword parameter named "LOAD" assigned the value of the function STATION.

ASSIGN   DTIME,100,FN$EXPONT,PH

Entering transaction will have its halfword parameter named "DTIME" assigned the product of 100 and the function EXPONT.

Block	Primary Purposes	Operand(s)
BLET	Changes the value of an ampervariable	A = Operand 'A' contains an expression for assigning the value of an ampervariable. It takes the form: &ampervariable=new__value.

Examples:

BLET   &TRUCK=SEMI

Entering transaction will change the value of an ampervariable, &TRUCK, to the value of a synonym called SEMI.

TABLE 7.4

(*Continued*)

Block	Primary Purposes	Operand(s)

BLET   &SPEED=&VSPEED(3)/60

Entering transaction will change the value of an ampervariable, &SPEED, to the value of another subscripted ampervariable, &VSPEED(3) divided by 60.

BPUTPIC	This block allows information to be printed to a computer screen or external file.	A = The 'A' operand contains information such as File for output, number of lines to be output and the variables whose values are desired as output data. It takes the form: FILE=fname,Lines=n,v1,v2,v3

Example:

BPUTPIC   FILE=SERCOM,LINES=1,PF$DTIME

Transaction Delay Time = *****

Entering transaction will cause the message "Transaction Delay Time = 20" to be printed on the computer screen (SERCOM). The value of its parameter PF$DTIME is 20 in this example.

BUFFER	Causes the order of transactions on the current events chain to be reordered in terms of priorities.	No Operands

Example:

BUFFER

It may be desireable to use the BUFFER Block after an ALTER Block has changed some transaction priority levels.

COUNT	U NU I NI FV FNV SE SNE SF SNF SV SNV LR LS	Examines a range of entities and based on their attributes determines a count. This count reflects the number of entities satisfying a condition specified by the simulation analyst.	A = Parameter of entering transaction into which the count is to be placed. B = Lower limit of range of entity members. C = Upper limit of range of entity members. The entity ranges being counted are based on the auxiliary operators which immediately follow the word COUNT. The definitions for the auxiliary operators are: U = Facility in use NU = Facility not in use I = Facility preempted NI = Facility not preempted FV = Facility available (FAVAIL) FNV = Facility unavailable (FUNAVAIL)

(*continues*)

TABLE 7.4
(Continued)

Block	Primary Purposes	Operand(s)
		SE = Storage empty
		SNE = Storage not empty
		SF = Storage full
		SNF = Storage not full
		SV = Storage available (SAVAIL)
		SNV = Storage unavailable (SUNAVAIL)
		LR = Logic switch reset
		LS = Logic switch set

Example:
        COUNT LS   10,500,550
Parameter 10 on the entering transaction will be assigned the number of logic switches in the range from 500 to 550 that are currently set.

Block	Primary Purposes	Operand(s)
DEPART	Transaction decrements the contents of queue.	A = Name or number of queue to decrement.
		B = Number of units the queue's contents are reduced.

Example:
        DEPART   WAIT,5
The queue, WAIT, has its contents decremented by 5 every time a transaction moves through this block.

Block	Primary Purposes	Operand(s)
ENTER	A transaction increments the contents of a storage.	A = Name or number of storage to increment.
		B = Number of units to increase storage contents.

Example:
        ENTER   ROOM,1
A transaction increments the contents of the storage ROOM by one. If ROOM is full (storage capacities can be defined with the STORAGE statement), the transaction is denied entry to the block and must wait for space to become available.

Block	Primary Purposes	Operand(s)
EXAMINE	Checks to see if entering transaction or specified numeric value belongs to a group.	A = Name or number of group to be examined.
		B = If this value is used, the group is assumed to be in the numeric mode. In the numeric mode, the value contained by 'B' is compared to see if it is a member. If no 'B' operand is used, the group is assumed to be in the transaction mode. In this case the current transaction checks to see if it belongs to the group.
		C = If condition checked in 'B' is

TABLE 7.4

(*Continued*)

Block	Primary Purposes	Operand(s)
		false, the name or number contained by 'C' represents a block to which the transaction will be routed.

Example:

EXAMINE   ZSET,,ZEXIT

A transaction checks to see if it belongs to the group ZSET. If it belongs, it will move to the next sequential block. If the transaction does not belong to the group ZSET, it will be routed to the block ZEXIT.

Block	Primary Purposes	Operand(s)
FAVAIL	Makes a facility available after a FUNAVAIL Block has made it unavailable.	A = Name, number or range of facilities to be made available.

Example:

FAVAIL   20

Facility 20 is made available by the entering transaction.

Block	Primary Purposes	Operand(s)
FUNAVAIL	Makes a facility unavailable for use. Overrides SEIZE & PREEMPT Blocks. In this mode of operation, if a transaction is currently controlling a facility when FUNAVAIL is executed, its use will be suspended until a FAVAIL has been executed.	A = Name, number or range of facilities to be made unavailable. (See *GPSS/H Reference Manual* for other functions of FUNAVAIL.)

Example:

FUNAVAIL   20

Facility 20 is made unavailable by the entering transaction.

Block		Primary Purposes	Operand(s)
GATE	LS LR	This block is used to monitor the state of a logic switch. If the switch is not in the state specified by the auxiliary operator, the transaction is either denied entry to the block or routed to a nonsequential block.	A = Name or number of a logic switch B = Optional nonsequential block the transaction is routed to if the condition specifed by the auxiliary operator is false. The auxiliary operators are LS (logic set) and LR (logic reset).

Examples:

GATE LR   57

If logic switch 57 is set, a transaction will be denied entry to the block. When 57 is logic reset, the entering transaction will pass through the block.

GATE LS   ZCPU,567

If logic switch ZCPU is in the reset state, the entering transaction will move to block 567. If logic switch ZCPU is set, the entering transaction will fall through to the next sequential block.

(*continues*)

TABLE 7.4

(*Continued*)

Block		Primary Purposes	Operand(s)
GATE	I NI U NU FV FNV FS FNS	This block is used to monitor the state of a facility. If the facility is not in the state specified by the auxiliary operator, the transaction is either denied entry to the block or routed to a nonsequential block.	A = Name or number of a Facility B = Optional nonsequential block the transaction is routed to if the condition specified by the auxiliary operator is false. The auxiliary operators are I (preempted), NI (not preempted), U (seized or preempted), NU (not seized or preempted), FV (available), FNV (unavailable), FS (seizeable), and FNS (not seizeable).

Example:

    GATE NU   MACHINE

If the facility MACHINE is in use (seized or preempted) a transaction will be denied entry to the block. When MACHINE is released, the entering transaction will pass through the block.

Block		Primary Purposes	Operand(s)
GATE	SE SNE SF SNF SV SNV	This block is used to monitor the state of a storage. If the storage is not in the state specified by the auxiliary operator, the transaction is either denied entry to the block or routed to a nonsequential block.	A = Name or number of a Facility B = Optional nonsequential block the transaction is routed to if the condition specified by the auxiliary operator is false. The auxiliary operators are SE (empty), SNE (not empty), SF (full), SNF (not full), SV (available), SNV (not available).

Example:

    GATE SV   PARKLOT,STREET

If the storage PARKLOT is available, the entering transaction will proceed to the next sequential block. If PARKLOT has been made unavailable with the SUNAVAIL Block, the transaction will be routed to the block STREET.

Block	Primary Purposes	Operand(s)
GATHER	Transactions from the same assembly set are delayed at this block until a specified count has been reached. Many simultaneous gathers for different assembly sets can be taking place at one time.	A = Number of transactions from the same assembly set to be gathered.

Example:

    GATHER   &PARTS

The ampervariable &PARTS specifies the number of transactions that need to be gathered before they are allowed to proceed to the next sequential block.

Block	Primary Purposes	Operand(s)
GENERATE	Transactions are created with this block.	A = Mean rate between transaction creations.

TABLE 7.4

(Continued)

Block	Primary Purposes	Operand(s)
		B = Spread to be used with the mean specified by 'A'. (i.e. A + or − B). If 'B' is coded as a function, then its value is multiplied by 'A' and the product becomes the transaction interarrival rate.
		C = Time of first transaction creation.
		D = Limit count for number of transactions created. Defaults to infinite.
		E = Priority to be assigned to created transactions.
		F = Specifies the number and type of parameters created transactions will have. Fullword (PF), Halfword (PH), Byte (PB), or Floating Point (PL) can be used.

Examples:

GENERATE   3600

A transaction will be created every 3600 time units.

GENERATE   3600,200,1000,100,50,20PF

Transactions will be generated every 3600+/−200 time units. The first one will be created at time 1000. After 100 transactions have been generated, no more will be created. The transactions will have a priority level of 50 and will have 20 fullword parameters.

Block	Primary Purposes	Operand(s)
INDEX	The value of the 'B' operand is added to the value of the parameter specified by the 'A' operand and stored in the parameter specified by the 'A' operand.	A = Name or number of the transaction parameter to be operated on. B = Value to be added to the contents of the parameter specified by 'A'.

Example:

INDEX   2,1

One is added to the value currently residing in parameter number two of the entering transaction.

Block	Primary Purposes	Operand(s)
JOIN	Causes a transaction or numeric value to become a member of a group.	A = Name or number of the group to be joined. B = Value to become a member of a numeric group. This parameter is omitted when the group is operating in the transaction mode.

Example:

JOIN   FLEET

The entering transaction becomes a member of the group FLEET.

(*continues*)

TABLE 7.4

(Continued)

Block	Primary Purposes	Operand(s)
LEAVE	Causes a transaction to decrement a storage's contents by a specified amount.	A = Name or number of a storage to be operated on. B = Number of units to decrement storage contents. If left empty, one unit is assumed for the decrement count.

Example:

    LEAVE   YARD
The entering transaction decrements the storage YARD by a count of one.

Block	Primary Purposes	Operand(s)
LINK	Causes a transaction to be added to a user chain.	A = Name or number of the user chain to be operated on. B = Can be a FIFO (measuring transactions are added to the chain in a first in first out fashion), LIFO (last in first out), or a parameter number. If a parameter number is referenced, the transactions are linked in ascending order based on their value of this parameter. C = If the chain's link indicator is off, this operand specifies a block to which the entering transaction will be routed. The link indicator is turned off when an UNLINK Block is executed on an empty chain.

Example:

    LINK   WAIT,FIFO,WSTAT
The entering transaction is linked to the user chain named WAIT in FIFO fashion. If another transaction had executed an UNLINK Block on WAIT while it was empty, WAIT's link indicator would have been turned off. If this were the case, then the entering transaction would not be placed on the user chain. Instead it would be routed directly to the block WSTAT.

Block		Primary Purposes	Operand(s)
LOGIC	S R I	Changes state of a logic switch entity.	A = Name or number of the logic switch to be operated on. If the auxiliary operator is S, the switch will be 'set'. If it is R, the switch will be 'reset'. If the operator is I, the switch will be toggled to the opposite state.

Example:

    LOGIC I   TOGGLE
The entering transaction will cause the logic switch named TOGGLE to be changed to the opposite state.

TABLE 7.4

(*Continued*)

Block	Primary Purposes	Operand(s)
LOOP	Used to route a transaction through a series of blocks a specified number of times.	A = Name or number of a parameter which is to be decremented and compared to zero. B = Block to which the transaction is routed if 'A' is not yet zero.

Example:

    LOOP   2,AGAIN

The entering transaction will have the value in parameter 2 decremented by one and compared to zero. If the value is zero, the transaction will move to the next sequential block. If the value is not zero, the transaction will be routed to the block, AGAIN.

Block	Primary Purposes	Operand(s)
MARK	Used to time stamp a transaction.	A = Name or number of a parameter which is to be time stamped. If left blank, current time is stored in Mark Time word of the entering transaction.

Example:

    MARK   2

The entering transaction will have the value in parameter 2 set to AC1, which is the current value of the absolute clock.

Block	Primary Purposes	Operand(s)
MATCH	Used to synchronize the flow of two transactions.	A = Specifies a conjugate block which is usually another MATCH Block (it can be a GATHER or ASSEMBLE Block). As soon as the matching condition (i.e. another transaction arrives at conjugate MATCH or completes GATHER or ASSEMBLE operation) the entering transaction can move on.

Example:

    MATCH   ZMATCH

The entering transaction will wait until a transaction from the same assembly set arrives at the conjugate MATCH Block called ZMATCH.

Block	Primary Purposes	Operand(s)
MSAVEVALUE	Used to save data in a matrix.	A = Specifies the name or number of matrix savevalue to be operated on. If this number or name is followed by a + or −, the value in the matrix will be incremented or decremented by the value of 'D'. B = A row or range of rows to be operated on.

(*continues*)

TABLE 7.4

(*Continued*)

Block	Primary Purposes	Operand(s)
		C = A column or range of columns to be operated on.
		D = The value to be placed into the matrix element or the value the matrix element will be incremented or decremented by.
		E = The type of matrix being operated on. Can be MX (fullword), MH (halfword), MB (byte), or ML (floating point).

Example:

MSAVEVALUE ZLIST,10,11,PF$CLOC,MX

The contents of the entering transaction's parameter PF$CLOC will be stored in row 10, column 11 of the fullword matrix savevalue named ZLIST.

Block	Primary Purposes	Operand(s)
PREEMPT	Allows a transaction to preempt a facility that is currently in use.	A = Specifies the name or number of a facility to be preempted. When only the 'A' operand is specified, the transaction entering the PREEMPT Block is given control of the facility. The transaction that was controlling the facility is placed on an interrupt chain. Consult the *GPSS/H Reference Manual* for other operands and functions of the PREEMPT Block.

Example:

PREEMPT   WORKS

The entering transaction representing a machine breakdown preempts the work station (facility named WORKS) from a transaction representing a worker.

Block	Primary Purposes	Operand(s)
PRIORITY	Gives a new priority level to the entering transaction.	A = The new priority level is specified by this operand.
		B = If the word 'BUFFER' is used for the 'B' operand, the current events chain is reordered. (See the BUFFER Block description.)

Example:

PRIORITY   HIGH

The entering transaction is given a priority level of HIGH. HIGH is a synonym previously defined by the simulation analyst.

Block	Primary Purposes	Operand(s)
QUEUE	Allows a transaction to specify a number of units that will become part of a queue.	A = The name or number of the queue to be operated on.
		B = Number of units to be added to the contents of a queue. If left blank, defaults to one.

TABLE 7.4

(*Continued*)

Block	Primary Purposes	Operand(s)
Example:		

QUEUE   ZLINE

The entering transaction becomes a member of the queue ZLINE. One unit is added to the current contents.

RELEASE	Entering transaction relinquishes control of a facility it had previously seized.	A = The name or number of the facility to be operated on.

Example:

RELEASE   MACHINE

The entering transaction relinquishes control of the facility MACHINE.

Block		Primary Purposes	Operand(s)
REMOVE	(none) G GE L LE E NE MAX MIN	Causes a transaction or numeric value to be removed from membership in a group.	A = The name or number of the group to be operated on. If only the 'A' operand is used, the entering transaction will be removed from the group if it is member. B = Specifies the maximum number of transactions to be removed from the group. Omitted if operating in the numeric mode. C = Used only if the group is operating in the numeric mode. In this case, the numeric value to be removed from the group is specified. D = Used in the transaction mode only. This parameter specifies a transaction attribute to be used as a condition for removing group members. It operates in conjunction with the G (greater), GE (greater or equal), L (less), LE (less or equal), E (equal), NE (not equal), MAX (maximum), and MIN (minimum) auxiliary operators. If no auxiliary operator is specified, E is assumed. E = Value used for the comparison with the parameter cited in 'D'. F = Block name or number to be used as an alternate exit if the conditions for removal are not met.

Example:

REMOVE   ROOMFUL,2,,PR,100,NEXTRM

The entering transaction attempts to remove two transactions with priority levels

(*continues*)

TABLE 7.4
(*Continued*)

Block	Primary Purposes	Operand(s)
	higher than 100 from the group ROOMFUL. If the attempt is not successful, the entering transaction will be routed to the block NEXTRM.	
RETURN	Entering transaction returns control of a preempted facility.	A = The name or number of the facility to be operated on.

Example:

    RETURN   WORKS

The entering transaction relinquishes control of the preempted facility WORKS.

Block	Primary Purposes	Operand(s)
SAVAIL	Entering transaction makes a storage available after having made it unavailable with a SUNAVAIL Block.	A = The name or number of a storage or range of storages to make available.

Example:

    SAVAIL   MCAGE

The entering transaction makes the storage MCAGE available for use again.

Block	Primary Purposes	Operand(s)
SAVEVALUE	Entering transaction adds to, subtracts from, or places a value into a permanent global location called a savevalue.	A = The name or number of a savevalue or range of savevalues to be operated on. If a trailing '+' or '−' is used, the current contents of the savevalue storage is to be incremented or decremented.
		B = The value to be either added, subtracted, or placed in the savevalue.
		C = Specifies the data type of the savevalue. May be X or XF (fullword), H or HX (halfword), XB (byte), or XL (floating point).

Example:

    SAVEVALUE   ZSTORE-,1,X

The entering transaction will cause the fullword value stored in the savevalue, ZSTORE, to be decremented by one.

Block		Primary Purposes	Operand(s)
SCAN	(none) G GE L LE E NE MAX MIN	Allows the entering transaction to look at the attributes of transactions belonging to a specified group.	A = The name or number of a group to be scanned. B = Specifies an attribute of the transactions belonging to the group being scanned. Based on the auxiliary operator of G (greater), GE (greater or equal), L (less), LE (less or equal), E (equal), or NE (not equal); this operand will be compared to the value specified in the 'C' operand. If MAX (max-

TABLE 7.4
(Continued)

Block	Primary Purposes	Operand(s)
		imum) or MIN (minimum) are used as auxiliary operators, the attribute with either the lowest or highest value as specified by 'B' will be selected.
		C = Comparand value used in conjunction with 'B'. With auxiliary operators MAX or MIN, this value should be omitted.
		D = Attribute to be obtained from the first transaction satisfying the SCAN requirements.
		E = Contains the name or number of the entering transaction's parameter where the information specified by 'D' will be stored.
		F = Name or number of a block to which the entering transaction will be routed if the scan is unsuccessful.

Example:

SCAN MIN   PICK,TIME$PF,,TOSTAT$PF,DESTIN$PF,ERR999

The entering transaction will look in the group PICK for the transaction having the minimum value in its parameter named TIME. When this transaction has been located, the value in its parameter TOSTAT will be placed in the DESTIN parameter of the transaction entering the SCAN Block.

Block	Primary Purposes	Operand(s)
SEIZE	Entering transaction captures or seizes a facility.	A = The name or number of the facility to be seized.

Example:

SEIZE   ZCHECK

The entering transaction will seize the facility ZCHECK.

Block	Primary Purposes	Operand(s)
SELECT	G GE L LE E NE U NU I NI FV FNV	The entering transaction stores the number of the first entity satisfying a specific condition, in one of its parameters. (See the description of the COUNT Block for definitions of these auxiliary operators.)	A = The name or number of a parameter that the entering transaction uses to store the appropriate entity number. B = Lower bound in range of entities to be checked. C = Upper bound in range of entities to be checked. D = Only used with the G (greater), GE (greater or equal), L (less), LE (less or equal), E (equal), or NE (not equal) auxiliary opera-

(continues)

TABLE 7.4

(Continued)

Block	Primary Purposes	Operand(s)
FS FNS SE SNE SF SNF SV SNV LR LS MIN MAX		tors. Its value is compared to a value specified by operand 'E'. E = Specifies an SNA/SNL which is evaluated over the specified range and compared to the comparand in 'D'. The first entity satisfying the test is stored in the parameter identified by 'A'. It is also used for the MAX (maximum) and MIN (minimum) auxiliary operators in addition to the ones mentioned in the description of 'D'. F = Contains the name or number of a block to which the entering transaction will be routed if unsuccessful.

Example:

> SELECT LS   1,1,10,,,ALTXIT
>
> The entering transaction will examine the logic switches in the range 1 through 10. When one is found to be logic set, its number will be stored in parameter one of the entering transaction. If none of the switches examined are set, the transaction will proceed to the block named ALTXIT.

Block	Primary Purposes	Operand(s)
SPLIT	Entering transaction produces offspring.	A = The number of offspring to be created. B = Block to which offspring will be sent. C-G = (See *GPSS/H Reference Manual* for definitions of these operands.)

Example:

> SPLIT   1,ZROUTE
>
> The entering transaction will produce one offspring which will be sent to a block called ZROUTE.

Block	Primary Purposes	Operand(s)
SUNAVAIL	Entering transaction causes a storage to become unavailable to transactions that attempt to enter it.	A = The name or number of the storage or range of storages to be made (unavailable. Transactions currently using the storage remain unaffected.

Example:

> SUNAVAIL   ROOM
>
> The entering transaction will cause the storage ROOM to be unavailable until a SAVAIL Block is executed.

Block	Primary Purposes	Operand(s)
TABULATE	Entering transaction causes an entry to be made in a Table statistics.	A = The name or number of a table to be operated on. B = Optional weighting factor.

TABLE 7.4

(*Continued*)

Block	Primary Purposes	Operand(s)
Example:		

TABULATE   ZTABLE
ZTABLE has an entry added to its contents.

Block	Primary Purposes	Operand(s)
TERMINATE	Entering transaction is destroyed.	A = An optional operand's value is decremented from the simulation termination counter. The initial value of this counter is set with the START control statement. When its value is zero or less, the simulation is terminated.

Example:

TERMINATE
Entering transaction is destroyed.

Block	Primary Purposes	Operand(s)
TEST	G GE L LE E NE	Entering transaction compares two values and based on the comparison proceeds sequentially, proceeds nonsequentially, or is denied entry to the block.	A = Expression used as a comparison to the value in 'B'. B = Expression used as a comparison to the value in 'A'. C = Optional block to which the transaction proceeds if it fails the test of G (greater), GE (greater or equal), L (less), LE (less or equal), E (equal), or NE (not equal). If 'C' is not used, the entering transaction will be denied entry to the block until the test is true.

Examples:

TEST E   PF$DESTIN,12,ZT20
Entering transaction will determine if its fullword parameter called DESTIN is equal to 12. If it is equal to 12, the transaction will proceed to the next sequential block. If it is not 12, it will proceed to the nonsequential block called ZT20.

TEST E   BV$TEST1,TRUE
Entering transaction will determine if the value of Boolean Variable TEST1 is equal to the value of the synonym 'TRUE'. If the two values are equal, then the entering transaction will proceed to the next sequential block. If the values are not equal, the transaction will be denied entry to the TEST Block and will wait until the value of TEST1 becomes equal to the value of 'TRUE'.

Block	Primary Purposes	Operand(s)
TRANSFER	Entering transaction unconditionally transfers to a specified block.	A = Omitted. B = Block name or number for unconditional transfer.
Example:		

TRANSFER   ,ZERR0
Entering transaction will always go to the block ZERR0.

(continues)

TABLE 7.4

(*Continued*)

Block	Primary Purposes	Operand(s)
TRANSFER	Entering transaction is sent to one of two blocks based on a percentage.	A = Percentage compared to a random sample drawn from RN1 (random number stream 1). B = Name or number of block that the entering transaction will proceed to if the value of RN1 is greater than the percentage specified by 'A'. C = Name or number of block that the entering transaction will proceed to if the value of RN1 is less than the percentage specified by 'A'.

Example:

    TRANSFER   .5,ZERR0,ZERR1

Entering transactions go to the block ZERR0 and to the block ZERR1 each approximately 50% of the time.

Block	Primary Purposes	Operand(s)
TRANSFER	Entering transaction is sent to one of a range of blocks based on block's availability.	A = The word 'ALL'. B = The name or number of the first block in a range of blocks. C = Name or number of the last block in a range of blocks. D = A number specifying that every nth block within the range specified by 'A' and 'B' should be tried for entry.

Example:

    TRANSFER   ALL,10,20,5

Entering transaction will attempt to transfer to one of blocks 10, 15, and 20. The first block among these three that is available for entry will admit the transaction. If none are available, the transaction will attempt the transfer each scan cycle of the GPSS/H current events chain until one of the blocks becomes available.

Block	Primary Purposes	Operand(s)
TRANSFER	Entering transaction is randomly sent to one of a range of blocks without regard to block availability.	A = The word 'PICK'. B = The name or number of the lower block in a range of blocks. C = Name or number of the upper block in range of blocks.

Example:

    TRANSFER   PICK,10,20

Entering transaction will attempt to transfer to one of the blocks in a range from 10 to 20. The block will be chosen randomly.

Block	Primary Purposes	Operand(s)
TRANSFER	Entering transaction is sent to a block while retaining the number of the block it transferred from.	A = The word 'SBR' (stands for subroutine). B = The name or number of the block the transaction will transfer to.

TABLE 7.4

(Continued)

Block	Primary Purposes	Operand(s)
		C = Name or number of a parameter that is to hold the number of the current block.

Example:

TRANSFER   SBR,GPPATH,9PH

Entering transaction transfers to the block GPPATH. The number of the TRANSFER Block will be stored in parameter 9 of the entering transaction.

Block	Primary Purposes	Operand(s)
TRANSFER	Entering transaction is sent to a block specified by one of its parameters added to a value in the 'C' operand.	A = Either PF (fullword parameter), PH (halfword parameter), PB (byte parameter), or PL (floating point parameter). B = Parameter number. C = The value to be added to the block's number. Referenced by the parameter specified in the 'B' operand.

Example:

TRANSFER   PH,4,1

Entering transaction transfers to the block number contained in parameter 4 added to one.

Block	Primary Purposes	Operand(s)
UNLINK	Causes a transaction to be removed from a user chain.	A = Name or number of the user chain to be operated on. B = Name or number of the block that unlinked transactions are sent to. C = Maximum number of transactions to be unlinked. Can be specified as 'ALL' so all transactions are unlinked. D = If omitted, transactions are unlinked from front of chain. If the word 'BACK' is used, transactions are unlinked from the back of the chain. (See the *GPSS/H Reference Manual* for other uses of the UNLINK Block.) E = Left Blank. F = Alternate block to be used by transaction if the unlink operation fails.

Example:

UNLINK   WAIT,ZOFF,1,BACK,ALTXIT

The entering transaction will attempt to unlink one transaction from the back of the user chain, WAIT. The unlinked transaction will go to the block ZOFF. If no transaction can be unlinked, the entering transaction will proceed to the block ALTXIT.

TABLE 7.5
Control Statements and Compiler Directives

Statement	Statement Type	Brief Description of Use
BVARIABLE	Control Statement	Defines a Boolean variable
CHAR*N	Compiler Directive	Declaration of character string variables
CLEAR	Control Statement	Clears statistics and removes transactions
DO	Control Statement	Used for construction of DO loops (beginning)
ELSE	Control Statement	Used with IF statement for testing sets of conditions
ELSEIF	Control Statement	Used with IF statement for testing sets of conditions
END	Control Statement	Indicates end of model
ENDDO	Control Statement	Used for construction of DO loops (end)
ENDIF	Control Statement	Signals end of group of statements associated with IF
ENDMACRO	Compiler Directive	Indicates end of a MACRO definition
EQU	Compiler Directive	Assigns entities to numeric values
FUNCTION	Control Statement	Defines a function
FVARIABLE	Control Statement	Defines a floating point variable
GETLIST	Control Statement	Gets data from keyboard or external file
GETSTRING	Control Statement	Gets an entire record from keyboard or external file
GOTO	Control Statement	An unconditional branching statement
HERE	Control Statement	Used as a Target for the GOTO statement
IF	Control Statement	Provides for conditional execution of control statements
INITIAL	Control Statement	Initializes savevalues, matrix savevalues, and logic switches
INTEGER	Compiler Directive	Declares an ampervariable as an integer
LET	Control Statement	Used to assign a value to an ampervariable
MACRO	Compiler Directive	Tells compiler to insert code defined as a MACRO
MATRIX	Control Statement	Defines a matrix
NOXREF	Compiler Directive	Inhibits generation of a cross reference file
OPERCOL	Compiler Directive	Defines outmost column that the first operand can be located
PUTPIC	Control Statement	Used to write data to a file or screen
PUTSTRING	Control Statement	Used to write data to a file or screen
QTABLE	Control Statement	Defines a Qtable
REAL	Compiler Directive	Declares an ampervariable as real
REALLOCATE	Compiler Directive	Changes the allocation of memory for various entity classes
RESET	Control Statement	Allows "pre-steady state" statistics to be discarded

TABLE 7.5
(*Continued*)

Statement	Statement Type	Breif Description of Use
RMULT	Control Statement	Changes the random number stream and value
SIMULATE	Control Statement	Tells simulation to run : specifies maximum run time allowed
START	Control Statement	Begins execution of simulation
STARTMACRO	Compiler Directive	Used to indicate the beginning of a macro
STORAGE	Control Statement	Defines a storage
SYN	Compiler Directive	Declares and defines a constant (synonym)
TABLE	Control Statement	Defines a table
UNLIST	Compiler Directive	Tells compiler to turn off portions of the output listing
VARIABLE	Control Statement	Defines a variable statement
VCHAR*N	Compiler Directive	Declares a variable length string

7.7 Running a Simulation with GPSS/H

Running a simulation with GPSS/H involves instructing a computer to execute a combination of blocks, compiler directives, and control statements. Although the actual execution command typed in at the keyboard is dependent on the computer system being used, there are certain statements that must be present to run a GPSS/H simulation. The model shown in Figure 7.3 contains the minimum GPSS/H statements and blocks required to run a model.

7.7.1 Clock

GPSS/H maintains two floating point clocks that are used by the simulation. The first and primary clock is called the absolute clock (AC1). The value of AC1 is equal to the amount of simulated time that has passed since the model run initially began or since a CLEAR statement was executed. The second clock is called the relative clock (C1). C1 maintains the time elapsed since the model run started, since a CLEAR statement was executed, or since a RESET statement

```
SIMULATE   1   Model can execute for up to one minute of CPU time
START      1   Set termination counter to one and start execution

GENERATE   1   Create transactions every one time unit
TERMINATE  1   Destroy transaction & decrement termination counter

END            End of model
```

Figure 7.3 Minimum requirements in a GPSS/H simulation.

TABLE 7.6
SCAs, SNAs, and SLAs

Attribute	Entity Type or Classification	Brief Description of Function
ABS(x)	Mathematical	Yields the absolute value of 'x'
AC1	System Status	Absolute clock time
ACOS(x)	Mathematical	Arc cosine of 'x'
AN1	System Status	# transactions in current transaction's assembly set
ASIN(x)	Mathematical	Arc sine of 'x'
ATAN(x)	Mathematical	Arc tangent of 'x'
BVx	Boolean Variable	Yields true (1) or false (0) value of Boolean variable 'x'
C1	System Status	Relative clock time
CAx	User Chain	Average contents of user chain 'x'
CCx	User Chain	Total # of transactions placed on user chain 'x'
CHx	User Chain	Current # of transactions on user chain 'x'
CM(x)	User Chain	Maximum number of transactions on user chain 'x'
COS(x)	Mathematical	Cosine of 'x'
CTx	User Chain	Average time per transaction on user chain 'x'
EXP(x)	Mathematical	Natural log base (e) raised to the xth power
Fx	Facility	True (1) if facility 'x' seized or preempted
FCx	Facility	Count of time facility is seized or preempted
FIx	Facility	True (1) if facility 'x' is currently preempted
FIX(x)	Conversion	Value of 'x' changed to fixed data type
FLT(x)	Conversion	Value of 'x' changed to floating point data type
FNx	Function	Value of function 'x'
FNIx	Facility	True (1) if facility 'x' is not preempted
FNSx	Facility	True (1) if facility 'x' can't be seized
FNUx	Facility	True (1) if facility 'x' is not seized or preempted
FNVx	Facility	True (1) if facility 'x' is not available
FPUx	Facility	Percent time facility 'x' is unavailable
FPVx	Facility	Percent time facility 'x' is available
FRx	Facility	Percent utilization of facility 'x'
FRNx	Random Number	Floating point pseudorandom number from stream 'x'
FRUx	Facility	Average utilization of facility 'x' while unavailable
FNVx	Facility	Average utilization of facility 'x' while available
FSx	Facility	True (1) if facility 'x' may be seized
FTx	Facility	Average period of time facility 'x' remains captured
FUx	Facility	True (1) if facility 'x' is seized or preempted
FUAx	Facility	Average period of time facility 'x' remains unavailable

TABLE 7.6

(*Continued*)

Attribute	Entity Type or Classification	Brief Description of Function
FUNx	Facility	Number of periods facility 'x' is unavailable
FUTx	Facility	Total time facility 'x' was unavailable
FVx	Facility	True (1) if facility 'x' is available
Gx	Group	Number of transactions or numeric numbers in group 'x'
LEN(x)	Character String	Returns length of string 'x'
LOG(x)	Mathematical	Natural log of 'x'
LRx	Logic Switch	True (1) if logic switch 'x' is reset
LSx	Logic Switch	True (1) if logic switch 'x' is set
M1	Transaction	Transaction Mark Time deducted from AC1
MBx(r,c)	Matrix	Value in byte matrix 'x' at Row (r) and Column (c)
MHx(r,c)	Matrix	Value in halfword matrix 'x' at Row (r) and Column (c)
MLx(r,c)	Matrix	Value in floating point matrix 'x' at Row (r) and Column (c)
MPx	Transaction	Difference between AC1 and parameter 'x'
MPBx	Transaction	Difference between AC1 and byte parameter 'x'
MPFx	Transaction	Difference between AC1 and fullword parameter 'x'
MPHx	Transaction	Difference between AC1 and halfword parameter 'x'
MPLx	Transaction	Difference between AC1 and floating point parameter 'x'
MXx(r,c)	Matrix	Value in fullword matrix 'x' at Row (r) and Column (c)
Mx	Block	Number of transactions to have entered block 'x'
MACx	System State	Next value of AC1. Next event occurs at this time
PBx	Transaction	Value of transaction byte parameter 'x'
PFx	Transaction	Value of transaction fullword parameter 'x'
PHx	Transaction	Value of transaction halfword parameter 'x'
PLx	Transaction	Value of transaction floating point parameter 'x'
PR	Transaction	Current transaction priority level
Qx	Queue	Current members in queue 'x'
QAx	Queue	Average number of member in queue 'x'
QCx	Queue	Total entries in queue 'x'
QMx	Queue	Maximum members of queue 'x'
QTx	Queue	Average time spent in queue 'x'
QXx	Queue	Average time spent in queue 'x' when more than zero time was spent
QZx	Queue	Number of members spending zero time in queue
Rx	Storage	Remaining capacity in storage 'x'

(*continues*)

TABLE 7.6

(Continued)

Attribute	Entity Type or Classification	Brief Description of Function
RNx	Random Number	A sample pseudorandom number from stream 'x'
RNXx	Random Number	Position of next sample from stream 'x'
RVEXPO	Distribution	Sample from exponential distribution using RVEXPO (Random Number Stream, Mean)
RVNORM	Distribution	Sample from normal distribution using RVNORM (Random Number Stream, Mean, Standard Deviation)
RVTRI	Distribution	Sample from triangular distribution using RVTRI (Random Number Stream, Min, Mode, Max)
Sx	Storage	Number of units using storage 'x'
SAx	Storage	Average number of units using storage 'x'
SCx	Storage	Total units to have used storage 'x'
SEx	Storage	True (1) if storage 'x' is empty
SFx	Storage	True (1) if storage 'x' is full
SIN(x)	Mathematical	Returns sine of 'x'
SMx	Storage	Maximum units in storage 'x' at any one time
SNEx	Storage	True (1) if storage 'x' is not empty
SNFx	Storage	True (1) if storage 'x' is not full
SNVx	Storage	True (1) if storage 'x' is not available
SPUx	Storage	Percentage that storage 'x' was unavailable
SPVx	Storage	Percentage that storage 'x' has been available
SQRT(x)	Mathematical	Square root of 'x'
SRx	Storage	Utilization of storage 'x'
SRUx	Storage	Utilization of storage 'x' while unavailable
SRVx	Storage	Utilization of storage 'x' while available
SSG(c,x)	Character String	Substring of 'c' from position x to end
SSG(c,x,j)	Character String	Substring of 'c' from position x for j characters
STx	Storage	Average time per unit in storage 'x'
SUAx	Storage	Average duration time or period of unavailability for storage 'x'
SUNx	Storage	Number of unavailable periods for storage 'x'
SUTx	Storage	Total time unavailable for storage 'x'
SVx	Storage	True (1) if storage 'x' is available
TAN(x)	Mathematical	Tangent of 'x'
TBx	Table	Unweighted mean of table 'x'
TBWx	Table	Weighted mean of table 'x'
TCx	Table	Number of unweighted entries in table 'x'
TCWx	Table	Number of weighted entries in table 'x'

TABLE 7.6

(Continued)

Attribute	Entity Type or Classification	Brief Description of Function
TDx	Table	Unweighted standard deviation of table 'x'
TDWx	Table	Weighted standard deviation of table 'x'
TG1	System Status	Value of termination counter
Vx	Variable	Value of variable 'x'
Wx	Block	Number of transactions currently in block 'x'
Xx	Savevalue	Value of fullword savevalue 'x'
XBx	Savevalue	Value of byte savevalue 'x'
XFx	Savevalue	Value of fullword savevalue 'x'
XHx	Savevalue	Value of halfword savevalue 'x'
XID1	System Status	Transaction ID number
XLx	Savevalue	Value of floating point savevalue 'x'

was executed. In a model that contains no RESET statements, the value of C1 will always be equal to the value of AC1 (see Figure 7.4).

The time units represented by the clocks are chosen implicitly by the simulation analyst and implemented through the selection of operands for the ADVANCE and other blocks.

7.7.2 Starting and Stopping

As seen in Figure 7.3, a model is "given permission" to be executed with the SIMULATE statement. The START statement tells actual execution to begin and defines the length of run or conditions for execution to be terminated. The TERMINATE block, when it has a value in its 'A' operand, is used to "count down" toward the model's completion time.

In general, two termination methods are used in GPSS/H. The first requires using a TERMINATE block with a value in its 'A' operand located at only one place in the model. A special GENERATE block is used in conjunction with this TERMINATE block. The combination of these two blocks plays no part in the model other than to signal when execution is over. This piece of code and the

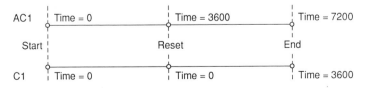

Figure 7.4 GPSS/H absolute clock (AC1) versus relative clock (C1).

```
*:============================================================*
*                   Timing Transactions                     *
*:============================================================*
*
      START       8
      GENERATE    3600
      TERMINATE   1
*:============================================================*
```

          Explanation : After 100 customer transactions have
          been serviced by the BARBER resource and pass through
          the TERMINATE Block, the START count of 100 will have
          been decremented to 0 and the model will stop executing.

Figure 7.5 Timing transaction method of model termination.

transactions created therein are known as the "timing transaction" section of the model (Figure 7.5).

The other method used to stop model execution involves placing a TERMINATE block (with its 'A' operand coded) at a strategic location in the model logic. This TERMINATE block becomes a counter and after a desired number of transactions are destroyed, model execution is halted (Figure 7.6).

The END statement is used to tell the simulation that no more control statements are to be executed. It indicates that the model is completely ended, both from a block standpoint and from a control statement standpoint.

7.7.3 Reset

Simulations often require a period of time to reach a steady state of operation. This may happen because the model needs to "fill up" with transactions or a certain occurrence needs to take place. Unless special care is taken, this start-up period may skew the statistics being gathered and lead the simulation analyst to draw false conclusions.

A tool provided by GPSS/H specifically to combat this problem is the RESET statement. The RESET statement allows the analyst to discard all statistics gath-

```
*============================================================*
         Start        100
*============================================================*
ATBARB SEIZE      BARBER
       ADVANCE    FN$BTIME
       RELEASE    BARBER
       TERMINATE  1
*============================================================*
```

          Explanation: After eight transactions have been created
          by the GENERATE Block and pass through the TERMINATE
          Block, the START count of 8 will be reduced to zero. Model
          execution will be stopped at this time.

Figure 7.6 Transaction count method of model termination.

```
XAMPLE STARTMACRO MACH,300          Start of macro named XAMPLE
       ENTER      #A
       ADVANCE    #B                Body of macro
       LEAVE      #A
       ENDMACRO                     End of macro
```

Figure 7.7 Example of a macro.

ered for blocks, facilities, queues, storages, tables, and user chains. After the reset has been executed, the collection of these statistics restarts, providing a nondistorted picture of model operation under steady-state conditions.

7.7.4 Clear

The CLEAR statement is used when multiple experiments are conducted on a model. The CLEAR statement removes all transactions from the model, discards all statistics, sets the clock to zero, and clears all entity contents. The CLEAR statement does not zero ampervariables or return the random number streams to their initial seed values.

7.8 Macros

GPSS/H contains a provision for defining frequently used sequences of blocks as single units. These units of code are known as macros. The beginning of a macro definition is indicated by the STARTMACRO statement and terminated with the ENDMACRO statement (Figure 7.7).

The operands following the STARTMACRO statement are represented within the body of the macro by #A for the first operand and #B for the second operand. Operands from 'A' to 'J' are allowable.

Macros have many uses including a reduction of coding time, forcing of uniformity, and code standardization. Macros can be used in the development of an application specific "mini-language" of analyst-created blocks. Chapter 9 goes into more detail in the creation of a user defined macro language.

7.9 Summary

This chapter has provided the reader with an overview of a leading simulation language. Hopefully enough information has been presented to make the example programs found in Chapters 8–11 more meaningful. The reader is encouraged to obtain a comprehensive tutorial guide to the computer simulation language of choice if a greater level of detail is desired.

References and Reading

Banks, Jerry, John S. Carson II, and John Ngo Sy. 1989. *Getting Started with GPSS/H*. Wolverine Software Corporation, Annandale, Virginia.

Bobillier, P. A, B. C. Kahn, and A. R. Probst. 1976. *Simulation with GPSS and GPSS/V*. Prentice-Hall, Englewood Cliffs, New Jersey.

Crain, Robert C., and Daniel T. Brunner. 1990. "Modeling Efficiently with GPSS/H." *Proc. 1990 Winter Simulation Conf.* (New Orleans, Dec. 9–12). SCS, San Diego, pp. 89–93.

Gordon, G. 1962. "A General Purpose System Simulator." *IBM Systems Journal* **1**(1).

Gordon, G. 1975. *The Application of GPSS/V to Discrete System Simulation*. Prentice-Hall, Englewood Cliffs, New Jersey.

Gordon, G. 1978. *System Simulation,* Second Edition. Prentice-Hall, Englewood Cliffs, New Jersey.

Henriksen, James O., and R. C. Crain. 1989. *GPSS/H Reference Manual,* Third Edition. Wolverine Software Corporation, Annandale, Virginia.

Neelamkavil, Francis. 1987. *Computer Simulation and Modelling*. Wiley, New York.

Schriber, Thomas J. 1988. "Perspectives on Simulation Using GPSS." *Proc. 1988 Winter Simulation Conf.* (San Diego, Dec. 12–14). SCS, San Diego, pp. 71–84.

Schriber, Thomas J. 1990. *An Introduction to Simulation Using GPSS/H*. Wiley, New York.

CHAPTER 8

Simple Queuing Systems

The primary focus of discrete event simulation has often been the study of queuing systems (Figure 8.1). Most discrete event simulation languages, including GPSS/H, are specifically designed to facilitate the modeling of systems with constrained resources and queues. When a resource is completely occupied, an entity wishing to use it must either wait (queue) or move on to an alternate course of action. The logic used by entities waiting to use a resource is known as the system's queuing discipline.

The order in which entities use resources and therefore enter and leave queues can be based on any number of different factors. A queue might be constructed in a first in first out (FIFO) or last in first out (LIFO) format (Figure 8.2). It may be built to allow entities to enter and leave based on a priority level. An example is a hospital emergency room. Patients with high priority (life threatening injuries) will not be left in queue waiting for the doctor (resource) as long as the boy with a sprained ankle will. Special features of certain entities may be used as a criterion for leaving queues in a particular order. For example, a fast car may be able to bypass a slower truck in a tollbooth queue.

The purpose of this chapter is to provide the reader with an introductory simulation based on the concept of a single resource and simple queue model. Initially, the model will be developed using a conventional programming language. The purpose of this exercise is to help familiarize the reader with the underlying concepts and workings of a simulation program.

The second part of Chapter 8 will look at the same type of model but will use the GPSS/H simulation language for construction. The reasons for using simulation languages and the theory behind their operation should become apparent through a comparison made between these two modeling approaches.

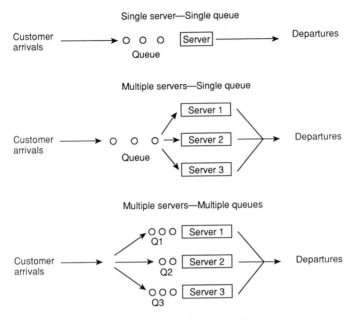

Figure 8.1 Various arrangements of servers and queues.

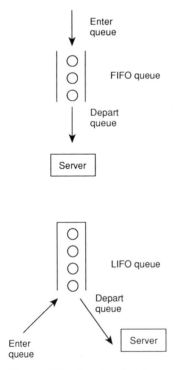

Figure 8.2 Queuing disciplines.

8.1 Queuing Systems

Queuing systems consist of entities vying for the use of constrained resources. An entity that arrives to find a resource completely occupied must either join a queue or take an alternate course of action. In everyday terms, a queuing system is a single or multiple set of servers that provide some type of assistance to arriving customers. A customer that cannot immediately receive service is forced to either enter a line in front of the server or move on to another part of the system (Figure 8.3).

Nearly all discrete event simulations contain subsystems that can be represented in terms of queuing systems. Some typical examples of queuing systems can be found in Table 8.1.

8.2 Pascal Program of a Simple Queuing System

This section illustrates how a simulation model can be developed using a standard programming language. The subject of this simulation will be a simple queuing system, and Turbo Pascal (Borland International, 1985) will be used to code the model.

8.2.1 Setting Up the Model

In a queuing system, events occur as time proceeds. Within the context of a single server queue model, events are defined as the arrival of a customer, the initiation of service, and the completion of service. Each of these events and their impacts on system operation must be reflected through logic imbedded in the simulation. As a means of allowing time-related sequences of events to occur, a simulation clock must be created. This clock functions as a chronological index or schedule instructing the model when certain events will occur.

In order to create a Turbo Pascal model for illustrative purposes, two questions need to be addressed.

1. *How often do customers arrive?* A variable will be created in the model to represent customer interarrival time. A random variable uniformly distributed between 2 and 20 minutes will be used for this parameter.

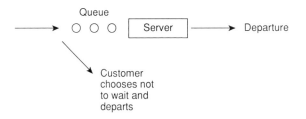

Figure 8.3 Customers may move to a different part of the system rather than queue.

TABLE 8.1
Examples of Queuing Systems

System to Be Modeled	Resource (Server)	Entity (Customer)
AGV System	Pick/Drop Stand	Automatic Guided Vehicle
Airport	Baggage Conveyor	Suitcase
Hospital Emergency Room	Doctor	Accident Victim
Highway Toll Booth	Booth	Automobile
Airport	Runway	Airplane
Parking Lot	Parking Space	Automobile
Manufacturing Plant	Assembly Operator	Engine Being Assembled
Supermarket	Checkout Counter	Shopper
21-Club	Doorman	College Student
Bowling Alley	Lane	Bowler
Stacker System	Crane	Pallet of Material
Barber Shop	Barber	Haircut Customer

2. How long will the server require to deal with each customer? Again, a uniformly distributed random variable will be used. However, its range will be from 8 to 14 minutes.

8.2.2 Model Operation

The model will start operation with the random generation of an arrival time for the first customer (Figure 8.4). The occurrence of this event will trigger a service initialization event and will necessitate the scheduling of a service completion time. Customer arrival is termed a primary event and service initialization is termed a secondary event. The start of a secondary event is dependent on the time of the primary. This model will also consider service completion to be a primary event since its occurrence is based on a randomly selected value. Table 8.2 lists the primary events in the system to be modeled and describes the subsequent consequences associated with each one's occurrence.

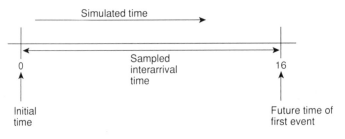

Figure 8.4 First primary event in simulation.

TABLE 8.2
Primary Event List

Primary Event	Consequences
Customer Arrival	(1) Schedule Next Arrival
	(2) Test Server's Status, Idle?
	No : Put Customer on Waiting Line
	Yes : Initiate Customer Service and
	Schedule Completion
Completion of Service	(1) Is a Customer Waiting?
	No : Server's Status Becomes Idle
	Yes : Put Next Customer into Service
	and Schedule Next Service
	Completion

8.2.3 Model Construction

In addition to the mechanisms required to model the queuing system and its activities, several other functions will be added to the Turbo Pascal simulation. First, a data initialization routine is needed. Start-up and termination provisions will also be required by the model. Finally, a procedure to generate an output report will be added. Figure 8.5 depicts the system in a general flowchart form.

8.2.4 Turbo Pascal Source Code Listing

A model of a single server and single queue was developed using Turbo Pascal and an event orientation approach. The source listing of this simulation program is shown in Figure 8.6.

8.2.5 Description of Functions and Variables

The following list describes the variables and functions used by the *single server–single queue* model listed in Section 8.2.4.

BeyondEnd Number equal to the simulation clock termination value plus one. This value is used to indicate no service completions are pending and the server is currently idle.

Clock This value is used to keep track of the current simulation clock time. It is advanced to the scheduled time of the next event that will occur.

Idle This Boolean variable is used as a flag to indicate whether the server is currently busy or not in use. When Idle is 'true' the server is not in use.

IdleTimer Keeps track of the amount of time the server spends occupied between idle periods. This variable is used in conjunction with ServerUtil to keep track of server utilization.

InterArrivalTimeAverage Constant used as the average customer interarrival time.

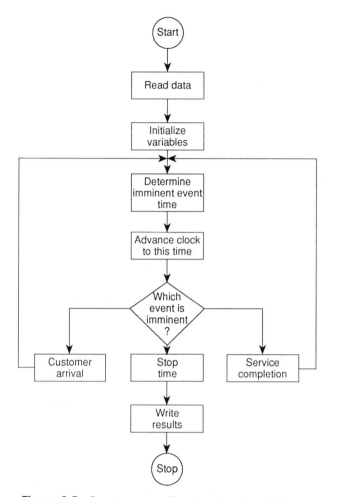

Figure 8.5 Queuing system flowchart (Schriber, 1974).

InterArrivalTimeRange Constant used to indicate the range of the possible customer interarrival times. This number is added to and subtracted from the interarrival time average to produce the range.

LengthofWaitingLine This variable maintains the current number of customers waiting to be serviced.

Max A function that returns the larger of two integers. It is used by this program to determine whether the current waiting line has exceeded the previous maximum waiting line length.

Min A function that returns the smallest of three integers. It is used by this program to determine whether service completion, customer arrival or simulation termination is the next event to occur.

```
{This is a program designed to model a single server with a single queue.}
Program Model(Input,Output,Lst);
{==================================================================================}

{Initialize the constants to be used in this run}
Const
{==================================================================================}
    InterArrivalAverage    = 11;   {Average Customer Interarrival Rate, Minutes}
    InterArrivalRange      = 9;    {Range of Customer Interarrival Rate, Minutes}
    ServiceAverage         = 11;   {Average Service Completion Time, Minutes}
    ServiceRange           = 3;    {Range of Service Completion Time, Minutes}
    StopTime               = 480;  {Simulation Runs for This Many Minutes}
{==================================================================================}

{Define Global Variable Types}
Var
{==================================================================================}
    Idle                         : Boolean;  {Flag Indicating Server is Idle}
    TimeofNextServiceCompletion  : Integer;  {Time for Next Service Completion}
    Clock                        : Integer;  {Simulation Clock Time}
    LengthofWaitingLine          : Integer;  {Current length of Server Queue}
    MxQueue                      : Integer;  {Maximum Queue Length}
    TimeofArrival                : Integer;  {Time of Next Customer Arrival}
    ServerUtil                   : Integer;  {Server Utilization Statistics}
    IdleTimer                    : Integer;  {Keeps Track of Server Idle Time}
    BeyondEnd                    : Integer;  {One Minute Past End of Simulation}
{==================================================================================}

{Function That Returns the Greater of Two Integers}
{==================================================================================}
Function Max(X,Y : Integer) : Integer;
    Var
    Z : Integer;
    Begin
    If (X>Y) Then Z := X Else Z := Y;
    Max := Z;
    End;
{==================================================================================}

{Function That Returns The Smallest of Three Integers}
{==================================================================================}
Function Min(X,Y,Z : Integer) : Integer;
    Var
    u,w : Integer;
    Begin
    If (X<Y) Then w := X Else w := Y;
    If (w<Z) Then u := w Else u := Z;
    Min := u;
    End;
{==================================================================================}

{Function That Returns A Random Number Uniformly From the Range A+/- B}
{==================================================================================}
Function Sample(A,B : Integer) : Integer;
    Var
    SampledValue : Integer;
    Begin
    If (B=0) Then Sample := A Else
        Begin
        SampledValue := Random(2*B+1);
        Sample := SampledValue + A-B;
        End
    End;
{==================================================================================}


{Begin the Main Program}
Begin
```

Figure 8.6 Turbo Pascal source code for single queue–single server model.

```
{==============================================================================}
{Initialize Variables}
Clock                            := 0;             {Clock Time = Zero}
Idle                             := True;          {Server is Idle}
LengthofWaitingLine              := 0;             {Waiting Line is Empty}
MxQueue                          := 0;             {Maximum Queue Has Been Zero}
ServerUtil                       := 0;             {Server Utilization is Zero}
BeyondEnd                        := StopTime+1;    {One Minute past End of Simulation}
TimeofNextServiceCompletion      := BeyondEnd;     {No Service Completion Scheduled}
{==============================================================================}

{Schedule First Customer Arrival}
TimeofArrival                    := Sample(InterArrivalAverage,InterArrivalRange);
{==============================================================================}

{Simulation Runs For Specified Length of Time}
While (Clock<StopTime) Do

  Begin
    {Find Next Event}
    Clock := Min(TimeofArrival,TimeofNextServiceCompletion,Stoptime);

{==============================================================================}
    {If Next Event is Customer Arrival Perform This Logic}
    If (Clock=TimeofArrival) Then
      Begin
        {Determine Next Arrival Time}
        TimeofArrival := Clock + Sample(InterArrivalAverage,InterArrivalRange);

        {If Server is Idle Seize Server Until Service Complete}
        If (Idle=True) Then
          Begin
            Idle := False;
            IdleTimer := Clock;   {Gather Idle Server Statistics}
            TimeofNextServiceCompletion := Clock + Sample(ServiceAverage,ServiceRange);
          End

        {If Server is Not Idle, Join Queue}
        Else If (Idle=False) Then
          Begin
            LengthofWaitingLine := LengthofWaitingLine + 1;
            MxQueue := Max(MxQueue,LengthofWaitingLine);
          End

      End
{==============================================================================}
    {If Next Event is A Service Completion Perform This Logic}
    Else If (Clock=TimeofNextServiceCompletion) Then
      Begin

        {If Queue for Server is Empty, Server Becomes Idle}
        If (LengthofWaitingLine<=0) Then
          Begin
            Idle := True;
            ServerUtil := ServerUtil + (Clock - IdleTimer); {Server Statistics}
            TimeofNextServiceCompletion := BeyondEnd;
          End

        {If Queue for Server is Not Empty, Server Gets New Waiting Customer}
        Else If (LengthofWaitingLine>0) Then
          Begin
            LengthofWaitingLine := LengthofWaitingLine-1;
            TimeofNextServiceCompletion := Clock + Sample(ServiceAverage,ServiceRange);
          End

      End
{==============================================================================}
    Else If (Clock=StopTime) Then Writeln ('End Of Simulation ',Clock);
  End;

{Output Report}
Writeln('Maximum Queue Length Observed Was ',MxQueue);
Writeln('Current Queue Length Is ',LengthofWaitingLine);
If (Idle=False) Then ServerUtil := ServerUtil + (Clock - IdleTimer);
Writeln('Server Utilization Is ',Round(ServerUtil/StopTime*100),' %');
{==============================================================================}
End.
```

Fig. 8.6 (*continued*)

MXQueue Used to maintain the maximum length of the customer queue.

Sample This function is used to randomly return a value in the range specified by the parameters it reads in. The range of values eligible for selection will be defined as its 'A' parameter + or − its 'B' parameter.

ServerUtil This variable is used to keep track of the percentage of time the server is in use.

ServiceTimeAverage Constant used as the average service completion time.

ServiceTimeRange Constant used to indicate the range of the possible service times. This number is added to and subtracted from the interarrival time average to produce the range.

StopTime The termination time for the simulation (in minutes). This simulation is set to run for 480 minutes (8 hours).

TimeofArrival The next scheduled time that a customer will enter the model and either receive service or be queued while waiting for service.

TimeofServiceCompletion The next scheduled time that a service completion will occur. If no customers are being served, this number value is set to StopTime + 1 (BeyondEnd).

8.2.6 Running the Model

The primary information provided by this model is server utilization and maximum waiting queue length. Since the simulated queuing system is stochastic, the results of one run alone will not provide an accurate picture of how the system is functioning. In order to reduce experimental variation, 100 runs will be completed. The results of each run will be tabulated and collectively analyzed to provide a better understanding of the queuing system's operation. Table 8.3 summarizes the results of 100 runs of the model. Figures 8.7 and 8.8 graphically display the same information.

8.2.7 Analyzing the Output

Upon inspection, Table 8.3 reveals that a considerable amount of variability exists between replications. Maximum queue sizes range from a low of 1 to a

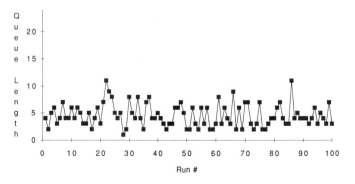

Figure 8.7 Maximum queue length for the Turbo Pascal queuing model.

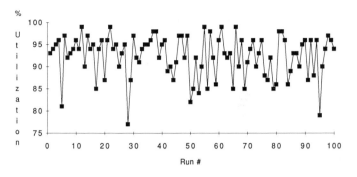

Figure 8.8 Percentage server utilization for the Turbo Pascal queuing model.

TABLE 8.3
Results of Pascal Queuing Model

Runs 1–25		Runs 26–50		Runs 51–75		Runs 76–100	
Max Queue	Server Util. %	Max Queue	Server Util. %	Max Queue	Server Util. %	Max Queue	Server Util. %
4	93	4	93	2	85	2	88
2	94	5	95	6	92	2	87
5	95	1	77	3	84	3	92
6	96	2	87	2	90	4	85
3	81	8	97	6	99	4	86
4	97	5	92	3	85	6	98
7	92	4	91	6	98	7	98
4	93	8	94	2	92	4	96
4	94	4	95	2	86	3	86
6	96	2	95	3	96	3	89
4	94	7	96	8	99	11	93
6	99	8	98	3	93	4	93
5	90	4	98	6	92	5	90
3	97	4	92	4	93	4	95
3	94	5	95	3	85	4	96
5	95	4	96	9	99	4	87
2	85	3	89	2	90	3	96
4	94	2	90	6	96	4	88
6	96	3	87	2	85	6	96
3	87	3	91	7	91	3	79
7	96	6	97	7	94	5	90
11	99	6	97	3	96	4	94
9	94	7	92	2	90	3	97
8	95	5	97	3	93	7	96
5	90	2	82	7	96	3	94

```
 4.53 = AVERAGE VALUE OF MAX QUEUE
92.37 = AVERAGE SERVER UTILIZATION

2.08 = STANDARD DEVIATION OF MAX QUEUE
4.73 = STANDARD DEVIATION OF SERVER UTILIZATION
```

Figure 8.9 Simple queue compiled output for the Turbo Pascal model.

high of 11. Server utilization ranges from a low of 77% to a high of 99%. This variance, found in the model's output, emphasizes the importance of recognizing a simulation as a controlled sampling experiment. Each replication is only one sample from the set of all possible system responses. The analyst must realize that inferences cannot be based on a single run.

In order to produce a more credible result, a mean and standard deviation for the runs tabulated in Table 8.3 were calculated. Figure 8.9 lists the values that were obtained.

Additional statistical tests can be performed to set up confidence intervals for the data.

8.3 GPSS Program of a Simple Queuing System

The same simple queuing system model can be developed using a simulation language. Use of a language such as GPSS/H offers the simulation analyst many advantages. Included among these are:

1. Constructs to facilitate the modeling of queuing systems.
2. Built in statistics gathering capability.
3. Output report creation tools.
4. Facilities for performing multiple repetitions.
5. Reduction of model coding time.
6. Reduction of debug and testing time.

By taking advantage of the tools provided by a simulation language, the analyst is able to produce a better model consisting of fewer lines of code.

8.3.1 Setting Up the Model

The GPSS/H simulation language takes a process orientation approach to modeling. Transactions representing customers are created. These transactions move through the blocks that represent various processes forming the system. In terms of an actual system (see Figure 8.10) this would be represented as follows.

1. Customer enters the system.
2. Customer enters queue and waits if server is currently busy.

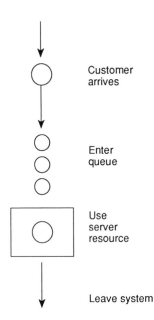

Customer
arrives

Enter
queue

Use
server
resource

Leave system

Figure 8.10 Actual system flow.

3. If server is available and customer is at head of queue, server is exclusively claimed by customer.
4. Customer leaves queue.
5. Service is completed and customer relinquishes server.
6. Customer leaves system.

In terms of a GPSS/H model it would be represented as follows.

1. Transaction representing customer is generated.
2. Transaction enters queue and waits if server resource is currently busy.
3. If server resource is available and customer transaction is at head of queue, server resource is exclusively claimed by customer transaction.
4. Customer transaction leaves queue (transaction may have spent zero time in queue if server resource was immediately available).
5. Service time passes and customer transaction relinquishes server resource.
6. Customer transaction is terminated and leaves model.

Like the Turbo Pascal model of this system, two distributions of time are needed as input data. These distributions will represent:

1. *Customer Arrival Time.* A random variable uniformly distributed between 2 and 20 minutes will be used for this parameter. It is the same distribution as used in the Turbo Pascal model.
2. *Service Completion Time.* Again, a uniformly distributed random variable

will be used. Its range will be the same as the range used in the Turbo Pascal model, from 8 to 14 minutes.

8.3.2 Model Operation

The model will start operation with the random generation of a customer transaction. This transaction will proceed to move through the model until it arrives at a block statement that inhibits its forward progress. In the case of the first transaction, this will occur at the block representing the service time. With subsequent transactions, forward progress through the block diagram may cease if the server is busy and/or while the transaction is being serviced. Table 8.4 lists the processes that can occur in the system being modeled and describes the causes associated with each one's occurrence.

8.3.3 Model Construction

In addition to the processes described in Table 8.4, the GPSS/H model of the system will include provisions for running multiple repetitions and printing out pertinent statistics. Figure 8.11 depicts a GPSS/H block diagram of the model.

TABLE 8.4
Process List

Process	Cause
Entering Model	Customer transaction is generated. A new transaction will enter the system randomly based on a uniform distribution ranging from 2 to 20 minutes.
Entering Waiting Queue (Transaction may be delayed in this block until server is available.)	Customer transaction enters the waiting line. Is the server resource idle and customer at head of queue? No : The customer contines to wait. Yes : Customer moves on to receive service.
Capturing Server	Customer captures server resource, preventing any other transactions from gaining access.
Leaving Waiting Queue	Customer transaction leaves waiting line. The time spent in queue may have been zero.
Receiving Service (Transaction will be delayed in this block until service time elapses.)	Server resource is used by customer transaction. The service is complete after a time period randomly chosen from the range of 8 to 14 minutes.
Relinquishing Server	After completion of service, the customer transaction relinquishes control over the server resource.
Departing Model	Customer transaction leaves simulation model.

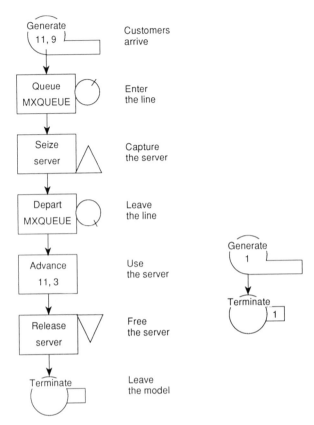

Figure 8.11 GPSS/H block diagram for a queuing system model.

8.3.4 GPSS/H Source Code Listing

The source code listing for the GPSS/H model of a simple queuing system is presented in Figure 8.12.

8.3.5 Description of Entities and Variables

This section summarizes each entity and variable used in the GPSS/H model of the queuing system.

Server The resource representing the server is named SERVER in the GPSS/H model. SERVER is a facility and allows only one customer transaction access at any given time. An automatically maintained statistic is printed at the end of each run to provide the modeler with SERVER's utilization. The standard numeric attribute (SNA) FRV provides this data.

MXQUEUE The waiting line used by customer transactions when the server resource is busy is named MXQUEUE. MXQUEUE gathers statistics describ-

```
        SIMULATE   2            SIMULATION CAN RUN FOR UP TO 2 MINUTES
*                               OF CPU TIME
*
        INTEGER    &REPIT       DECLARE AN AMPERVARIABLE TO BE USED
*                               FOR COUNT MULTIPLE RUNS
*
*===================================================================*
*                   SIMULATION - MAIN SEGMENT                       *
*===================================================================*
*
        GENERATE   11,9         CREATE A CUSTOMER TRANSACTION
*                               EVERY 2 TO 20 MINUTES
*
        QUEUE      MXQUEUE      CUSTOMER TRANSACTION JOINS THE
*                               WAITING LINE CALLED MXQUEUE
*
        SEIZE      SERVER       CUSTOMER TRANSACTION CAPTURES
*                               SERVER RESOURCE WHEN POSSIBLE
*
        DEPART     MXQUEUE      CUSTOMER TRANSACTION MOVES OUT
*                               OF WAITING LINE
*
        ADVANCE    11,3         CUSTOMER TRANSACTION RECEIVES
*                               SERVICE FROM 8 TO 14 MINUTES LONG
*
        RELEASE    SERVER       CUSTOMER TRANSACTION RELINQUISHES
*                               SERVER
*
        TERMINATE               CUSTOMER TRANSACTION LEAVES MODEL
*===================================================================*
*                     TIMING TRANSACTION                            *
*===================================================================*
*
        GENERATE   1            A TIMING TRANSACTION GENERATED EVERY
*                               ONE MINUTE OF SIMULATED TIME
*
        TERMINATE  1            EACH TRANSACTION DECREMENTS THE START
                                BLOCK COUNTER BY ONE
*===================================================================  *
*              CONTROL ROUTINE & OUTPUT GENERATION                  *
*===================================================================*
*
        DO         &REPIT=1,100  DO ONE HUNDRED REPETITIONS OF THE
*                                SIMULATION
*
        CLEAR                    ON EACH NEW RUN, REMOVE ALL OLD
*                                TRANSACTIONS AND STATISTICS
*
*
        START      480,NP        EACH RUN LAST FOR 480 MINUTES
*                                (8 HOURS)
*
*       AT THE END OF EACH RUN PRINT MAXIMUM QUEUE LENGTH AND SERVER
*       UTILIZATION STATISTICS.
        PUTPIC     FILE=RESULTS,LINES=1,QM$MXQUEUE,FRV$SERVER
        ****       ****.****
*
        ENDDO                    END OF REPETITION LOOP
*
        END                      END OF MODEL
*===================================================================*
```

Figure 8.12 GPSS/H source code for single server–single queue model.

TABLE 8.5

Results of GPSS/H Queuing Model

Runs 1–25		Runs 26–50		Runs 51–75		Runs 76–100	
Max Queue	Server Util. %	Max Queue	Server Util. %	Max Queue	Server Util. %	Max Queue	Server Util. %
4	92	5	89	6	96	6	93
3	95	4	96	3	88	6	97
4	96	4	94	4	92	3	90
4	90	5	97	4	92	3	96
3	89	5	88	2	87	4	96
2	94	2	94	5	99	3	92
4	91	4	96	4	95	6	97
4	91	3	91	4	96	5	93
3	94	3	91	9	99	5	97
5	95	3	95	2	92	7	94
4	97	3	89	6	98	3	91
6	91	3	89	2	89	8	94
7	96	4	94	2	93	4	91
4	92	5	96	2	85	3	90
4	95	4	99	6	92	3	96
3	89	4	92	3	88	4	97
2	93	4	94	2	96	3	93
2	94	3	93	3	92	5	93
2	87	3	91	3	89	5	92
6	94	5	91	6	95	5	87
3	93	3	93	3	94	4	97
5	96	6	94	1	81	3	86
2	78	3	92	3	90	4	97
2	95	7	90	5	96	5	89
5	94	3	92	3	79	2	89

ing characteristics of the waiting line. The SNA QM is printed at the end of each model run to provide the modeler with the maximum length MXQUEUE ever attained.

&REPIT This ampervariable is used as a counter enabling 100 repetitions of the model to be run.

8.3.6 Running the Model

The intent of this model is to provide the simulation analyst with values for maximum queue length and server utilization. One hundred repetitions of the model have been tabulated in Table 8.5. Server utilization has been rounded to the nearest integer value. Figures 8.13 and 8.14 graphically depict the same information.

8.3.7 Analyzing the Output

Table 8.5, like Table 8.3, reveals that a considerable amount of variability exists between replications. Maximum queue sizes range from a low of 1 to a high of 9.

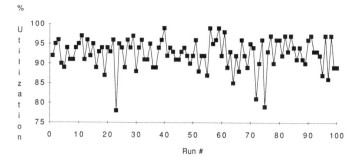

Figure 8.13 Percentage server utilization for the GPSS/H queuing model.

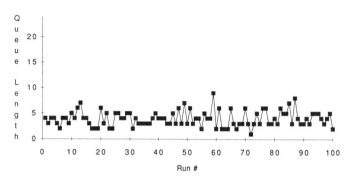

Figure 8.14 Maximum queue length for the GPSS/H queuing model.

Server utilization ranges from a low of 78% to a high of 99%. Again, the variance found in a model's output emphasizes the importance of recognizing a particular run of a simulation as only one sample from the set of all possible system responses. It would be unwise to base a decision on a single run.

The means and standard deviations for Table 8.5 were calculated and the values are given in Figure 8.15.

8.4 Summary

This chapter has provided the reader with examples of a simple queuing model using both a traditional programming language and a specialized simulation

```
 3.93 = AVERAGE VALUE OF MAX QUEUE
92.51 = AVERAGE SERVER UTILIZATION

1.48 = STANDARD DEVIATION OF MAX QUEUE
3.86 = STANDARD DEVIATION OF SERVER UTILIZATION
```

Figure 8.15 Simple queue compiled output for the GPSS/H model.

language. The example of a queuing system modeled in Turbo Pascal was developed to promote an understanding of the logic and concepts that can be taken for granted when using a language such as GPSS/H.

The built in GPSS/H simulation clock, statistic gathering tools, and general language construction all facilitate model coding and use. These features must be added by the analyst when a traditional programming language is used.

In addition to being made aware of the advantages of using simulation language for modeling, the reader should realize that runs of a model are not definitive within themselves. Instead, each run is a sample taken from the set of all possible model results. This fact emphasizes the importance of taking enough samples to provide an *average result* with which the simulation analyst can feel comfortable.

References and Reading

Borland International. 1985. *Turbo Pascal Reference Manual, Version 3.0.* Borland International, Scotts Valley, California.

Schriber, Thomas J. 1974. *Simulation Using GPSS.* Krieger Books, Melbourne, Florida. (Originally published by J. Wiley & Sons).

Shoup, Terry E., Leroy S. Fletcher, and Edward U. Mochel. 1981. *Engineering Design.* Prentice-Hall, Englewood Cliffs, New Jersey.

Thesen, Arne. 1987. "Writing Simulations from Scratch: Pascal Implementation." *Proc. 1987 Winter Simulation Conf.* (Atlanta, Dec. 14–16). SCS, San Diego, pp. 152–164.

CHAPTER 9

Advanced Topics

This chapter is written specifically for the person who expects to use simulation on a regular basis. Its purpose is to provide the simulation analyst with a toolkit of time-saving techniques and procedures to help streamline the modeling process. At the same time, end users will be provided with better, more usable data.

Included in this toolkit are methods for enhancing output with commercially available graphics and spreadsheet software. In addition, the advantage of computer animation is explored using the simple queuing model originally presented in Chapter 8.

Another useful tool for the modeler's kit bag is a custom developed macro language or a library of reusable software modules. When many similar models are developed using standard simulation languages (simulator packages essentially provide these macros), this can become an extremely useful and time-saving application technique.

The final topic covered in this chapter deals with logic transfer. After a simulation has been developed, the importance of insuring that the logic used in the model is also used in the real world system cannot be emphasized enough. A methodology for accomplishing this task is discussed.

9.1 Post-Processing Output

All models must provide some type of output. This output can be communicated or presented to the end user in many different ways. Traditionally, simulation output data took the form of hard-to-understand stacks of numerical data. Some simulation analysts thrive on reams of paper covered with statistics. Coupled with this overkill tendency of the analyst is the ease with which most simulation languages allow data to be gathered and reported. Nearly all simulation software products automatically make an abundance of data available at the end of each run.

A challenge for the simulation analyst is knowing what data to report, what data to omit, and what type of report format to use. A good rule of thumb is to make the data as readable as possible and limit the quantity to the essentials.

Two types of output data are usually available from a simulation. The first type describes the model itself and will help the analyst verify the simulation. This does not need to appear in an output report given to the end user. The second type of data is the output that describes characteristics of the system being modeled. This data will be of interest to the end user and should appear in some type of output report. Tables, graphs, and bar charts can all be used to make the raw data more readable.

Although many simulation products contain data analysis tools, it may still be desirable to explore some commercially available software. The reason for this is twofold. First, the function of a simulation software product is usually modeling, not data presentation. Second, excellent data presentation software is available. This software has been developed specifically for putting data into a form that can be easily understood and communicated. The simulation analyst can use these types of packages to great advantage.

Many different data analysis and presentation software packages are currently available. Two of these are briefly profiled in Sections 9.1.1 and 9.1.2.

9.1.1 Lotus 1-2-3

A very popular method of transforming raw simulation data into an easy-to-read report is through the use of a spreadsheet software package. Many spreadsheet programs are currently available from a wide variety of sources. This section concentrates on one of the most popular of these programs, Lotus 1-2-3 (Harvey, 1987).

Spreadsheets are programs that allow the user to manipulate data that has been entered into a series of cells organized into rows and columns. Although it is possible to enter the data into the spreadsheet from the computer keyboard, the simulation analyst will probably be interested in transporting a raw simulation output data file into the spreadsheet. Lotus 1-2-3 provides the capability of performing this function through the "/File/Import" menu selection or through use of its command language key words of "{READLN}" or "{READ}" (Lotus Development Corporation, 1986).

As an example of the different types of operations that spreadsheet software can offer the simulation analyst, the output data from the GPSS/H model described in Chapter 8 will be imported into Lotus 1-2-3. Figure 9.1 shows how the Lotus 1-2-3 spreadsheet appears after using the "/File/Import" menu selection to import Table 8.5. The first six lines of Table 8.5 were imported as text, and the rest of the table was imported as numbers.

	A	B	C	D	E	F	G	H
1	==================		==================		==================		==================	
2	Runs 1–25		Runs 26–50		Runs 51–75		Runs 76–100	
3	==================		==================		==================		==================	
4	Max	Server	Max	Server	Max	Server	Max	Server
5	Queue	Util %	Queue	Util %	Queue	Util %	Queue	Util %
6	==================		==================		==================		==================	
7	4	92	5	89	6	96	6	93
8	3	95	4	96	3	88	6	97
9	4	96	4	94	4	92	3	90
10	4	90	5	97	4	92	3	96
11	3	89	5	88	2	87	4	96
12	2	94	2	94	5	99	3	92
13	4	91	4	96	4	95	6	97
14	4	91	3	91	4	96	5	93
15	3	94	3	91	9	99	5	97
16	5	95	3	95	2	92	7	94
17	4	97	3	89	6	98	3	91
18	6	91	3	89	2	89	8	94
19	7	96	4	94	2	93	4	91
20	4	92	5	96	2	85	3	90
21	4	95	4	99	6	92	3	96
22	3	89	4	92	3	88	4	97
23	2	93	4	94	2	96	3	93
24	2	94	3	93	3	92	5	93
25	2	87	3	91	3	89	5	92
26	6	94	5	91	6	95	5	87
27	3	93	3	93	3	94	4	97
28	5	96	6	94	1	81	3	86
29	2	78	3	92	3	90	4	97
30	2	95	7	90	5	96	5	89
31	5	94	3	92	3	79	2	89

Figure 9.1   Data from Table 8.5 after being imported into Lotus 1-2-3.

Once the data has been transported into the Lotus 1-2-3 spreadsheet, any of the data manipulations offered by the software may be performed. For instance, the following Lotus 1-2-3 command is entered into cell A33.

$$AVG(A7. \, . \, . A31, C7..C31, E7..E31, G7..G31)$$

Cell A33 will provide the average maximum queue size for the data in Table 8.5. The contents of cell A33 is now 3.93.

By using Lotus 1-2-3 commands and features, professional reports and formats for data can be designed. Lotus 1-2-3 spreadsheets may be developed specifically to automate the report creation process. This is especially helpful when numerous simulation outputs consisting of similar data formats will be generated.

In addition to data manipulation, performing calculations, and report generation, spreadsheets may be used for their graphic capabilities. Figure 9.2 is a point diagram plotting the different maximum queue sizes observed in Table 8.5.

Spreadsheets can be useful tools in the analysis and presentation of data. All the features and power available in state-of-the-art packages such as Lotus 1-2-3 can be harnessed and used by the simulation analyst.

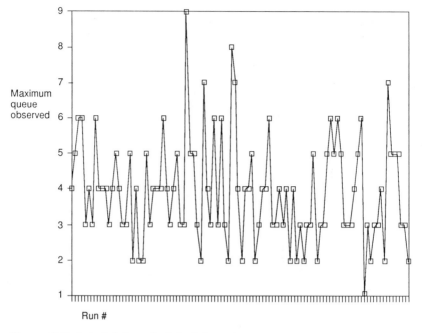

Figure 9.2 Lotus 1-2-3 graph of simulation output.

9.1.2 Graph-in-the-Box

Another commercially available software package that can be used as a simulation output data post-processor is Graph-in-the-Box (New England Software, 1987). Graph-in-the-Box is typical of low-cost, user friendly graphics generators. Graph-in-the-Box allows data to be loaded directly from the PC screen into a data base and displayed graphically. Like Lotus 1-2-3, Graph-in-the-Box can be set up with generic formats to automate graph production.

Figures 9.3, 9.4, and 9.5 give examples of the types of graphs that can be generated with Graph-in-the-Box.

9.2 Macro Language Development

One of the most powerful tools that can be added to the simulation analyst's toolkit is a library of simulation macros. These macros are subroutines or groupings of code that represent a generic process (see Section 9.2.6). When simulations of similar systems or simulations of systems containing many repetitive processes are written, macros can be used to great advantage. Not only are coding and debugging times significantly reduced but if changes are needed in the model, the macro code can be altered in a single place. If macros are not

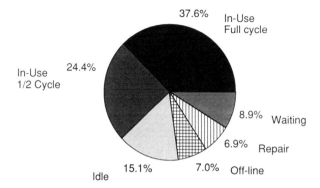

Figure 9.3   Resource analysis pie graph.

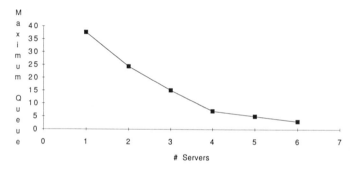

Figure 9.4   Cross-plot of servers versus maximum queue size.

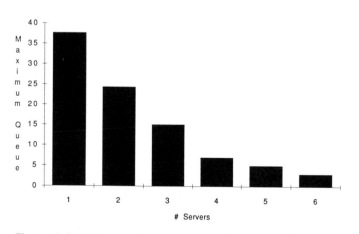

Figure 9.5   Histogram of servers versus maximum queue size.

used, the analyst is faced with searching throughout the entire model to make numerous changes.

In order to identify processes that should be represented by macros, the simulation analyst needs to verify the presence of two characteristics:

1. Similar processes occur repeatedly in the system(s) being modeled.
2. The processes are functionally the same but may have differing attributes that can be described as inputs to the macro.

When these two criteria are met, the simulation analyst may begin coding the macro. A good method for accomplishing this is to first identify the elements that will vary between different processes using the macro. These elements can be coded as variable parameters or values that are read into the macro with each specific application. The next step is to create the code for the macro.

9.2.1 Macro Development Process

With GPSS/H, a special provision for using macros has been built into the language. The STARTMACRO and ENDMACRO statements are used to define a grouping of code that can be accessed in the model through a single MACRO statement. As an illustration of the macro development process, consider the case of Rider's Packaging Corporation.

Rider's Packaging Corporation

Rider's Packaging Corporation is a company that performs assembly and packaging operations for a variety of different manufacturing plants. As a part of their ongoing modernization, Rider's plans to produce an overall model of their plant. Of immediate interest to the modeling team are the seven different assembly lines that form the main artery for plant output.

Due to the large number of assembly stations in the plant and the similarities they share, the modeling team decided to develop an assemble macro. This macro was to be named "ASSEM" in their models.

The first step Rider's took in the macro development process was to identify all common attributes of the assembly process. They listed the following items.

1. Either one or two operators work at each station. These operators may be shared by several stations. Some stations require two operators who must both be present before work can begin.
2. The assembly operation takes a finite amount of time per operator.
3. A main workpiece on a pallet moves through a sequence of assembly stations. At each station, components are added to the part. When the operation has been completed, the operator pushes a button that moves the palletized workpiece along a rail to the next station. The pallet cannot move to the next station if it is occupied.

4. Each station has a unique identification number.

Several variable parameters can be derived from the list of common attributes. A listing of these is as follows.

1. Number of station operators (1 or 2).
2. Whether both operators are needed before work begins (in two operator stations).
3. Time per assembly operation for each operator.
4. Pallet move time to next station.
5. Current station identification number.
6. Next station identification number (or 99 for last station).

The "ASSEM" macro needs to consider the preceding five items as variable input parameters. The simulation analysts from Rider's developed the macro shown in Figure 9.6 to incorporate the necessary logic at the assembly stations.

9.2.2 A Macro Mini-Language

In the same way that the macro was developed in Section 9.2.1, additional macros can be coded and used together as a "mini-language." The development of a mini-language to be used in conjunction with normal simulation block statements can provide the analyst with a powerful tool that is responsible for a great reduction in model coding time. The Rider's Packaging Corporation case study is continued in the following example.

Reader's Mini-Language

Rider's simulation department was impressed with the amount of coding time that was saved by using a macro for their assembly stations. After the completion and some use of their new ASSEM macro, a decision was made to develop a company specific macro-based mini-language. It was felt that a macro language approach could be used as an additional time-saving technique for this and future simulation projects. Three more commonly used processes were identified by Rider's simulation department as likely candidates for inclusion in the soon to be developed macro language. Figure 9.7 shows a flow diagram for the work being done at Rider's Corporation. This work flow can be represented in terms of the following additional processes:

1. The packaging operation
2. The shipping operation
3. Materials handling (via forklift trucks)

```
*=============================================================*
* LIST OF MACRO INPUT PARAMETERS AND ASSOCIATED DEFINITIONS    *
*=============================================================*
* #A - I.D. NUMBER OF CURRENT ASSEMBLY STATION                 *
* #B - NUMBER OF STATION OPERATORS                             *
* #C - TRUE IF BOTH OPERATORS ARE REQUIRED TO START WORK. FALSE IF ONLY *
*      ONE OPERATOR AT STATION OR IF TWO OPERATORS CAN WORK INDEPENDENTLY *
*      ON PART.                                                *
* #D - OPERATOR #1 ASSEMBLY TIME                               *
* #E - OPERATOR #2 ASSEMBLY TIME (0 IF ONLY ONE OPERATOR REQUIRED) *
* #F - NEXT STATION I.D. NUMBER                                *
*      - MAY BE 99 TO INDICATE LAST STATION IN A SERIES        *
* #G - MOVE TIME TO NEXT STATION                               *
* #H - OPERATOR #1 I.D.                                        *
* #I - OPERATOR #2 I.D. (1 IF ONLY ONE OPERATOR REQUIRED)      *
* #J - TRUE IF THIS IS THE FIRST STATION IN AN ASSEMBLY SEQUENCE *
*=============================================================*
* LIST OF GPSS/H ENTITIES USED IN MACRO                       *
*=============================================================*
*
TRUE    SYN     1                   SYNONYM FOR (1) MEANING TRUE
*
WAITS   EQU     000(99),Q           QUEUE TO DETERMINE HOW LONG LOADS WAIT FOR
*                                   A PARTICULAR STATION
*
STAT    EQU     100(99),F           FACILITY USED TO REPRESENT THE PHYSICAL WORK
*                                   STATION RESOURCE
*
WAITO   EQU     200(99),S           STORAGE TO DETERMINE HOW LONG LOADS WAIT
*                                   AT A STATION FOR AN OPERATOR
*
OPER    EQU     300(99),S           STORAGE TO REPRESENT OPERATOR RESOURCES
*=============================================================*
        STORAGE S((OPER+1))-S((OPER+98)),1    STORAGE CAPACITY OF ONE
*=============================================================*
*
*
*=============================================================*
*                   MACRO DEFINITION                          *
*=============================================================*
ASSEM   STARTMACRO
*
        TEST E   #J,TRUE,*+4        IF THIS IS THE FIRST STATION IN A SEQUENCE
*                                   PERFORM THIS CODE
*
*=============================================================*
*         FIRST STATION IN SEQUENCE OF ASSEMBLY OPERATIONS     *
*=============================================================*
*
        QUEUE    WAITS+#A           ENTER A QUEUE WHILE WAITING FOR
*                                   STATION TO BECOME AVAILABLE
*
        SEIZE    STAT+#A            ATTEMPT TO RESERVE STATION FOR EXCLUSIVE
*                                   USAGE
*
        DEPART   WAITS+#A           STATION QUEUE CAN BE LEFT
*=============================================================*
*
        TEST E   #B,2,*+34          DETERMINE WHETHER ONE OR TWO ASSEMBLY
*                                   WORKERS ARE REQUIRED
*=============================================================*
*               TWO STATION OPERATORS BEING USED              *
*=============================================================*
```

Figure 9.6 ASSEM Macro as developed by Rider's Packaging Corporation simulation department.

```
        TEST E      #C,TRUE,*+18  DETERMINE WHETHER WORK IS DONE INDEPENDENTLY
*                                 BY EACH ASSEMBLY OPERATOR OR IF BOTH WORKERS
*                                 ARE REQUIRED PRIOR TO STARTING
*=========================================================================*
*           BOTH STATION OPERATORS REQUIRED TO START OPERATION        *
*=========================================================================*
*
        ENTER       WAITO+#A,2    STATISTIC THAT KEEPS TRACK OF TIME PALLET
*                                 WAITS FOR BOTH OPERATORS TO BECOME AVAILABLE
*
        GATE SNF    OPER+#H       ATTEMPT TO RESERVE BOTH OPERATORS AT THE
        GATE SNF    OPER+#I       SAME TIME BEFORE BEGINNING ASSEMBLY OPERATION
        TRANSFER    SIM,,*-2
*
        ENTER       OPER+#H       BOTH OPERATORS ARE AVAILABLE SO RESERVE
        ENTER       OPER+#I       THEM FOR USE
*
        LEAVE       WAITO+#A,2    AFTER BOTH OPERATORS HAVE BECOME AVAILABLE
*                                 THE ASSEMBLY OPERATION CAN BEGIN;
*
        SPLIT       1,*+2         A TRANSACTION REPRESENTING FIRST OPERATOR
*                                 IS CREATED
*
        TRANSFER    ,*+7          PARENT TRANSACTION IS SENT TO ASSEMBLE BLOCK
*                                 TO WAIT FOR BOTH OPERATORS TO COMPLETE
*
        SPLIT       1,*+4         SECOND OPERATOR TRANSACTION IS CREATED
*
        ADVANCE     #D            FIRST OPERATOR SPENDS TIME WORKING ON TASK
*
        LEAVE       OPER+#H       FIRST OPERATOR COMPLETE, RESOURCE AVAILABLE
*                                 TO OTHER USERS
*
        TRANSFER    ,*+3          GO TO ASSEMBLE BLOCK
*
        ADVANCE     #E            SECOND OPERATOR SPENDS TIME WORKING ON TASK
*
        LEAVE       OPER+#I       SECOND OPERATOR COMPLETE, RESOURCE AVAILABLE
*                                 TO OTHER USERS
*
        ASSEMBLE    3             TRANSACTION REPRESENTING PALLET WAITS FOR
*                                 BOTH OPERATORS TO FINISH ASSEMBLY OPERATION,
*                                 THEN CAN MOVE ON.
*
        TRANSFER    ,*+21         PALLET READY TO LEAVE WORK STATION
*=========================================================================*
*           STATION OPERATORS WORK INDEPENDENTLY ON WORK PIECE        *
*=========================================================================*
*
        ENTER       WAITO+#A,2    WORK PIECE WAITS FOR OPERATORS TO BECOME
*                                 AVAILABLE
*
        SPLIT       1,*+2         A TRANSACTION REPRESENTING FIRST OPERATOR
*                                 IS CREATED
*
        TRANSFER    ,*+11         PARENT TRANSACTION IS SENT TO ASSEMBLY BLOCK
*                                 TO WAIT FOR BOTH OPERATORS TO COMPLETE THEIR
*                                 DUTIES
*
        SPLIT       1,*+6         SECOND OPERATOR TRANSACTION IS CREATED
*
        ENTER       OPER+#H       AS SOON AS ASSEMBLY OPERATOR RESOURCE IS
*                                 AVAILABLE, USE IT.
*
        LEAVE       WAITO+#A,1    OPERATOR IS READY TO BEGIN WORK ON PALLET
*
        ADVANCE     #D            FIRST OPERATOR SPENDS TIME WORKING ON TASK
```

(Figure 9.6 continued)

181

```
*
        LEAVE      OPER+#H      FIRST OPERATOR COMPLETE, RESOURCE AVAILABLE
*                               TO OTHER USERS
*
        TRANSFER   ,*+5         GO TO ASSEMBLE BLOCK
*
        ENTER      OPER+#I      AS SOON AS SECOND OPERATOR RESOURCE IS READY,
*                               USE IT
*
        LEAVE      WAITO+#A     NO LONGER WAITING FOR OPERATOR RESOURCE
*
        ADVANCE    #E           SECOND OPERATOR SPENDS TIME WORKING ON TASK
*
        LEAVE      OPER+#I      SECOND OPERATOR COMPLETE, RESOURCE AVAILABLE
*                               TO OTHER USERS
*
        ASSEMBLE   3            TRANSACTION REPRESENTING PALLET WAITS FOR
*                               BOTH OPERATORS TO FINISH ASSEMBLY OPERATION,
*                               THEN CAN MOVE ON.
*
        TRANSFER   ,*+6         PALLET READY TO LEAVE WORK STATION

*===============================================================================*
*                ONLY ONE STATION OPERATOR IS REQUIRED                          *
*===============================================================================*
*
        ENTER      WAITO+#A,1   WORK PIECE WAITS FOR OPERATOR TO BECOME
*                               AVAILABLE
*
        ENTER      OPER+#H      AS SOON AS ASSEMBLY OPERATOR RESOURCE IS
*                               AVAILABLE, USE IT.
*
        LEAVE      WAITO+#A,1   OPERATOR IS READY TO BEGIN WORK ON PALLET
*
        ADVANCE    #D           OPERATOR SPENDS TIME WORKING ON TASK
*
        LEAVE      OPER+#H      OPERATOR COMPLETE, RESOURCE AVAILABLE TO
*                               OTHER USERS
*===============================================================================*
*    ASSEMBLY OPERATION COMPLETE MOVE TO NEXT STATION OR TERMINATE              *
*===============================================================================*
*
        TEST NE    #F,99,*+6    DETERMINE IF THIS IS THE LAST STATION.
*===============================================================================*
*      PALLET READY TO MOVE ON TO NEXT ASSEMBLY STATION IN SEQUENCE             *
*===============================================================================*
*
        QUEUE      WAITS+#F     ENTER A QUEUE WHILE WAITING FOR NEXT
*                               STATION TO BECOME AVAILABLE
*
        SEIZE      STAT+#F      ATTEMPT TO RESERVE STATION FOR EXCLUSIVE
*                               USAGE
*
        DEPART     WAITS+#F     STATION QUEUE CAN BE LEFT
*
        RELEASE    STAT+#A      RELINQUISH CURRENT ASSEMBLY STATION
*
        ADVANCE    #G           TIME DELAY FOR MOVE TO NEXT STATION IN
*                               SEQUENCE
*
        ENDMACRO                END OF MACRO CODE
*===============================================================================*
```

(Figure 9.6 continued)

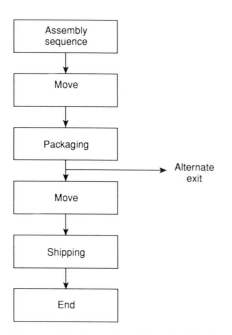

Figure 9.7 General work flow for Rider's Packaging Corporation.

Pack Macro

The first macro to be developed was the PACK MACRO. It would be used to represent the packaging operation at Rider's. The standard macro development procedure they used in the creation of the ASSEM MACRO was adopted again. The first step in this procedure was identification of all common attributes of the packaging process. The following elements were listed:

1. One packaging operator works at each station. This operator may be shared by several stations.
2. The packaging operation takes a finite amount of time.
3. The packaging operation takes place on a special packing stand.
4. Only one packaging operation takes place per assembled workpiece.
5. Workpiece may leave the system either directly from packaging or by first going to shipping.

Several variable parameters can be derived from the previous list of common attributes. Included are:

1. Station operator identification number
2. Packaging operation time
3. Packaging stand identification number

Figure 9.8 illustrates the packaging macro developed by the simulation department at Rider's Packaging Corporation.

Ship Macro

The next statement to be included as part of Rider's macro language was the SHIP MACRO. It would be used to represent the shipping operation. Rider's simulation analysts identified all common attributes used in this operation. Their list included the following.

1. One shipping clerk works at several shipping stations. This clerk may only service one pallet at a time.
2. The shipping operation occupies the clerk for a finite amount of time.
3. Several empty trucks are always waiting at the shipping docks to receive pallets.
4. The workpiece permanently leaves the system after completing the shipping operation.

The variables needed for the SHIP MACRO are:

1. Shipping clerk identification number
2. Shipping operation time

Figure 9.9 illustrates the shipping macro developed by the simulation department at Rider's Packaging Corporation.

Handle Macro

The final macro in Rider's mini-language would be one to represent its materials handling system. The simulation analysts compiled the following list:

1. Up to three different forklift trucks may be used to pick up and move pallets from assembly to packaging or from packaging to shipping.

2. The travel time between the different stations is predictable and can be represented in terms of an input distribution.

3. The forklift trucks have terminals onboard that indicate which stations have pallets requiring moves. When an operator decides to pick up a pallet, a code is entered at the terminal. This notifies the other trucks that this particular move is being worked on.

4. The load pick-up time (not including travel time) is station dependent.

5. The load drop-off time (not including travel time) is station dependent.

6. The average time a forklift truck takes to arrive at a station calling for a move will be input. This value reflects the time from pallet assignment to forklift truck until arrival at station.

7. When a pallet is to be moved using the materials handling system, the central computer will verify that the next station is reserved for the pallet. Only then will a forklift truck be called to perform the move.

```
*=============================================================================*
* LIST OF INPUT PARAMETERS AND ASSOCIATED DEFINITIONS                         *
*=============================================================================*
* #A -- I.D. NUMBER OF CURRENT PACKAGING STATION                              *
* #B -  PACKAGING OPERATION TIME                                              *
* #C -- OPERATOR I.D. NUMBER                                                  *
* #D -  IF '99' THEN THIS IS THE LAST STATION IN THE PALLET'S SEQUENCE        *
*=============================================================================*
* LIST OF GPSS/H ENTITIES USED IN MACRO                                       *
*=============================================================================*
*
TRUE   SYN       1                 SYNONYM FOR (1) MEANING TRUE
*
WAITS  EQU       000(99),Q         QUEUE TO DETERMINE HOW LONG LOADS WAIT FOR
*                                  A PARTICULAR STATION
*
STAT   EQU       100(99),F         FACILITY USED TO REPRESENT THE PHYSICAL WORK
*                                  STATION RESOURCE
*
WAITO  EQU       200(99),S         STORAGE TO DETERMINE HOW LONG LOADS WAIT
*                                  AT A STATION FOR AN OPERATOR
*
OPER   EQU       300(99),S         STORAGE TO REPRESENT OPERATOR RESOURCES
*=============================================================================*
       STORAGE   S((OPER+1))-S((OPER+98)),1   STORAGE CAPACITY OF ONE
*=============================================================================*
*
*
*=============================================================================*
*                     MACRO DEFINITION                                        *
*=============================================================================*
PACK   STARTMACRO                  MACRO DEFINITION BEGINS
*
       ENTER     WAITO+#A,1         WORK PIECE WAITS FOR OPERATOR TO BECOME
*                                  AVAILABLE
*
       ENTER     OPER+#C            AS SOON AS PACKAGING OPERATOR RESOURCE IS
*                                  AVAILABLE, USE IT.
*
       LEAVE     WAITO+#A,1         OPERATOR IS READY TO BEGIN WORK ON PALLET
*
       ADVANCE   #B                 OPERATOR SPENDS TIME WORKING ON TASK
*
       LEAVE     OPER+#C            OPERATOR COMPLETE, RESOURCE AVAILABLE
*                                  TO OTHER USERS
*=============================================================================*
* PACKAGING OPERATION COMPLETE MOVE TO NEXT STATION OR TERMINATE              *
*=============================================================================*
*
       TEST E    #D,99,*+2          DETERMINE IF THIS IS THE LAST STATION.

*=============================================================================*
*                 CODE FOR LAST STATION IN AN SEQUENCE                        *
*=============================================================================*
*
       RELEASE   STAT+#A            RELEASE WORK STATION
*=============================================================================*
*
       ENDMACRO                     END OF MACRO CODE
*=============================================================================*
```

Figure 9.8 Rider's packaging macro.

Based on this list, the simulation analysts at Rider's were able to determine a need for the following variables in the HANDLE MACRO.

1. Pick-up station identification number
2. Drop-off station identification number
3. Identification numbers for up to three forklift trucks
4. Travel time from pick-up to drop-off station
5. Load pick-up time
6. Load drop-off time
7. Average time for a forklift truck to arrive at a calling station

Figure 9.10 illustrates the materials handling macro developed by the simulation department at Rider's Packaging Corporation.

Mini-Language Simulation Run with Output Report

Rider's Packaging Corporation now had a usable macro mini-language to aid in model development. In addition to the regular GPSS/H block statements, the following macros were now available:

```
ASSEM     The assembly operations
PACK      The packaging operations
SHIP      The shipping operations
HANDLE    Materials handling (currently forklift
          trucks)
```

The simulation department decided to test their new macro mini-language by modeling an existing operation in the plant. Figure 9.11 illustrates the line to be modeled.

After collecting input data and doing some preliminary analytical work, Rider's simulation team put together the segment of GPSS/H code shown in Figure 9.12 to represent the system being modeled.

As demonstrated by the relatively simple and short segment of code found in Figure 9.12, a macro mini-language dramatically reduces simulation coding time. Different scenarios can be pieced together in building block fashion using the four statements in the macro mini-language.

Figure 9.13 shows a finished simulation listing that includes the macro code and an output section to create a results file.

The simulation produces the following results when run (Figure 9.14).

9.2.3 Using Functions and Variables as Input Parameters

The example of Rider's Packaging Corporation illustrates how a macro mini-language might be conceived and used to help reduce model development time,

```
*=============================================================================*
* LIST OF INPUT PARAMETERS AND ASSOCIATED DEFINITIONS                         *
*=============================================================================*
* #A - I.D. NUMBER OF SHIPPING CLERK ASSIGNED TO STATION                      *
* #B - SHIPPING OPERATION TIME                                                *
*=============================================================================*
* LIST OF GPSS/H ENTITIES USED IN MACRO                                       *
*=============================================================================*
*
TRUE    SYN     1               SYNONYM FOR (1) MEANING TRUE
*
SHIPS   SYN     98              SYNONYM FOR SHIPPING OPERATION ALWAYS
*                               STATION #98
*
WAITO   EQU     200(99),S       STORAGE TO DETERMINE HOW LONG LOADS WAIT
*                               AT A STATION FOR AN OPERATOR
*
OPER    EQU     300(99),S       STORAGE TO REPRESENT OPERATOR RESOURCES
*=============================================================================*
        STORAGE S((OPER+1))-S((OPER+98)),1   STORAGE CAPACITY OF ONE
*=============================================================================*
*
*
*=============================================================================*
*                         MACRO DEFINITION                                    *
*=============================================================================*
SHIP    STARTMACRO              MACRO DEFINITION BEGINS
*
        ENTER   WAITO+SHIPS     WORK PIECE WAITS FOR CLERK TO BECOME
*                               AVAILABLE AT SHIPPING
*
        ENTER   OPER+#A         AS SOON AS SHIPPING CLERK RESOURCE IS
*                               AVAILABLE, USE IT.
*
        LEAVE   WAITO+SHIPS,1   CLERK IS READY TO BEGIN WORK ON PALLET
*
        ADVANCE #B              CLERK SPENDS TIME WORKING ON TASK
*
        LEAVE   OPER+#A         CLERK COMPLETE, RESOURCE AVAILABLE TO
*                               OTHER PALLETS
*
        RELEASE STAT+SHIPS      SHIPPING STATION IS RELEASE TO ANOTHER PALLET
*=============================================================================*
*          SHIPPING OPERATION TERMINATE LOAD TRANSACTION                      *
*=============================================================================*
*
        TERMINATE               LOAD IS TERMINATED
*
        ENDMACRO                END OF MACRO CODE
*=============================================================================*
```

Figure 9.9 Rider's shipping macro.

standardize code, and provide a vehicle for gathering specific statistics. The power of this tool becomes evident upon using it. Although the Rider's example did not point this fact out, it is important to note that the macro input parameters do not need to be numbers or constants. They can be distributions, transaction parameters, functions, variables, or any GPSS/H standard numerical attributes. These inputs can be deterministic or stochastic. This wide range of possibilities gives the simulation analyst a variety of methods for inputting macro data.

```
*=========================================================================*
* LIST OF INPUT PARAMETERS AND ASSOCIATED DEFINITIONS                     *
*=========================================================================*
* #A - PICK-UP STATION                                                    *
* #B - DROP-OFF STATION                                                   *
* #C - TRAVEL TIME FROM PICK-UP TO DROP-OFF STATION                       *
* #D - LOAD PICK-UP TIME                                                  *
* #E - LOAD DROP-OFF TIME                                                 *
* #F - AVERAGE TIME FOR A FORK TRUCK TO ARRIVE AT A CALLING STATION       *
*=========================================================================*
* LIST OF GPSS/H ENTITIES USED IN MACRO                                   *
*=========================================================================*
*
TRUE    SYN       1                SYNONYM FOR (1) MEANING TRUE
*
WAITS   EQU       000(99),Q        QUEUE TO DETERMINE HOW LONG LOADS WAIT FOR
*                                  A PARTICULAR STATION
*
STAT    EQU       100(99),F        FACILITY USED TO REPRESENT THE PHYSICAL WORK
*                                  STATION RESOURCE
*
FORK    EQU       400(3),F         FACILITY USED TO REPRESENT THE FORK TRUCKS
*
WFORK   EQU       405,Q            QUEUE TO DETERMINE HOW LONG LOADS WAIT AT
*                                  A STATION FOR AN OPERATOR
*=========================================================================*
TEST1   BVARIABLE FNU(401)+FNU(402)+FNU(403)  BOOLEAN VARIABLE TO DETERMINE
*                                  IF A FORK TRUCK IS AVAILABLE
*=========================================================================*
*
*
*=========================================================================*
*                        MACRO DEFINITION                                 *
*=========================================================================*
HANDLE  STARTMACRO                 MACRO DEFINITION BEGINS
*
        QUEUE     WAITS+#B         ENTER A QUEUE WHILE WAITING FOR STATION
*                                  TO BECOME AVAILABLE
*
        SEIZE     STAT+#B          ATTEMPT TO RESERVE STATION FOR EXCLUSIVE USAGE
*
        DEPART    WAITS+#B         STATION QUEUE CAN BE LEFT
*=========================================================================*
*           WAIT FOR A FORK TRUCK TO BECOME AVAILABLE                     *
*=========================================================================*
*
        QUEUE     WFORK            STATISTIC THAT KEEPS TRACK OF TIME PALLET
*                                  WAITS FOR A FORK TRUCK TO BECOME AVAILABLE
*
        TEST E    BV$TEST1,TRUE    DETERMINE IF A FORK TRUCK IS AVAILABLE
*
        SELECT NU 1,FORK+1,FORK+3  RESERVE AN ELIGIBLE FORK TRUCK RESOURCE
*
        SEIZE     PF1              THE FORK TRUCK IS AVAILABLE SO USE IT
*
        DEPART    WFORK            AFTER FORK TRUCK IS AVAILABLE,
*                                  LOAD CAN BE MOVED
*
        ADVANCE   #F               FORK TRUCK MOVES TO STATION FOR LOAD PICK-UP
*
        ADVANCE   #D               LOAD IS REMOVED FROM PICK-UP STATION
*
        RELEASE   STAT+#A          PALLET RELEASES CURRENT WORK STATION
*
        ADVANCE   #C               TIME DELAY FOR MOVE TO NEXT STATION IN SEQUENCE
*
        ADVANCE   #E               TIME DELAY FOR PALLET DROP OFF AT STATION
*
        RELEASE   PF1              FORK TRUCK IS FREE
*
        ENDMACRO                   END OF MACRO CODE
*=========================================================================*
```

9.2.4 Advantages of Using Subroutines in GPSS/H Macros

A disadvantage of using macros in a simulation is the resulting bulk of code that can occur when the GPSS/H compiler expands all the macro calls. A simple technique that can be employed to reduce the effects of this problem is to embed a subroutine in the macro. The subroutine code will appear only once in the compiled program rather than once for every macro call. The resulting simulation will be more efficient and, depending on the number of macro calls, will contain fewer blocks.

9.2.5 Macro Mini-Language versus a Simulator Package

In Chapter 1, a simulator was defined as a class of simulation software package that is prewritten, user friendly, and application specific. A macro mini-language is very similar to commercially available simulator packages. In fact macro mini-languages can be thought of as custom designed and written simulators.

Since the two are so similar, the question comes to mind, *"When should a simulator be purchased, and when should a macro mini-language be used?"* Figure 9.15 provides an answer.

9.2.6 Generic Simulation

A generic simulation is defined as a reusable model that can be made application specific through the use of a macro mini-language, subroutines, variables, or a series of software modules. A generic simulation is highly desirable in situations where many similar systems need to be modeled under tight time constraints. Many materials handling and industrial equipment vendors employ a generic simulation to reduce new model development time.

Rather than redevelop the entire system from scratch for each model, a base system is maintained and application specific code is added to form a completed simulation.

9.2.7 Automatic Code Generator

Taking the concept of a generic simulation and macro mini-language one step further logically leads to the topic of an automatic code generator. A tool such as this can be developed to provide a method of piecing together a simulation from prewritten software modules or macros.

A traditional programming language can be used to write a user interface that prompts the simulation analyst for data as the model is pieced together. Based on the answers to various questions, the automatic code generator will pull different simulation modules from a library, thereby creating an application specific model that can be run like a regular simulation.

Figure 9.10 Materials handling macro.

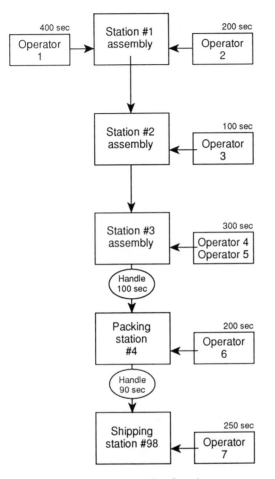

Figure 9.11 Rider's existing line flow diagram.

An automatic code generator gives the simulation analyst the advantage of standardization, faster development time, and user friendliness. Tools such as code generators have not yet been fully exploited in industry and business. Eventually they will provide a better means for nontechnical people to obtain quick answers to complex questions.

9.3 Custom Generated Animation

Chapter 2 provided a description of animation and graphics as a means of bringing a simulation to life. In this section, a simple program written in GW-BASIC (Microsoft Corporation, 1988) is developed to further illustrate some of the useful features that a tool such as this has to offer the simulation analyst.

```
*===================================================================*
*     MACRO LANGUAGE CODE TO REPRESENT RIDER'S OPERATION #1 LINE    *
*===================================================================*
*
        GENERATE   500,100,,,,1PF          A PALLET ENTERS THE SYSTEM
*                                          EVERY 500 +/- 100 SECONDS
*
ASSEM   MACRO      1,2,0,400,200,2,30,1,2,1    ASSEMBLY STATION NUMBER ONE
*
ASSEM   MACRO      2,2,0,200,100,3,30,2,3,0    ASSEMBLY STATION NUMBER TWO
*
ASSEM   MACRO      3,2,1,300,300,99,0,4,5,0    ASSEMBLY STATION NUMBER THREE
*
HANDLE  MACRO      3,4,100,10,10,45        FORK TRUCK TRANSPORTS PALLET
*                                          FROM ASSEMBLY THREE TO PACKAGING
*
PACK    MACRO      4,200,6,0               PACKAGING OPERATION
*
HANDLE  MACRO      4,SHIPS,90,10,10,45     FORK TRUCK TRANSPORTS PALLET
*                                          FROM PACKAGING TO SHIPPING
*
SHIP    MACRO      7,250                   SHIPPING OPERATION
*===================================================================*
*                  END OF MACRO MINI-LANGUAGE CODE                  *
*===================================================================*
```

Figure 9.12 Simulation code for Rider's operation.

Most simulation products include some type of animation software. Sometimes this software can be very expensive. In many applications, a fancy "I'll buy it!" animation is not necessary. The techniques used in this example of a low-cost, do-it-yourself animation can be applied to nearly any model regardless of the simulation language being used. As long as an external ASCII file can receive data from the simulation, the animation data can be shown on the screen in a post-processor mode.

9.3.1 The Model To Be Illustrated

The model to be animated as an example is similar to the one discussed in Chapter 8. It is a serial queuing system consisting of two servers and two queues. This configuration (commonly used in fast-food drive through window arrangements) is illustrated in Figure 9.16.

The GPSS/H source code for the model is shown in Figure 9.17. By inspecting the code in Figure 9.17, it can be observed that a BPUTPIC block is being used to enter data into an ASCII file after the occurrence of each event. These events include entering a queue, leaving a queue, seizing a server, and releasing a server. The data entered into the ASCII file consists of four elements:

1. *AC1*. Simulated time of the event's occurrence.
2. *Special Entity Number.* A number that represents the entity (queue or facility) in the animation layout file.
3. *Queue Length.* If the event involves a queue, enter its length. If the event involves a facility, enter a 0.

```
        SIMULATE    15
*
        UNLIST      MACX            INHIBIT MACRO EXPANSIONS IN LIST FILES
*==============================================================================*
* LIST OF GPSS/H ENTITIES USED IN MACROS                                       *
*==============================================================================*
*
TRUE    SYN         1               SYNONYM FOR (1) MEANING TRUE
*
SHIPS   SYN         98              SYNONYM FOR SHIPPING OPERATION ALWAYS
*                                   STATION #98
WAITS   EQU         000(99),Q       QUEUE TO DETERMINE HOW LONG LOADS WAIT FOR
*                                   A PARTICULAR STATION
*
STAT    EQU         100(99),F       FACILITY USED TO REPRESENT THE PHYSICAL WORK
*                                   STATION RESOURCE
*
WAITO   EQU         200(99),S       STORAGE TO DETERMINE HOW LONG LOADS WAIT
*                                   AT A STATION FOR AN OPERATOR
*
OPER    EQU         300(99),S       STORAGE TO REPRESENT OPERATOR RESOURCES
*
FORK    EQU         400(3),F        FACILITY USED TO REPRESENT THE FORK TRUCKS
*
WFORK   EQU         405,Q           QUEUE TO DETERMINE HOW LONG LOADS WAIT AT
*                                   A STATION FOR AN OPERATOR
*==============================================================================*
        STORAGE     S((OPER+1))-S((OPER+98)),1    STORAGE CAPACITY OF ONE
*==============================================================================*
TEST1   BVARIABLE   FNU(401)+FNU(402)+FNU(403)    BOOLEAN VARIABLE TO DETERMINE
*                                   IF A FORK TRUCK IS AVAILABLE
*==============================================================================*
*
*
*
*==============================================================================*
*               LISTING OF MACROS USED IN SIMULATION                           *
*==============================================================================*


*==============================================================================*
*                         ASSEM MACRO                                          *
*==============================================================================*
ASSEM   STARTMACRO
*
        TEST E      #J,TRUE,*+4     IF THIS IS THE FIRST STATION IN A SEQUENCE
*                                   PERFORM THIS CODE

*==============================================================================*
*          FIRST STATION IN SEQUENCE OF ASSEMBLY OPERATIONS                    *
*==============================================================================*
*
        QUEUE       WAITS+#A        ENTER A QUEUE WHILE WAITING FOR
*                                   STATION TO BECOME AVAILABLE
*
        SEIZE       STAT+#A         ATTEMPT TO RESERVE STATION FOR EXCLUSIVE
*                                   USAGE
*
        DEPART      WAITS+#A        STATION QUEUE CAN BE LEFT
*==============================================================================*
*
        TEST E      #B,2,*+34       DETERMINE WHETHER ONE OR TWO ASSEMBLY
*                                   WORKERS ARE REQUIRED
*==============================================================================*
*               TWO STATION OPERATORS BEING USED                               *
*==============================================================================*
*
```

Figure 9.13 Example simulation code from Rider's Packaging Corporation case study.

```
        TEST E    #C,TRUE,*+18  DETERMINE WHETHER WORK IS DONE INDEPENDENTLY
*                               BY EACH ASSEMBLY OPERATOR OR IF BOTH WORKERS
*                               ARE REQUIRED PRIOR TO STARTING
*==========================================================================*
*          BOTH STATION OPERATORS REQUIRED TO START OPERATION         *
*==========================================================================*
*
        ENTER     WAITO+#A,2    STATISTIC THAT KEEPS TRACK OF TIME PALLET
*                               WAITS FOR BOTH OPERATORS TO BECOME AVAILABLE
*
        GATE SNF  OPER+#H       ATTEMPT TO RESERVE BOTH OPERATORS AT THE
        GATE SNF  OPER+#I       SAME TIME BEFORE BEGINNING ASSEMBLY OPERATION
        TRANSFER  SIM,,*-2
*
        ENTER     OPER+#H       BOTH OPERATORS ARE AVAILABLE SO RESERVE
        ENTER     OPER+#I       THEM FOR USE
*
        LEAVE     WAITO+#A,2    AFTER BOTH OPERATORS HAVE BECOME AVAILABLE
*                               THE ASSEMBLY OPERATION CAN BEGIN;
*
        SPLIT     1,*+2         A TRANSACTION REPRESENTING FIRST OPERATOR
*                               IS CREATED
*
        TRANSFER  ,*+7          PARENT TRANSACTION IS SENT TO ASSEMBLE BLOCK
*                               TO WAIT FOR BOTH OPERATORS TO COMPLETE
*
        SPLIT     1,*+4         SECOND OPERATOR TRANSACTION IS CREATED
*
        ADVANCE   #D            FIRST OPERATOR SPENDS TIME WORKING ON TASK
*
        LEAVE     OPER+#H       FIRST OPERATOR COMPLETE, RESOURCE AVAILABLE
*                               TO OTHER USERS
*
        TRANSFER  ,*+3          GO TO ASSEMBLE BLOCK
*
        ADVANCE   #E            SECOND OPERATOR SPENDS TIME WORKING ON TASK
*
        LEAVE     OPER+#I       SECOND OPERATOR COMPLETE, RESOURCE AVAILABLE
*                               TO OTHER USERS
*
        ASSEMBLE  3             TRANSACTION REPRESENTING PALLET WAITS FOR
*                               BOTH OPERATORS TO FINISH ASSEMBLY OPERATION,
*                               THEN CAN MOVE ON.
*
        TRANSFER  ,*+21         PALLET READY TO LEAVE WORK STATION
*==========================================================================*
*          STATION OPERATORS WORK INDEPENDENTLY ON WORK PIECE         *
*==========================================================================*
*
        ENTER     WAITO+#A,2    WORK PIECE WAITS FOR OPERATORS TO BECOME
*                               AVAILABLE
*
        SPLIT     1,*+2         A TRANSACTION REPRESENTING FIRST OPERATOR
*                               IS CREATED
*
        TRANSFER  ,*+11         PARENT TRANSACTION IS SENT TO ASSEMBLY BLOCK
*                               TO WAIT FOR BOTH OPERATORS TO COMPLETE THEIR
*                               DUTIES
*
        SPLIT     1,*+6         SECOND OPERATOR TRANSACTION IS CREATED
*
        ENTER     OPER+#H       AS SOON AS ASSEMBLY OPERATOR RESOURCE IS
*                               AVAILABLE, USE IT.
*
        LEAVE     WAITO+#A,1    OPERATOR IS READY TO BEGIN WORK ON PALLET
```

(Figure 9.13 continued)

193

```
*
       ADVANCE    #D             FIRST OPERATOR SPENDS TIME WORKING ON TASK
*
       LEAVE      OPER+#H        FIRST OPERATOR COMPLETE, RESOURCE AVAILABLE
*                                TO OTHER USERS
*
       TRANSFER   ,*+5           GO TO ASSEMBLE BLOCK
*
       ENTER      OPER+#I        AS SOON AS SECOND OPERATOR RESOURCE IS READY,
*                                USE IT
*
       LEAVE      WAITO+#A       NO LONGER WAITING FOR OPERATOR RESOURCE
*
       ADVANCE    #E             SECOND OPERATOR SPENDS TIME WORKING ON TASK
*
       LEAVE      OPER+#I        SECOND OPERATOR COMPLETE, RESOURCE AVAILABLE
*                                TO OTHER USERS
*
       ASSEMBLE   3              TRANSACTION REPRESENTING PALLET WAITS FOR
*                                BOTH OPERATORS TO FINISH ASSEMBLY OPERATION,
*                                THEN CAN MOVE ON.
*
       TRANSFER   ,*+6           PALLET READY TO LEAVE WORK STATION
*=======================================================================*
*            ONLY ONE STATION OPERATOR IS REQUIRED                      *
*=======================================================================*
*
       ENTER      WAITO+#A,1     WORK PIECE WAITS FOR OPERATOR TO BECOME
*                                AVAILABLE
*
       ENTER      OPER+#H        AS SOON AS ASSEMBLY OPERATOR RESOURCE IS
*                                AVAILABLE, USE IT.
*
       LEAVE      WAITO+#A,1     OPERATOR IS READY TO BEGIN WORK ON PALLET
*
       ADVANCE    #D             OPERATOR SPENDS TIME WORKING ON TASK
*
       LEAVE      OPER+#H        OPERATOR COMPLETE, RESOURCE AVAILABLE TO
*                                OTHER USERS
*=======================================================================*
*   ASSEMBLY OPERATION COMPLETE MOVE TO NEXT STATION OR TERMINATE       *
*=======================================================================*
*
       TEST NE    #F,99,*+6      DETERMINE IF THIS IS THE LAST STATION.
*=======================================================================*
*    PALLET READY TO MOVE ON TO NEXT ASSEMBLY STATION IN SEQUENCE       *
*=======================================================================*
*
       QUEUE      WAITS+#F       ENTER A QUEUE WHILE WAITING FOR NEXT
*                                STATION TO BECOME AVAILABLE
*
       SEIZE      STAT+#F        ATTEMPT TO RESERVE STATION FOR EXCLUSIVE
*                                USAGE
*
       DEPART     WAITS+#F       STATION QUEUE CAN BE LEFT
*
       RELEASE    STAT+#A        RELINQUISH CURRENT ASSEMBLY STATION
*
       ADVANCE    #G             TIME DELAY FOR MOVE TO NEXT STATION IN
*                                SEQUENCE
*
       ENDMACRO                  END OF MACRO CODE
*=======================================================================*
*=======================================================================*
*                         PACK MACRO                                    *
*=======================================================================*
```

(Figure 9.13 continued)

194

```
* LIST OF INPUT PARAMETERS AND ASSOCIATED DEFINITIONS                         *
*===========================================================================*
* #A - I.D. NUMBER OF CURRENT PACKAGING STATION                               *
* #B - PACKAGING OPERATION TIME                                               *
* #C - OPERATOR I.D. NUMBER                                                   *
* #D - IF '99' THEN THIS IS THE LAST STATION IN THE PALLET'S SEQUENCE         *
*===========================================================================*
PACK    STARTMACRO              MACRO DEFINITION BEGINS
*
        ENTER   WAITO+#A,1      WORK PIECE WAITS FOR OPERATOR TO BECOME
*                               AVAILABLE
*
        ENTER   OPER+#C         AS SOON AS PACKAGING OPERATOR RESOURCE IS
*                               AVAILABLE, USE IT.
*
        LEAVE   WAITO+#A,1      OPERATOR IS READY TO BEGIN WORK ON PALLET
*
        ADVANCE #B              OPERATOR SPENDS TIME WORKING ON TASK
*
        LEAVE   OPER+#C         OPERATOR COMPLETE, RESOURCE AVAILABLE
*                               TO OTHER USERS
*
*===========================================================================*
*      PACKAGING OPERATION COMPLETE MOVE TO NEXT STATION OR TERMINATE        *
*===========================================================================*
*
        TEST E  #D,99,*+2       DETERMINE IF THIS IS THE LAST STATION.
*===========================================================================*
*        CODE FOR LAST STATION IN AN SEQUENCE                                *
*===========================================================================*
*
        RELEASE STAT+#A         RELEASE WORK STATION
*===========================================================================*
*
        ENDMACRO                END OF MACRO CODE
*===========================================================================*


*===========================================================================*
*                          SHIP MACRO                                        *
*===========================================================================*
* LIST OF INPUT PARAMETERS AND ASSOCIATED DEFINITIONS                        *
*===========================================================================*
* #A - I.D. NUMBER OF SHIPPING CLERK ASSIGNED TO STATION                     *
* #B - SHIPPING OPERATION TIME                                               *
*===========================================================================*
SHIP    STARTMACRO              MACRO DEFINITION BEGINS
*
        ENTER   WAITO+SHIPS     WORK PIECE WAITS FOR CLERK TO BECOME
*                               AVAILABLE AT SHIPPING
*
        ENTER   OPER+#A         AS SOON AS SHIPPING CLERK RESOURCE IS
*                               AVAILABLE, USE IT.
*
        LEAVE   WAITO+SHIPS,1   CLERK IS READY TO BEGIN WORK ON PALLET
*
        ADVANCE #B              CLERK SPENDS TIME WORKING ON TASK
*
        LEAVE   OPER+#A         CLERK COMPLETE, RESOURCE AVAILABLE TO
*                               OTHER PALLETS
*
        RELEASE STAT+SHIPS      SHIPPING STATION IS RELEASE TO ANOTHER PALLET

*===========================================================================*
*         SHIPPING OPERATION TERMINATE LOAD TRANSACTION                      *
*===========================================================================*
```

(Figure 9.13 continued)

195

```
*
          TERMINATE                      LOAD IS TERMINATED
*
          ENDMACRO                       END OF MACRO CODE
*===============================================================================*


*===============================================================================*
*                              HANDLE MACRO                                     *
*===============================================================================*
* LIST OF INPUT PARAMETERS AND ASSOCIATED DEFINITIONS                           *
*===============================================================================*
* #A - PICK-UP STATION                                                          *
* #B - DROP-OFF STATION                                                         *
* #C - TRAVEL TIME FROM PICK-UP TO DROP--OFF STATION                            *
* #D - LOAD PICK--UP TIME                                                       *
* #E - LOAD DROP--OFF TIME                                                      *
* #F - AVERAGE TIME FOR A FORK TRUCK TO ARRIVE AT A CALLING STATION             *
*===============================================================================*
HANDLE STARTMACRO                       MACRO DEFINITION BEGINS
*
          QUEUE      WAITS+#B            ENTER A QUEUE WHILE WAITING FOR STATION
                                        TO BECOME AVAILABLE
*
          SEIZE      STAT+#B            ATTEMPT TO RESERVE STATION FOR EXCLUSIVE USAGE
*
          DEPART     WAITS+#B            STATION QUEUE CAN BE LEFT
*===============================================================================*
*            WAIT FOR A FORK TRUCK TO BECOME AVAILABLE                           *
*===============================================================================*
*
          QUEUE      WFORK               STATISTIC THAT KEEPS TRACK OF TIME PALLET
*                                        WAITS FOR A FORK TRUCK TO BECOME AVAILABLE
*
          TEST E     BV$TEST1,TRUE       DETERMINE IF A FORK TRUCK IS AVAILABLE
*
          SELECT NU  1,FORK+1,FORK+3     RESERVE AN ELIGIBLE FORK TRUCK RESOURCE
*
          SEIZE      PF1                 THE FORK TRUCK IS AVAILABLE SO USE IT
*
          DEPART     WFORK               AFTER FORK TRUCK IS AVAILABLE,
*                                        LOAD CAN BE MOVED
*
          ADVANCE    #F                  FORK TRUCK MOVES TO STATION FOR LOAD PICK-UP
*
          ADVANCE    #D                  LOAD IS REMOVED FROM PICK--UP STATION
*
          RELEASE    STAT+#A             PALLET RELEASES CURRENT WORK STATION
*
          ADVANCE    #C                  TIME DELAY FOR MOVE TO NEXT STATION IN SEQUENCE
*
          ADVANCE    #E                  TIME DELAY FOR PALLET DROP OFF AT STATION
*
          RELEASE    PF1                 FORK TRUCK IS FREE
*
          ENDMACRO                       END OF MACRO CODE
*===============================================================================*


*===============================================================================*
*    SIMULATION CODE BEGINS                                                     *
*===============================================================================*
*===============================================================================*
*    MACRO LANGUAGE CODE TO REPRESENT RIDER'S OPERATION #1 LINE                 *
*===============================================================================*
*
          GENERATE   500,100,,,,1PF           A PALLET ENTERS THE SYSTEM
*                                             EVERY 500 +/- 100 SECONDS
```

(*Figure 9.13 continued*)

```
*
ASSEM   MACRO      1,2,0,400,200,2,30,1,2,1      ASSEMBLY STATION NUMBER ONE
*
ASSEM   MACRO      2,2,0,200,100,3,30,2,3,0      ASSEMBLY STATION NUMBER TWO
*
ASSEM   MACRO      3,2,1,300,300,99,0,4,5,0      ASSEMBLY STATION NUMBER THREE
*
HANDLE  MACRO      3,4,100,10,10,45             FORK TRUCK TRANSPORTS PALLET
*                                               FROM ASSEMBLY THREE TO PACKAGING
*
PACK    MACRO      4,200,6,0                    PACKAGING OPERATION
*
HANDLE  MACRO      4,SHIPS,90,10,10,45          FORK TRUCK TRANSPORTS PALLET
*                                               FROM PACKAGING TO SHIPPING
*
SHIP    MACRO      7,250                        SHIPPING OPERATION
*=================================================================================*
*                  END OF MACRO MINI-LANGUAGE CODE                               *
*=================================================================================*
*============================================================================*
*                       TIMING TRANSACTION                       *
*============================================================================*
        GENERATE    3600
        TERMINATE   1
        START       5
*============================================================================*
*                       OUTPUT FILE CREATION                     *
*============================================================================*
        INTEGER     &C        DEFINE FOR USE IN OUTPUT FILE
*
        PUTPIC      FILE=RESULTS,LINES=9
 =
 =

                    WAITING FOR STATIONS
                    ====================
 =
STATION          NUMBER OF        AVERAGE              AVE TIME
   #             ENTRIES          QUEUE LENGTH         IN QUEUE (SEC)
=======          =========        ============         ==============
 =
        DO          &C=1,98,1
        IF          (QC(WAITS+&C)=0)
        GOTO        SKIP1
        ENDIF
        PUTPIC      FILE=RESULTS,LINES=1,(&C,_
                    QC(WAITS+&C),QA(WAITS+&C),QT(WAITS+&C))
    **           ****             ***.*                *****.*
SKIP1   HERE
        ENDDO
        PUTPIC      FILE=RESULTS,LINES=9
 =
 =

                    STATION RESOURCES
                    =================
 =
STATION          NUMBER OF        PERCENT TIME         AVE TIME
   #             ENTRIES          IN USE               PER USE  (SEC)
=======          =========        ============         ==============
 =
        DO          &C=1,98,1
        IF          (FC(STAT+&C)=0)
        GOTO        SKIP2
        ENDIF
        PUTPIC      FILE=RESULTS,LINES=1,(&C,_
                    FC(STAT+&C),FR(STAT+&C)/10,FT(STAT+&C))
    **           ****             **.**                *****.*
```

(Figure 9.13 continued)

```
SKIP2    HERE
         ENDDO
         PUTPIC      FILE=RESULTS,LINES=9
  =
  =
                           FORK TRUCK RESOURCES
                           ====================
  =
   TRUCK       NUMBER OF      PERCENT TIME      AVE TIME
     #         ENTRIES          IN USE        PER USE  (SEC)
  =======      =========      ============    ==============
  =
         DO          &C=1,3,1
         IF          (FC(FORK+&C)=0)
         GOTO        SKIP3
         ENDIF
         PUTPIC      FILE=RESULTS,LINES=1,(&C,_
                     FC(FORK+&C),FR(FORK+&C)/10,FT(FORK+&C))
       **          ****          **.**          *****.*


SKIP3    HERE
         ENDDO
         PUTPIC      FILE=RESULTS,LINES=9
  =
  =
                           WAITING FOR OPERATOR
                           ====================
  =
            OPERATOR       NUMBER OF      AVERAGE
               #           ENTRIES        LINE LENGTH
            =======        =========      ============
  =
         DO          &C=1,98,1
         IF          (SC(WAITO+&C)=0)
         GOTO        SKIP4
         ENDIF
         PUTPIC      FILE=RESULTS,LINES=1,(&C,_
                     SC(WAITO+&C),SA(WAITO+&C))
                      **          ****          ***.*
SKIP4    HERE
         ENDDO
         PUTPIC      FILE=RESULTS,LINES=9
  =
  =
                           OPERATOR USAGE
                           ==============
  =
  OPERATOR     NUMBER OF      PERCENT TIME      AVE TIME
     #         ENTRIES          IN USE        PER USE  (SEC)
  =======      =========      ============    ==============
  =
         DO          &C=1,98,1
         IF          (SC(OPER+&C)=0)
         GOTO        SKIP5
         ENDIF
         PUTPIC      FILE=RESULTS,LINES=1,(&C,_
                     SC(OPER+&C),SR(OPER+&C)/10,ST(OPER+&C))
       **          ****          **.**          *****.*
SKIP5    HERE
         ENDDO
         END
*
*
```

(*Figure 9.13 continued*)

```
=
=
```

WAITING FOR STATIONS
=====================

```
=
```

STATION #	NUMBER OF ENTRIES	AVERAGE QUEUE LENGTH	AVE TIME IN QUEUE (SEC)
1	35	0.0	0.0
2	34	0.0	0.0
3	34	0.0	26.4
4	33	0.0	7.6
98	32	0.0	0.0

```
=
=
```

STATION RESOURCES
=================

```
=
```

STATION #	NUMBER OF ENTRIES	PERCENT TIME IN USE	AVE TIME PER USE (SEC)
1	35	76.49	393.4
2	34	53.63	283.9
3	33	71.86	391.9
4	33	74.85	408.2
98	32	72.00	405.0

```
=
=
```

FORK TRUCK RESOURCES
=====================

```
=
```

TRUCK #	NUMBER OF ENTRIES	PERCENT TIME IN USE	AVE TIME PER USE (SEC)
1	47	40.57	155.4
2	18	16.50	165.0

```
=
=
```

WAITING FOR OPERATOR
=====================

```
=
```

OPERATOR #	NUMBER OF ENTRIES	AVERAGE LINE LENGTH
1	70	0.2
2	68	0.1
3	66	0.0
4	32	0.0
98	32	0.0

```
=
=
```

OPERATOR USAGE
==============

```
=
```

OPERATOR #	NUMBER OF ENTRIES	PERCENT TIME IN USE	AVE TIME PER USE (SEC)
1	35	76.49	393.4
2	69	76.29	199.0
3	34	18.89	100.0
4	33	55.00	300.0
5	33	55.00	300.0
6	32	35.56	200.0
7	32	44.44	250.0

Figure 9.14 Simulation output from Rider's Packaging Corporation model.

Simulator (Commercial)	Macro Mini-Language	Comments/Observations
One Time Purchase Cost	Development Cost	If only one model is to be written, a simulator may provide a more cost-effective solution. If multiple simulations will be written, the advantages of a macro language will offset the cost of development.
Difficult to Modify Underlying Algorithms	Easy to Modify Underlying Algorithms	The simulation analyst has full access and understanding of the underlying simulation code in the macro language. The simulator package may contain no provisions for customization.
No Debugging Time	Debugging Required	The simulator will be fully working and debugged upon purchase.
Generally Application Specific	Can Be Made Exact To In-House Application	Simulators have to account for all cases while macro languages can be made specific to the simulation analyst's case. For example, an Automatic Guided Vehicle (AGV) simulator has to be general enough to work with the AGV systems built by all vendors. One specific vendor may employ certain techniques to provide a competitive advantage. A simulator may not have the capability of providing this special technique, so a macro language approach should be used.
Inflexible	Very Flexible	Simulators are built to perform a particular function. A macro language can be changed to reflect exactly what is desired. A sediment expressed by a materials handling control system engineer concerning a simulator package was, "We're not going to limit our design to what this simulation package is capable of doing."
Simulation Analyst Is Not In Control Of What Is In The Code	Simulation Analyst Is In Control Of Code	Macro languages offer the advantage of being user designed. The simulation analyst does not have this control when a simulator is used.

Figure 9.15 When to use a simulator and when to use a macro language.

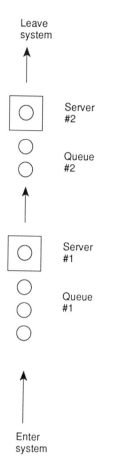

Figure 9.16　Serial queuing system.

　　4. *Special Code Character.* This character represents the following events:

　　　　1 = enter a queue
　　　　2 = leave a queue
　　　　3 = seize a server (facility)
　　　　4 = release a server (facility)

　　The data file that is created while the simulation runs is used to drive the post-processor animation program. A sampling of the information contained in this data file (called QUEUE.DAT) is shown in Figure 9.18.

9.3.2　The Animation Program

The program that creates the animation from the output ASCII file created by the GPSS/H simulation is written in GW-BASIC and runs on an IBM PC with a VGA card.

```
        SIMULATE   2          SIMULATION CAN RUN FOR UP TO 2 MINUTES
*                              OF CPU TIME
*==============================================================*
*
        GENERATE   11,9        CREATE A CUSTOMER TRANSACTION UNIFORMLY
*                              EVERY 2 TO 20 MINUTES
*
        QUEUE      MXQUEUE     CUSTOMER TRANSACTION JOINS THE WAITING
*                              LINE CALLED MXQUEUE
*
┌──────────────────────────────────────────────────────────────────┐
│*      PUT DATA TO THE ANIMATION FILE FOR QUEUE ENTRY               │
│       BPUTPIC    FILE=DATA,LINES=1,AC1,1,Q$MXQUEUE,1               │
│       ********   **       *****     *                              │
└──────────────────────────────────────────────────────────────────┘
*
        SEIZE      SERVER      CUSTOMER TRANSACTION CAPTURES SERVER
*                              RESOURCE WHEN POSSIBLE
*
┌──────────────────────────────────────────────────────────────────┐
│*      PUT DATA TO THE ANIMATION FILE FOR SEIZING SERVER           │
│       BPUTPIC    FILE=DATA,LINES=1,AC1,11,0,3                      │
│       ********   **       *****     *                              │
└──────────────────────────────────────────────────────────────────┘
*
        DEPART     MXQUEUE     CUSTOMER TRANSACTION MOVES OUT
*                              OF WAITING LINE
*
┌──────────────────────────────────────────────────────────────────┐
│*      PUT DATA TO THE ANIMATION FILE FOR DEPARTING QUEUE          │
│       BPUTPIC    FILE=DATA,LINES=1,AC1,1,Q$MXQUEUE,2               │
│       ********   **       *****     *                              │
└──────────────────────────────────────────────────────────────────┘
*
        ADVANCE    12,3        CUSTOMER TRANSACTION RECEIVES
*                              SERVICE FROM 8 TO 14 MINUTES LONG
*
        RELEASE    SERVER      CUSTOMER TRANSACTION RELINQUISHES SERVER
*
┌──────────────────────────────────────────────────────────────────┐
│*      PUT DATA TO THE ANIMATION FILE FOR RELEASING SERVER         │
│       BPUTPIC    FILE=DATA,LINES=1,AC1,11,0,4                      │
│       ********   **       *****     *                              │
└──────────────────────────────────────────────────────────────────┘
*
        QUEUE      MXQUEUE2    CUSTOMER TRANSACTION JOINS THE
*                              WAITING LINE CALLED MXQUEUE
*
┌──────────────────────────────────────────────────────────────────┐
│*      PUT DATA TO THE ANIMATION FILE FOR QUEUE ENTRY              │
│       BPUTPIC    FILE=DATA,LINES=1,AC1,12,Q$MXQUEUE2,1            │
│       ********   **       *****     *                              │
└──────────────────────────────────────────────────────────────────┘
*
        SEIZE      SERVER2     CUSTOMER TRANSACTION CAPTURES SERVER
*                              RESOURCE WHEN POSSIBLE
*
┌──────────────────────────────────────────────────────────────────┐
│*      PUT DATA TO THE ANIMATION FILE FOR SEIZING SERVER           │
│       BPUTPIC    FILE=DATA,LINES=1,AC1,13,0,3                      │
│       ********   **       *****     *                              │
└──────────────────────────────────────────────────────────────────┘
*
        DEPART     MXQUEUE2    CUSTOMER TRANSACTION MOVES OUT
*                              OF WAITING LINE
*

┌──────────────────────────────────────────────────────────────────┐
│*      PUT DATA TO THE ANIMATION FILE FOR DEPARTING QUEUE          │
│       BPUTPIC    FILE=DATA,LINES=1,AC1,12,Q$MXQUEUE2,2            │
│       ********   **       *****     *                              │
└──────────────────────────────────────────────────────────────────┘
*
        ADVANCE    18,3        CUSTOMER TRANSACTION RECEIVES
*                              SERVICE FROM 8 TO 14 MINUTES LONG
*
        RELEASE    SERVER2     CUSTOMER TRANSACTION RELINQUISHES SERVER
*
┌──────────────────────────────────────────────────────────────────┐
│*      PUT DATA TO THE ANIMATION FILE FOR RELEASING SERVER         │
│       BPUTPIC    FILE=DATA,LINES=1,AC1,13,0,4                      │
│       ********   **       *****     *                              │
└──────────────────────────────────────────────────────────────────┘
*
        TERMINATE             CUSTOMER TRANSACTION LEAVES MODEL
*==============================================================*
*             TIMING TRANSACTION & OUTPUT ROUTINE              *
*==============================================================*
*
        GENERATE   1          A TIMING TRANSACTION GENERATED EVERY
*                             ONE MINUTE OF SIMULATED TIME
*
        TERMINATE  1          EACH TRANSACTION DECREMENTS THE START
*                             BLOCK COUNTER BY ONE
*
        START      480,NP     EACH RUN LAST FOR 480 MINUTES (8 HOURS)
*
        END                   END OF MODEL
```

Figure 9.17 GPSS/H source code for simulation to be animated (boxed areas contain code that creates the animation file data).

```
                              Key:
  6      1      1      1      Column 1 - Time (AC1)
  6     11      0      3      Column 2 - Entity Number
  6      1      0      2      Column 3 - Queue Length
 17      1      1      1      Column 4 - Special Code Character
 20     11      0      4
 20     12      1      1
 20     13      0      3
 20     12      0      2
 20     11      0      3
 20      1      0      2
 23      1      1      1
 33      1      2      1
 33     11      0      4
 33     12      1      1
 33     11      0      3
```

Figure 9.18 Sample of data (QUEUE.DAT) used to drive post-processor animation program.

Figure 9.19 provides a source code listing of the GW-BASIC animation program that has been specifically designed to animate queuing systems. The placement of servers, the queues, their displayed lengths, and system labels are all controlled by an input file called "SIM.LAY" (simulation layout). Figure 9.20 displays and describes the contents of this file as used in this example.

9.3.3 Running the Animation

The process of running the animation post-processor involves the following steps:

1. Creating a GPSS/H (or other type) simulation program.
2. Putting in statements to create an ASCII output file after each event that changes the state of the simulation (Figure 9.17).
3. Creating an animation layout file that corresponds to a simulation program and uses the format described in Figure 9.20.
4. Running the GPSS/H simulation program to create an output animation data file (Figure 9.18).
5. Running the GW-BASIC program to animate the data as a post-processor. Figures 9.21 and 9.22 show how the animation appears at different points in simulated time.

9.3.4 Summary

The programs used in this example only scratch the surface of what can be done using animation. Many commercially available animation programs take full advantage of current graphics technology and produce exciting high-resolution animation to accompany simulation programs (see Chapter 2). The process illustrated in this chapter can be easily adapted to a number of queuing system examples. However, by investing in a commercial animation package, development time can be eliminated and many powerful features can be gained.

```
100 '**********************************************************************
110 '********** GW BASIC PROGRAM TO PRODUCE A SIMPLE ANIMATION **********
120 '**********************************************************************
130 '
140 ' SET SCREEN UP =========================================================
150 '
160 KEY OFF : CLS        ' CLEAR SCREEN
170 SCREEN 9             ' HIGH RESOLUTION GRAPHICS SCREEN
180 COLOR 3,4,3          ' SET FOREGROUND, BACKGROUND, AND BORDER COLORS
190 DIM PT(100)          ' LAYOUT CAN HAVE UP TO 100 POINTS
200 DIM XPT(100)         ' 100 SCREEN X COORDINATES
210 DIM YPT(100)         ' 100 SCREEN Y COORDINATES
220 DIM ZPT(100)         ' 100 ATTRIBUTES (EITHER ASSOCIATED QUEUE OR FACILITY)
230 ETIME = 480          ' SET A MAXIMUM END TIME FOR SIMULATION RUN
240 SIZE=10              ' SIZE OF ENTITIES TO BE ANIMATED
250 '
260 ON ERROR GOTO 1140 ' ERROR TRAP
270 '
280 ' INPUT ANIMATION LAYOUT SCREEN ====================================
290 '
300 OPEN "SIM.LAY" FOR INPUT AS #1        ' LAYOUT FILE NAME
310 INPUT #1,NUMPTS                       ' NUMBER OF POINTS TO INPUT
320 FOR I=1 TO NUMPTS                     ' INPUT ALL POINTS
330 INPUT #1,PT(I),XPT(I),YPT(I),ZPT(I)   ' POINT NUMBER, X-CORD, Y-CORD, ATTRIBUTE
340 NEXT I                                ' COMPLETE INPUT LOOP
350 '
360 INPUT #1,NUMTXT
370 FOR I=1 TO NUMTXT
380 INPUT #1,CR1,CR2,TXT$
390 LOCATE CINT(CR2/14),CINT(CR1/8):PRINT TXT$  'PIXEL TO TEXT SCREEN ADDRESS
400 NEXT I
410 LOCATE 4,5 :PRINT "TIME"       ' LABEL FOR ANIMATION TIME CLOCK
420 LOCATE 20,21: PRINT "ANIMATION PROGRAM" ' LABEL
430 '
440 ' OPEN AND PRIME ANIMATION WITH SIMULATION OUTPUT DATA ================
450 '
460 OPEN "QUEUE.DAT" FOR INPUT AS #2  ' POST PROCESS ANIMATION DATA FROM THIS FILE
470 INPUT #2,AC1,ENTITY,LGTH,SCODE     ' FILE CONTAINS TIME, ENTITY #, QUEUE LENGTH, SPECIA
    CODE
480 '
490 ' START MAIN PROCESSING LOOP OF ANIMATION ==============================
500 '
510 FOR ATIME=1 TO ETIME       ' ANIMATION TIMING LOOP IS STARTED
520 LOCATE 5,5:PRINT ATIME      ' PRINT TIME ON SCREEN AS ANIMATION PROGRESSES
530 FOR I=1 TO 500: NEXT I      ' TIMING LOOP TO SLOW DOWN ANIMATION
540 IF AC1=ATIME THEN GOTO 600 ELSE GOTO 850 'IF NO EVENT AT THIS TIME ADVANCE TIME
550 '
560 ' IF AN EVENT IS OCCURS AT THIS TIME, EXECUTE THE FOLLOWING STATEMENTS
570 '
580 ' LOOP THROUGH ALL POINTS TO SEE IF THE ENTITY REPRESENTED BY THAT
590 ' NEEDS SOME TYPE OF ANIMATION UPDATE
600 FOR I=1 TO NUMPTS
610 '
620 ' ANIMATE A QUEUE THAT HAS INCREASED ITS LENGTH
630 IF ((LGTH>(PT(I)+1-ENTITY)) OR (LGTH=(PT(I)+1-ENTITY))) AND ZPT(I)=ENTITY AND SCODE=1 T
    GOSUB 890
640 '
650 ' ANIMATE A QUEUE THAT HAS DECREASED ITS LENGTH
660 IF (((LGTH+1)>(PT(I)+1-ENTITY)) OR ((LGTH+1)=(PT(I)+1-ENTITY))) AND ZPT(I)=ENTITY AND
    SCODE=2 THEN GOSUB 960
670 IF ((LGTH>(PT(I)+1-ENTITY)) OR (LGTH=(PT(I)+1-ENTITY))) AND ZPT(I)=ENTITY AND SCODE=2 T
    GOSUB 890
680 '
690 ' ANIMATE A FACILITY BEING SEIZED
700 IF (SCODE=3 AND ZPT(I)=ENTITY) THEN GOSUB 1030
710 '
720 ' ANIMATE A FACILITY BEING RELEASED
730 IF (SCODE=4 AND ZPT(I)=ENTITY) THEN GOSUB 1100
```

Figure 9.19 Animation post-processor.

```
740 '
750 ' COMPLETE LOOP
760 NEXT
770 '
780 ' INPUT NEXT EVENT ==========================================================
790 '
800 INPUT #2,AC1,ENTITY,LGTH,SCODE
810 '
820 ' IF NEXT EVENT OCCURS IN SAME TIME FRAME DON'T ADVANCE CLOCK
830 IF AC1=ATIME THEN GOTO 600
840 '
850 NEXT ATIME  ' ADVANCE ANIMATION CLOCK
860 '**********************************************************************
870 '********** SUBROUTINE TO DRAW A FIGURE REPRESENTING A TRANSACTION **
880 '**********************************************************************
890 X=XPT(I):Y=YPT(I)
900 LINE (0+X,0+Y)-(SIZE+X,SIZE+Y),2,B
910 PAINT (SIZE/2+X,SIZE/2+Y),1,2
920 RETURN
930 '**********************************************************************
940 '********** SUBROUTINE TO ERASE FIGURE REPRESENTING A TRANSACTION **
950 '**********************************************************************
960 X=XPT(I):Y=YPT(I)
970 PAINT (SIZE/2+X,SIZE/2+Y),4,2
980 LINE (0+X,0+Y)-(SIZE+X,SIZE+Y),4,B
990 RETURN
1000 '**********************************************************************
1010 '********** SUBROUTINE TO DRAW A FIGURE REPRESENTING A SERVER *******
1020 '**********************************************************************
1030 X=XPT(I)-SIZE/2:Y=YPT(I)-SIZE/2
1040 LINE (0+X,0+Y)-(2*SIZE+X,2*SIZE+Y),2,B
1050 PAINT (SIZE/2+X,SIZE/2+Y),1,2
1060 RETURN
1070 '**********************************************************************
1080 '********** SUBROUTINE TO DRAW A FIGURE REPRESENTING AN IDLE SERVER**
1090 '**********************************************************************
1100 X=XPT(I):Y=YPT(I)
1110 PAINT (5+X,5+Y),4,2
1120 RETURN
1130 '**********************************************************************
1140 LOCATE 20,60
1150 IF ERL=800 THEN PRINT "END OF SIMULATION" : END
1160 PRINT "ERROR...PROGRAM ENDING LINE = ",B : END
```

(*Figure 9.19 continued*)

9.4 Transfer Methodology

When does a simulation project actually end? This question has been debated by simulation analysts and persons involved with the simulation process. Does it end after the model is complete or when the real world system has been installed, tested, and verified to work? (Figures 9.23 and 9.24). The answer to this question is dependent on the objectives of the simulation study. Some simulations are used solely as design tools while others are kept up to date and used to pretest desired system changes.

The transition from model to real world implementation is a very important aspect of the simulation process that is beginning to receive more attention in industrial applications of modeling. A simulation should not be coded, run, and

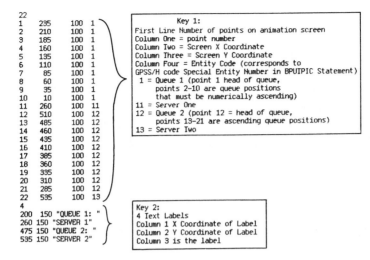

Figure 9.20 SIM.LAY input data file.

put on the shelf. Too many problems and inconsistencies can arise from the "gap" between simulation completion and design of a real world system.

The use of simulation in the design stages of complex manufacturing systems has warranted the development of new methodology for transferring logic from model to actual system. This section emphasizes the importance of maintaining simulation integrity during actual system implementation and presents four methods of accomplishing the transfer of logic.

9.4.1 Introduction to Logic Transfer

Discrete event simulation in manufacturing has traditionally been used as a tool for studying the behavior of dynamic real world systems (Law, 1986; Lajeunesse, 1984; Christy and Watson, 1983; Schriber, 1984). Some common applications use simulation to prove that proposed systems or system changes are feasible. Following development, validation, and verification of a simulation, specific questions can be answered using the model (Figure 9.25).

Another growing area of application for simulations is the modeling of control algorithms for complex materials handling systems. In these cases, it is essential that the actual system logic closely duplicates the logic used in the simulation (Figure 9.26). Otherwise, the simulation results will not be accurate and the actual system will not perform as expected. Often, after a model is developed and a proposed system is proven to work, the simulation phase is over. Control system development will then be turned over to a group of software design engineers who reformulate the control algorithms. The result can be changes in the operating characteristics of the system. Steps can be taken to minimize this potential pitfall and its effects. Examples of measures that can be taken to

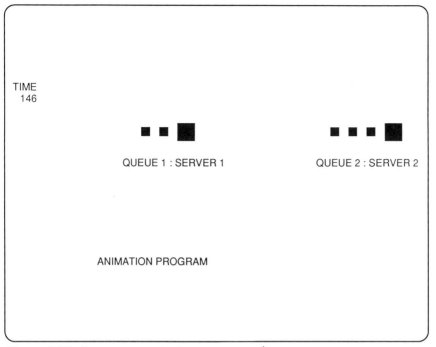

Figure 9.21 Post-processor animation screen, example one.

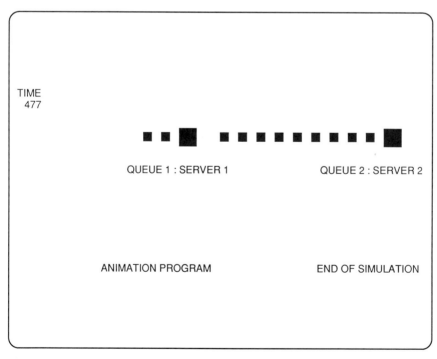

Figure 9.22 Post-processor animation screen, example two.

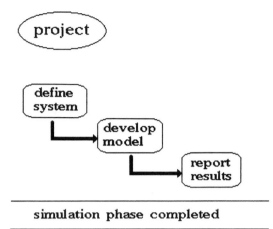

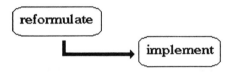

Figure 9.23   Traditional approach to modeling.

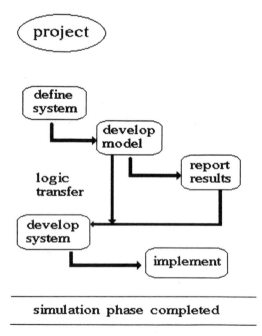

Figure 9.24   Desired approach to modeling, using a logic transfer.

Feasibility :

1. Proposed Systems

2. System Changes

Figure 9.25 Traditional uses of simulation.

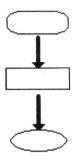

Figure 9.26 Modeling of control algorithms for materials handling systems.

preserve the integrity of the algorithms developed with simulation are explored in this chapter, as well as several different methods of transferring simulation logic.

9.4.2 Performing a Logic Transfer

The simulations being discussed here in Section 9.4 are being used as design tools. They are typically precursors to the actual system being built. It is the goal of the simulation team to identify all logic necessary to implement a controller for the system. In addition, the simulation team must effectively communicate its developed and debugged algorithms to the system design team. This insures that the required logic is incorporated into the actual controller. Four methods of facilitating logic transfer have been devised. These are philosophic transfer, pseudocode transfer, data base transfer, and actual code transfer (Figure 9.27). These four transfer methods are not completely independent, rather they can be thought to exist on a continuum as Figure 9.28 demonstrates.

It is possible to utilize a simulation logic transfer methodology that falls somewhere in between two categories on the continuum. To better understand what these categories entail, a detailed description of each is presented.

9.4.3 Philosophic Transfer

The most common and perhaps least efficient method of transporting simulation logic into actual system control logic is termed a philosophic transfer. Under this scenario, logic for the real world system is based on the key ideas and assumptions used in the simulation (Figure 9.29). This information is presented to the system design team verbally or in the form of a written report. The design team

Philosophic

Pseudocode

Database

Actual Code

(model) — logic → (system)

Figure 9.27 Four types of logic transfer.

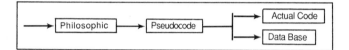

Figure 9.28 Transfer methodology continuum.

evaluates the simulation findings and uses them as a guide or criterion in implementing the actual system software.

In many simple cases, the philosophic transfer works quite well. However, there are some inherent shortcomings that can cause inefficiencies. One of these inefficiencies is duplication of effort. The system software is designed, coded, debugged, and tested. This same process has already been used in the development of the simulation. Another potential shortcoming is the possibility that a piece of information was not communicated properly, resulting in a misinterpreted or omitted portion of logic. A subtle difference in logic can produce a discrepancy that renders the simulation results invalid. The philosophic transfer method tends to make simulation validation a more complex task (Carson, 1986). Since the two softwares were developed in a somewhat independent fashion, the differences become harder to identify. Whether the simulation accurately depicts the actual system becomes a difficult question with an answer that is hard to prove.

The best way to insure that these problems do not occur when employing the philosophic transfer method is to form a system design team consisting of both simulation analysts and software engineers. A common design can be determined and ideas tested with a simulation. When the design is finalized and the simulation is complete, the system software can be written.

If the project has emphasized communication and structure, the transfer of the philosophy contained in the simulation should be successful. Duplication of effort has been minimized by doing the initial design work collectively. The ideal

ideas
assumptions

Verbal or Written

Communication

Figure 9.29 Philosophic transfer from simulation analyst to system engineer.

simulation   controller

Figure 9.30 Pseudocode transfer.

philosophic transfer approach to implementing a simulation in the real world is characterized by teamwork and communication.

9.4.4 Pseudocode Transfer

The second method of transferring data from a simulated controller to an actual controller is the pseudocode transfer method. This approach is similar to the philosophic transfer but it takes the level of detail a step further. It evolved from the need to insure that all assumptions incorporated into a simulation were addressed and made apparent to the actual system design team (Figure 9.30). In this scenario, pseudocode (Page-Jones, 1980) is generated by simulation personnel as a method of documenting what has been implemented. This pseudocode is analyzed and rewritten for the actual controller by system software engineers.

The pseudocode method of transfer offers the advantage of being more detailed. Therefore, the number of omissions and oversights occurring are expected to be fewer than would be seen when using the philosophic transfer method. Simulation validation is also made easier. The logic rules used in the control system can be examined and verified as identical to those in the simulation. Differences are identified readily and the pseudocode provides a common record for both the simulation and system software package.

A disadvantage associated with using this method of transfer is duplication of programming effort. The pseudocode has to be rewritten in the language of the controller, debugged, and tested. Some of the simulation team's time is also required to rewrite the logic in the form of pseudocode.

Communication between the simulation team and the system design team is important under this transfer scenario but not nearly as crucial as when using the philosophic transfer method. By placing a structured and detailed pseudocode document in the hands of the design team, little additional interaction will be required of the simulators. It is not until the verification and validation phase of the project, when the completed system software is compared to the simulation, that further communication will be required.

9.4.5   Data Base Transfer

The third method of transferring simulation logic to an actual system is known as a data base transfer. The essence of this transfer method is to transport a data base, that was developed in the simulation, and use it to drive the actual system controller. It is important to note that this method of data transfer is contingent upon software existing in both the simulation and controller (Figure 9.31). This requires that an initial development project must be undertaken to define the data base and delineate how it will be used. After this has been established, and the simulation and controller software have been developed, the data base can be transferred and utilized. This type of transfer will most commonly be used in cases where many similar systems are being designed using a generic simulation and a generic controller.

The advantages to using this transfer method are quite apparent. The debugging of the data base and its testing are all done in the simulation phase. Nearly all duplication of programming effort is eliminated (after the initial system has been created). Changes to the simulation and actual system can be done easily and consistently. Simulation validation and verification becomes much easier. In addition, communication and the passing of abstract concepts becomes less of an issue.

A potential drawback encountered when using the data base transfer method is the loss of flexibility. Although using a data base simplifies logic and provides the system engineers with a standard, unusual cases and exceptions become more difficult to incorporate. For this reason it is very important that the data bases be designed in a comprehensive manner.

9.4.6   Actual Code Transfer

The final method of data transfer to be examined is transporting actual code from simulation to system controller. This can be done either when the simulation has been written in a conventional language such as FORTRAN or when using a specialized simulation language such as GPSS/H (Henriksen and Crain, 1989) or GPSS/PC (Cox, 1984) that has the capability of calling FORTRAN subroutines. These subroutines contain code that will be used in the system controller. The FORTRAN subroutines can be written either by the simulation analysts or by the system design team prior to implementation in the simulation. Duplicated effort is reduced since the control logic is written only once in the simulation phase and then reused in the actual system (Figure 9.32).

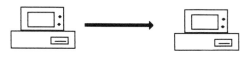

simulation 　　　　　　　　　　　 controller

Figure 9.31 Data base transfer between computer terminals.

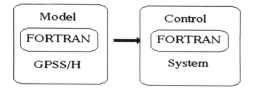

Figure 9.32 Actual code transfer.

Using this actual code transfer method requires that the simulation analysts and system designers work very closely together. It may be advantageous to form one team consisting of both simulation and design personnel. A disadvantage inherent when using this method is the requirement of a more concerted initial effort and additional time to debug the model. The simulation analyst may not be familiar with the control algorithm, and the system designer may not be familiar with the simulation. When the model is run and debugged, some learning time may be required. However, testing and debugging the simulation is also testing and debugging the actual system. Little duplication of effort will occur when the finished software is transported to the actual system software.

9.4.7　Transfer Method Comparisons

Table 9.1 compares two aspects of the four transfer methods previously described. These aspects are communication and duplication of effort. The first column in the chart refers to the level of communication that will be required to successfully implement each transfer method. The second column indicates the level of duplication of effort occurring between the simulation group and the system design team. These levels are rated on a scale from one to ten, with ten being the greatest amount of time required and one being the least. This scale is to be used only to compare the four methods of transfer and does not consider project complexity or any other issue.

9.4.8 Summary of Transfer Methodology

The widespread use of simulation in the design stages of complex control systems has warranted the development of new standards of communication and requires new techniques for the transfer of simulation logic for the following reasons.

TABLE 9.1

Comparison of Simulation Logic Transfer Methods

	Communication[a]	Duplication of Effort
Transfer of Philosophy	10	10
Transfer of Pseudocode	6	5
Transfer of Data Base	3	3
Transfer of Actual Code	7	1

[a] Communication is an important aspect in the success of any simulation. The author wishes to demonstrate that the time spent communicating information relating to the system can be reduced using different methods of simulation transfer.

1. Fewer mistakes
2. Fewer incorrect assumptions
3. Verifies simulation
4. System of checks and balances
5. Reduction of development time

This has become an issue for several reasons. First, it is essential that simulation integrity be maintained in the actual control system. Second, without a logic transfer methodology, subtle differences between the simulation and real world system are prone to emerge. Third, duplication of effort can be minimized when using a logic transfer. Section 9.4 has listed four methods that can be used for transporting simulation logic into actual system software. [This section on transfer methodology has been taken from McHaney (1991) with permission from ABLEX Publishing Corporation.]

9.5 Summary

This chapter has covered a number of different techniques that can be employed to make the modeling process more practical to the simulation analyst and to the eventual user of the system being modeled. The toolkit of time-saving techniques and procedures described in this chapter includes methods of enhancing output, how to use a macro language, the benefits of animation, and simulation logic transfer.

References and Reading

Carson, John S. 1986. "Convincing Users of a Model's Validity is Challenging Aspect of Modeler's Job." *Industrial Engineering* (June): 74–85.

Christy, David P., and Hugh J. Watson. 1983. "The Application of Simulation: A Survey of Industry Practice." *Interfaces* (Oct): 47–52.

Cox, Springer. 1984. *GPSS/PC*. Minuteman Software, Stow, Massachusetts.

Davis, Deborah A. 1986. "Modeling AGV Systems." *Proc. 1986 Winter Simulation Conf.* (Washington, D.C., Dec. 8–10). SCS, San Diego, pp. 568–574.

Harmonosky, Catherine M., and Randall P. Sadowski. 1984. "A Simulated Model and Analysis Integrating AGV's with Non-Automated Material Handling." *Proc. 1984 Winter Simulation Conf.* (Dallas, Nov. 28–30). SCS, San Diego, pp. 178–183.

Harvey, Greg. 1987. *Lotus 1-2-3 Desktop Companion.* Sybex, San Francisco.

Henriksen, James O., and Robert C. Crane. 1989. *GPSS/H Reference Manual,* Third Edition. Wolverine Software Corporation, Annandale, Virginia.

Lajeunesse, Jim. 1984. "Eleven Steps to Simulating an Automated System." *Modern Materials Handling* (Nov. 4): 45–49.

Law, Averill M. 1986. "Introduction to Simulation: A Powerful Tool for Analyzing Complex Manufacturing Systems." *Industrial Engineering* (May): 46–63.

Lotus Corporation. 1986. *The Lotus Guide to Learning 1-2-3 Macros.* Addison-Wesley, Reading, Massachusetts.

McHaney, Roger. 1988. "Bridging the Gap: Transferring Logic from a Simulation into an Actual System Controller." *Proc. 1988 Winter Simulation Conf.* (San Diego, Dec. 12–14). SCS, San Diego, pp. 583–590.

McHaney, Roger. 1990. "Simulation Control Algorithms: Design for Transportability." *Proc. 1990 Summer Simulation Conf.* (Calgary, July 16–18). SCS. San Diego, pp. 276–281.

McHaney, Roger. 1991. "Reusing Simulation Logic in System Development Projects." *Progress in Simulation,* Vol. I (George W. Zobrist and James V. Leonard, eds.). ABLEX Publishing Corporation, Norwood, New Jersey.

Microsoft Corporation. 1988. *Microsoft GW-BASIC User's Guide and User's Reference.* Phoenix Computer Products, Inc. Redmond, Washington (under license of Microsoft Corporation).

New England Softwave. 1987. *Graph-in-the-Box Owner's Handbook.* New England Software, Greenwich, Connecticut.

New England Software. 1987. *Graph-in-the-Box, Release 2, Owner's Handbook.* New England Software, Greenwich, Connecticut.

Newton, Dave. 1985. "Simulation Model Calculates How Many Automated Guided Vehicles Are Needed." *Industrial Engineering* (Feb.): 68–78.

Page-Jones, Meilir. 1980. *The Practical Guide to Structured Systems Design.* Yourdon Press, New York.

Quinn, Edward B. 1987. "Discrete Event Computer Simulation of AGV Networks." *Proc. AGVS 87* (Pittsburgh, Oct. 27–29). MHI, Charlotte, North Carolina, pp. 43–51.

Sadowski, Randall. 1987. "Computer Simulation of Automatic Guided Vehicles." *Proc. AGVS 87* (Pittsburgh, Oct. 27–29). MHI, Charlotte, North Carolina, pp. 21–41.

Schriber, Thomas J. 1984. "A GPSS/H Model for a Hypothetical Flexible Manufacturing System." *Proc. First ORSA/TIMS Spec. Interest Conf. Flexible Manufacturing Systems* (Ann Arbor, Michigan, Aug.) pp. 168–182.

Schroer, Bernard J. 1989. "A Simulation Assistant for Modeling Manufacturing Systems." *Simulation* (Nov.): 200–206.

CHAPTER 10

Applying the Process: Part I

This chapter is the beginning of the final section of the book. This section, consisting of Chapters 10 and 11, takes the reader through a simulation project. In Chapter 6, the simulation process was broken into 15 different activities or phases. This chapter illustrates the first eight phases in the context of an example case study. These eight phases follow:

- Phase (1): Model Users Define Study Objectives
- Phase (2): Resources Supporting Study Effort Made Available
- Phase (3): System Definition
- Phase (4): Model Scope and Level of Detail Determined
- Phase (5): Preferred Model View Chosen
- Phase (6): Model Inputs Collected
- Phase (7): Model Validation
- Phase (8): Concept Model Developed

The subject chosen for the simulation case study is not a high-tech, leading-edge manufacturing facility but rather a transportation system, a little on the nostalgic side. Although the system might seem antiquated, the thought process used in analysis, the applied modeling principles, and the methods of simulation development are not. The system to be analyzed provides a good framework for discussion and will be interesting to a wide variety of simulation (or potential simulation) analysts.

10.1 The System To Be Studied

Mackinac Island is a scenic resort island nestled between Michigan's upper and lower peninsulas in the Straits of Mackinac. The island has been declared Michigan's most historic site and has become a major tourist attraction.

To help keep Mackinac Island in its original state, the use of motor vehicles has been restricted to a firetruck and an ambulance. Other modes of allowable transportation on the island include foot travel, bicycles, and horse drawn carriages. The island is crisscrossed with roads and trails that provide access to different attractions and points of interest. Several horse carriage companies have set up tour routes to give people an enjoyable means of getting to these attractions.

The case study to be examined in this chapter is based on a fictional analysis of the horse carriage transportation system on Mackinac Island. Although transportation with horses is no longer common in most of the industrialized world, the methodology used in this study can be applied to bus routes, automatic guided vehicle traffic, or forklift truck usage. The analysis of carriage routes has been selected merely for illustrative purposes.

10.2 Setting the Stage

Northern Michigan Horse Company (NMHC) owns and operates about a dozen horse drawn carriages that take tourists on various routes around Mackinac Island. Established in the early 1960s, NMHC was run by its owner Lyle DePorres until his death in 1989. His youngest brother, a professor of operations research, inherited the business and decided to visit Mackinac Island and to see what he now owned.

Professor Patrick DePorres came ashore Mackinac Island after a ride on a small ferry boat. The first thing he noticed about the island was the dearth of automobiles. There was no exhaust, no running engines, and no honking. The second thing that came to his attention was a rapidly moving horse drawn carriage that skidded around the corner where he was standing and nearly knocked him off his feet. As it passed by he noticed red lettering on the back that spelled *Northern Michigan Horse Company*. "That's no way to treat your new owner," he thought.

Over the next few days, DePorres tried to familiarize himself with the operation at NMHC. He took very careful notes concerning the routes traveled, departure and arrival times, numbers of passengers on each ride, and the utilization of each carriage. He discovered through his detective work that several problems existed at NMHC. First, as a typical day progressed, the departures would miss their scheduled times by greater and greater margins, which tended to anger customers. DePorres thought that perhaps an additional carriage was needed to meet scheduled times promptly. Another problem was the variation in route completion times. On some days certain routes seemed to take much longer than on other days. The final problem was the number of potential customers that turned away. Route capacities were often exceeded, and people requesting trips to certain destinations could not be serviced.

DePorres decided that the operation of the horse drawn carriage transportation network would provide an excellent simulation case study. He knew more than an arithmetic model would be needed due to the stochastic nature of the process taking place. He felt that a discrete event simulation would be an ideal analysis tool. He began work immediately by trying to define his objectives for the study.

10.3 Phase (1): Model Users Define Study Objectives

The first phase in a simulation project is the definition of its objectives. Without this definition, a project will not have a sense of direction and may not provide the desired information in a timely fashion.

DePorres wanted to insure that his simulation project would successfully provide the desired information without wasting any time or financial resources. He developed the following definitions:

Simulation Customer Professor DePorres, Northern Michigan Horse Company.

Simulation Objective The purpose of this study is to build a general model of the tour route network that NMHC currently uses. This model will use an approach that will allow the modeler to alter various simulation parameters with minimal effort. The model will be set up so that routes, number of carriages, and dispatch times can be easily altered for experimentation. The model will help determine what factors cause the carriage tours to fall behind schedule.

10.4 Phase (2): Resources Supporting Study Effort Made Available

After having established the study's objectives, DePorres knew that certain resources would be necessary. Included among these are the following:

Computer System/Software The university employing DePorres has an active operations research department. Their mainframe computer is stocked with several simulation languages and simulator packages to which DePorres has access. He plans to contact the university and the appropriate simulation software vendors to obtain permission to complete his project using these resources. DePorres wants to make sure no licensing agreements will be breached by his project.

Time for Labor Another resource necessary for completion of the project is time for labor. Either DePorres or an assistant will have to gather data, design and construct the model, and then experiment to obtain results for analysis. This process is a labor intensive activity and will require a great deal of someone's time.

Incidental Expenses Computer print paper, phone line expenses (to the university computer), printer ribbon cartridges, floppy disks, and other incidental expenses need to be included in the budget.

Support from NMHC Staff (forming a simulation team) Although this resource cannot be given a specific price tag, support from the staff of NMHC is crucial to the success of the simulation project. In order to gather truly representative data from the daily operation of the system, the opinions and inputs from the carriage drivers and dispatchers will be required. It is important to avoid making these employees feel as though their jobs are threatened. They need to be made aware that simulation is being done to analyze the system not to pinpoint an individual who should be fired for poor performance.

Means of Gathering Data In a typical simulation study, it is up to management to establish a means of collecting data. DePorres plans to collect simulation data by riding the routes with a stopwatch, measuring the distances and analyzing the dispatcher's data log.

10.5 Phase (3): System Definition

Assured that the resources were in place to implement a simulation study, DePorres started working on the system definition phase of the project. He remembered from an operations research class that *a system can be viewed as a set of components that are related to each other in such a manner as to create a connected whole.* The connected whole he wanted to analyze was, in general terms, the physical operation of his carriage tour company. He needed to break the system into manageable component parts and identify the interactions between each. In addition, he wanted to develop a definition for the system's environment and boundary.

10.5.1 The System

DePorres decided to do some brainstorming and came up with the following list of system components:

Horse Carriages The central components of the system are the horse carriages. These entities include the carriage itself, the horse, and a driver. Each carriage has a fixed passenger capacity.

Roadways The roadways around Mackinac Island form part of the system being modeled. The roads may be paved, gravel, or dirt and have varying surface qualities.

Routes The routes are a logical system component that describe the best path to travel from destination to destination around the island. Routes may be the shortest path in some cases or the most scenic in others.

Destination Points Destination points are the locations on the island that tourists are interested in visiting. The destination points will have specific visiting or stopping times associated with them.

Stable Area The stable area is the homebase for the carriages. When the carriages are not in use, they will be stored in the stables.

Customers The individuals who wish to use the carriage tours are the customers. Customers may ride as singles but more often arrive with a companion or companions. Occasionally, customers who have to wait too long for service will get mad and leave.

Ticket Sales Tickets are sold to customers prior to boarding. The action of selling tickets takes place at a ticket booth near the stables.

Dispatch Schedule The dispatch schedule tells each carriage driver which route to take on the next trip. If no customers have signed up for the route, the driver will not be dispatched.

Loading and Unloading The loading and unloading operations occur when customers board or disembark from the carriages. The time this operation takes depends on the number of passengers involved.

10.5.2 Interactions between Components

In order to create an accurate system simulation, the individual components and their interactions need to be modeled. During his brainstorming session, De-Porres generated a list of system components. He then wanted to list the interactions that needed to be included in the model. He set up Table 10.1 to help organize his thoughts. The system components that will directly interact in terms of the model are correlated with a 'yes', and independent elements are correlated with a 'no'.

10.5.3 System Environment and Boundary

To complete the system's definition, an environment and boundary need to be identified. The environment is defined as *that which lies outside the system and has influence on its behavior but is not controlled by it in any way.*

DePorres identified the environment for the system as being the laws and customs of Mackinac Island, physical surroundings, characteristics of the land, and weather conditions. The boundary is the line separating the environment from the carriage system (see Figure 10.1).

10.5.4 Overview of System Operation

Customers enter the system and proceed to the ticket booth. They inquire about the tour routes and leave, inquire about the routes and purchase a ticket, or simply purchase a ticket.

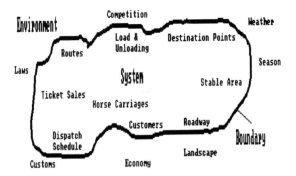

Figure 10.1 System environment and boundary.

TABLE 10.1
Interacting Components

System Components	Horse Carriages	Roadway	Routes	Destination Points	Stable Area	Customers	Ticket Sales	Dispatch Schedule	Loading/Unloading
Horse Carriages	—	yes	yes	yes	yes	yes	no	yes	yes
Roadway	yes	—	no	no	no	no	no	no	no
Routes	yes	no	—	no	no	no	no	yes	no
Destination Points	yes	no	no	—	no	no	no	no	no
Stable Area	yes	no	no	no	—	no	no	no	no
Customers	yes	no	no	no	no	—	yes	no	yes
Ticket Sales	no	no	no	no	no	yes	—	no	no
Dispatch Schedule	yes	no	yes	no	no	no	no	—	no
Loading/Unloading	yes	no	no	no	no	yes	no	no	—

After their tickets have been obtained, customers will either wait for the ride to begin or immediately board a carriage. If their scheduled departure is postponed because of a late carriage return, a percentage of the customers become irate, return to the ticket counter, and demand a refund.

When the departure time arrives and if a carriage is ready, customers will board. The carriage then travels along a predefined route making the appropriate sight-seeing stops.

When a carriage tour is complete, the passengers disembark at the stable area. The carriage returns to the stable, the horse is watered, and the carriage is either sent on another route immediately or waits for a another route to be dispatched. The horse must be watered even if the tours are running behind schedule.

10.6 Phase (4): Model Scope and Level of Detail Determined

Feeling confident that he had a working definition for the system to be modeled, DePorres decided to concentrate on the simulation's scope and level of detail.

As an overall philosophy regarding this topic, DePorres felt that a simulation ought to be scaled to a reasonable level of detail to balance system actuality with model practicality. It is easy to spend excessive time putting too much detail into a model and then receive very little extra knowledge in return.

It is important that a model's scope be limited to the parts of a system that have a direct bearing on the outcome of the study. For instance, a great deal of time and energy can be spent modeling the bearing assembly of the carriage's wheels. However, this exercise would be well outside the scope of the project. Going down to this level of detail is not necessary. All that is needed is a method for representing the time it takes a carriage to move from one point to the next. The actual mechanical means for accomplishing this is irrelevant to the objectives of the study.

DePorres arrived at the following conclusions concerning the model's scope and level of detail:

- The scope of the model includes simulating customer arrival, ticket purchase, customers waiting for the appropriate carriage dispatch, loading the carriage with passengers, driving the tour routes, making the sight-seeing stops, unloading the carriage, customer departure, and carriage storage or reuse. The activities falling within the scope of the model will be represented in terms of their times and interactions.
- The model will use the least amount of detail that is practical without making any blanket assumptions that lessen the usefulness of the model's output. The most detailed portion of the simulation will be the routes and roadways.

The reasons influencing the decision on the detail of the simulation in regard to routes and roadways are as follows:

1. The routes and number of carriages used are of primary interest to the study. Different types of carriages, faster horses, or new drivers are not within the scope of this project and will not be considered.
2. Carriages, horses, and drivers can be represented as a single entity. If it is found that the different drivers, horses, or carriages play significant roles in route completion times, then these differences will be represented in terms of attributes associated with each entity.
3. Loading and unloading carriages will be represented in terms of time based on the current number of customers interfacing with the carriage.

10.7 Phase (5): Preferred Model View Chosen

A discrete event simulation requires that the system being modeled is viewed in a manner that facilitates the modeling process. DePorres thought about the different ways the model could be viewed and developed.

One method would be to view the system as a series of events. (Events being defined as instantaneous occurrences that can change the state of the system.) Examples of different events for this simulation are customer arrivals, carriage departures, and ticket purchases.

Another method would be to view the system as a series of activities. The model would consist of code representing the conditions triggering the start or termination of each activity.

The third method considered and the one that appealed the most to DePorres was the process orientation view. When using this approach to modeling, the system is viewed as a series of processes. Processes are defined as interrelated events separated by passages of time. A transaction or active entity, in this case a customer or carriage, has all of its experiences described in terms of repeatable sequences of steps. Objects required by the transaction during its movement are passive entities or resources. The roadway and the carriages' passenger capacities are examples of these system resources. When different transactions desire to use the same resource simultaneously, one may be denied entry and have to wait until the other is finished.

Based on the information and his own opinions, DePorres decided to use the process orientation approach to develop his Northern Michigan Horse Company simulation.

10.8 Phase (6): Model Inputs Collected

The next phase of the modeling process is the collection of input data. Two types of input data are required for most modeling applications. These are quantitative and qualitative. Quantitative data consists of numerical or measurable values. Qualitative data is information describing the logic underlying system operation.

DePorres generated a list of the items requiring further definition through the collection of quantitative input data.

- Passenger arrival rates
- Percentage of potential customers purchasing tickets
- Percentage of potential customers that do not purchase tickets
- Time required to inquire about routes
- Ticket sale time
- Maximum time customers are willing to wait for service
- Percentage of customers demanding refunds after a delay
- Ticket refund time
- Capacity of each carriage
- Loading time per passenger
- Carriage travel speeds per each road surface type
- Unloading time per passenger
- Dwell time at each designated stop along tour route
- Roadway layout and distances
- Roadway surface types

Deporres also generated a list of the items requiring further definition through the collection of qualitative input data.

- Carriage dispatching rules
- Carriage route time schedule
- Carriage route designated stops
- Customer characteristics

Input data can be collected in several different ways. Among these are observation, estimation, interpolation, expert opinions, and projections. Most of the data needed by DePorres can be collected through observation or discussions with system experts. The system experts relevent to this simulation project are the staff members of the Northern Michigan Horse Company.

10.8.1 The Data Collection Process

DePorres began to collect the necessary data for the construction of the model. What follows is a brief description of the methodology he used for collection in each category.

Information from Ticket Booth

DePorres examined past records and discovered that the daily number of passengers was quite steady between the beginning of June and the end of August. He developed a log sheet that would be filled out by a person monitoring the ticket counter. This log was intended to provide the following information:

Passenger Arrival Rates The interarrival times between potential customers.
Percentage of Potential Customers Purchasing Tickets The percentage of people approaching the booth that end up purchasing a ticket.

Time of Day	# Tickets Purchased	# Tickets Returned	Information Requested?	Time to Inquire	Time to Buy/Refund Ticket	Ticket Numbers	Reason for Refund
8:30 AM	2	0	no	0:00:00	0:01:30	0112-0113	----
8:34 AM	0	0	yes	0:03:20	0:00:00	----	----
9:34 AM	0	2	yes	0:03:10	0:01:45	0112-0113	schedule delay

Figure 10.2 Example of ticket counter log sheet that will be used to collect data for several weeks, after which the data will be analyzed and put into a format that facilitates use in the model.

Percentage of Potential Customers That Do Not Purchase Tickets The percentage of people approaching the ticket booth that do not purchase a ticket.

Time Required to Inquire about Routes The amount of time spent by a person asking questions at the ticket booth. This person may or may not end up buying a ticket.

Ticket Sale Time The time the ticket booth attendant takes to sell a ticket.

Maximum Time Customers Are Willing to Wait for Service The amount of time a customer is willing to wait if the scheduled ride is late.

Percentage of Customers Demanding Refunds after a Delay The percentage of customers demanding a refund if their scheduled ride is late.

Ticket Refund Time The amount of time the ticket booth operator spends refunding a purchaser's money.

The log sheet is illustrated in Figure 10.2.

Information from the Carriage

DePorres decided to put an extra employee on each carriage for two weeks. This employee would carry a stopwatch, clipboard, and specially marked map. The employee would be responsible for tabulating data concerning the following items:

Loading Time per Passenger The amount of time it takes the carriage to be loaded. This number will be divided by the number of passengers to obtain an average loading time per passenger.

Carriage Travel Speeds per Each Road Surface Type DePorres had bicycle speedometers/odometers temporarily mounted on each carriage to allow the speeds on each road surface to be monitored.

Unloading Time per Passenger As in the passenger loading times, passenger unloading times will be determined by total unloading time divided by the number of passengers getting off the carriage.

Dwell Time at Each Designated Stop along Tour Route The amount of time the carriage spends stopped at each attraction along the route will be collected.

Other Information To Be Gathered

In addition to information gathered at the ticket booth and on the carriages, DePorres collected information concerning the following items:

Roadway Layout and Distances He obtained a Mackinac Island road map from the local Chamber of Commerce and used it as a source of information about roadway layout and distances.

Roadway Surface Types DePorres jogged around the island and noted the different road surface types.

Capacity of Each Carriage The capacity of each carriage was obtained by inspecting the carriages while they were in storage after hours.

Carriage Dispatching Rules The dispatching rules and logic were explained to DePorres by the stable manager. DePorres wrote these rules down and spent time observing operations to make sure his interpretation of the dispatching rules was correct.

Time Schedule The scheduled departure times were published in several flyers sent out by NMHC.

Designated Stops The same flyers contained listings of the different stops along the carriage routes.

10.8.2 The Input Data

Several weeks went by with DePorres and his crew collecting data. When it was felt that sufficient information was in hand, an analysis process was begun. The goal of the analysis was to take the raw data and produce inputs to the simulation. This transformation was accomplished using several methods including the *experience of the modeler* and *goodness-of-fit tests* (see Section 6.6).

After the analysis was complete, DePorres wrote an input data specification to formally document the information that would be used to build the model. A copy of this document follows.

Northern Michigan Horse Company

Carriage Tour Simulation
Input Data Specification

Prepared by

Professor Patrick DePorres
7-20-90

Introduction

This document contains a complete description of the data to be used as inputs in the Northern Michigan Horse Company carriage tour simulation.

Section I: Ticket Booth Input Data

The following data, based on observation and careful record keeping, will be used as input data for modeling customer arrivals and the ticket booth operations.

Customer Arrival Patterns

Description: Customers arrive either singly or in groups. They usually arrive in groups due to the fact that most are either families or several friends. The arrival of each customer group is based on an exponential distribution. The number of customers in each arriving group is represented in Table A.

Customer Personality Type

Description: Each group of customers is assumed to be headed up by an individual whose personality will influence how the group reacts to schedule delays. This dominant personality may be tolerant and likely to overlook delays or may be severe and not tolerate any delays. Table B contains a breakdown of personality types to be used in the model.

Customer Talkativeness

Description: When each group of potential customers arrives at the ticket booth, a spokesperson will spend a certain amount of time asking the clerk questions. Later, if the group's scheduled departure is delayed and a refund is requested, the spokesperson will again spend time talking to the ticket booth clerk. A talkativeness factor will randomly be assigned to each customer

TABLE A
Customer Arrival Patterns

Number of People per Group	Percentage of Arrivals
1	3.00
2	49.00
3	23.00
4	14.00
5	7.00
6	2.00
7	1.00
8	0.75
9	0.15
10	0.10

Note: since carriage passenger capacity is ten, groups having more than ten members are treated as more than one group.

TABLE B
Customer Personality Patterns

Personality Type per Group	Percentage of Groups	Description
1 = Severe	3.00	Demands refund immediately upon any departure delay
2 = Irritable	8.00	Will wait up to 10 minutes for a departure delay
3 = Moderate	59.0	Will wait up to 20 minutes for a departure delay
4 = Tolerant	21.00	Will wait up to 40 minutes for a departure delay
5 = Very Tolerant	9.00	Will wait indefinitely for a departure delay

group. This factor will play a part in determining time spent at the ticket counter. Table C describes the talkativeness factors to be assigned.

Ticket Counter Service Time

Description: This data represents the amount of service time required by the ticket booth clerk to issue a ticket and collect payment. The ticket counter service time does not include any time to answer questions asked by the customer. That time is included in the section entitled "Customer Talkativeness." Tickets will be sold until the route is filled or is scheduled to be dispatched. The booth closes after the last carriage for the day is dispatched.

TABLE C
Customer Talkativeness Patterns

Talkativeness Level per Group	Percentage of Groups	Description
1 = Very	12.00	Will talk approximately five minutes per visit
2 = Medium	35.00	Will talk approximately two minutes per visit
3 = Little	36.00	Will talk approximately one minute per visit
4 = None	17.00	Will not strike up any conversation with attendant

Ticket counter service time can be represented as a normal distribution with a mean of 25 seconds and a standard deviation of 3. In addition to this initial service time, 3 seconds per group member is added.

Ticket Refund Time

Description: This data represents the amount of time required for the ticket booth clerk to issue a refund. This time does not take into account any extra delay due to the comments made by the refundee.

Basic ticket refund time was found to be normally distributed with a mean of 46 seconds and a standard deviation of 4. In addition to this base time, 3 seconds per group member is added to the time.

Potential Customer Arrival Rate

Description: Groups of potential customers arrive based on an exponential distribution. This arrival time includes those who ask questions but decide not to buy tickets.

The group of potential customers and arrival rate is an exponential distribution and has a mean of 300 seconds.

Percent of Potential Customer Groups Not Purchasing Tickets

Description: Each potential customer group arrives at the ticket booth, examines the schedule and price, and makes a determination of whether they will buy a ticket or leave. The percentages of potential customer groups making each decision is shown in Table D.

Route Selected

Description: Each customer group deciding to purchase a ticket selects a desired carriage route. Table E lists the percentages of customers selecting each of the five available routes.

Route Filled

Description: If the potential customer group decides to buy a ticket but the desired route does not have the capacity to accommodate all members of the group, three courses of action can be taken. Table F describes these actions and the percentage of groups selecting each option.

Section II: Carriage Operations Input Data

The following input data describes the operation of the Northern Michigan Horse Company carriages including their speeds, loading and unloading times, time from stable to initial dispatch point, and travel.

TABLE D
Percentage of Potential Customer Groups
Purchasing Tickets

Percentage of Arrivals	Decision
87	Purchase Ticket
13	No Purchase Made

TABLE E
Routes Selected

Route Number and Name	Percentage of Customer Groups Selecting Route
1	20.00
2	20.00
3	20.00
4	20.00
5	20.00

TABLE F
Customer Action When Desired Route Is Filled

Plans of Action	Percentage of Groups Selecting Plan	Description
1 = New Route	75.00	Selects a new route that is not completely booked.
2 = Same Route Later	19.00	Waits for the next departure of desired route; Leaves system if all repetitions of this route are filled.
3 = Leave System	6.00	Does not purchase ticket and leaves system.

Speeds

Description: Carriages travel at different speeds based on the type of terrain being traversed. Table G lists the different speeds per each terrain to be used in the simulation. (The speeds will be represented in the simulation with a normal probability distribution.)

Load/Unload Time

Description: Every loading and unloading of the carriage will require a time delay for each passenger that will be boarding. The boarding time per pas-

TABLE G
Carriage Speeds

Terrain Number and Type	Carriage Speeds Used in Simulation (in feet per minute)
1 = Good Pavement	Mean = 500.00 Std. Dev. = 36
2 = Medium Pavement	Mean = 400.00 Std. Dev. = 28
3 = Poor Pavement	Mean = 300.00 Std. Dev. = 18
4 = Gravel	Mean = 200.00 Std. Dev. = 10
5 = Poor Gravel	Mean = 100.00 Std. Dev. = 4

senger was determined to be distributed between 30 and 70 seconds with a mode of 45. A triangular distribution, multiplied by the number of passengers, will be used to represent this delay.[1] Unloading will also be represented with the same delay time.

Stable to Dispatch Area

Description: A time delay used to represent the movement of a carriage from the stables to the dispatch area was determined to be approximately 1 minute. A triangular distribution with a mode of 1 minute and a range of 50 seconds to 5 minutes will be used to represent this time in the model. The same time delay will also be used to represent the time spent traveling from the unloading point back to the stables after the completion of a route.

Stable Area

Description: Another triangular distribution will be used to represent the time required to water and check the horse after each carriage ride. The mode for this delay will be 300 seconds, the minimum 250 seconds and the maximum 500 seconds.

Section III: Routes, Roadways, and Dispatch Times

The following data concerning the routes, roadways, and dispatching times has been collected for the Northern Michigan Horse Company simulation.

---

[1] A triangular distribution is frequently used in simulation when detailed knowledge of the distribution of a random variable is unavailable (Henriksen and Crain, 1989; Law and Kelton, 1982).

Routes and Roadways

Description: Five different routes are currently available through NMHC. Each route is designed to take passengers to different attractions on the island. Passengers are given time to get off the carriage at some of the stops and are asked to remain onboard at others. The time required to complete each route is dependent on several different factors including length of route, terrain traversed, dwell time at different attractions, passenger loading and unloading times, and number of attractions on each route. The accompanying map and Tables H–L describe the five routes offered by NMHC. Note that distances shown in Tables H–L are broken into segments based on roadway surface type.

Dispatch Times

Description: All routes are dispatched several times each day. Carriages are not dedicated to servicing specific routes but rather are called as needed from the stable area. Table M lists the dispatch times for each repetition of the five routes used by NMHC.

TABLE H
Route #1

Segment	Distance (feet)	Roadway Surface	Dwell Time at Destination	Passengers Unload Here?
Dispatch Point	890	Good Pavement		
to	890	Poor Pavement	3 Minutes	No
Grand Hotel	1785	Good Pavement		
Grand Hotel				
to	2228	Good Pavement	3 Minutes	No
West Bluff				
West Bluff	900	Good Pavement		
to	850	Poor Gravel	15 Minutes	Yes
Devil's Kitchen	1865	Poor Pavement		
Devil's Kitchen	1336	Poor Pavement		
to	1778	Medium Pavement	10 Minutes	Yes
Stonecliffe	2673	Gravel		
Stonecliffe	2673	Gravel		
to	1800	Medium Pavement	3 Minutes	No
The Annex	1113	Poor Pavement		
The Annex	1788	Poor Pavement		
to	4010	Good Pavement	—	Yes
Dropoff Point				

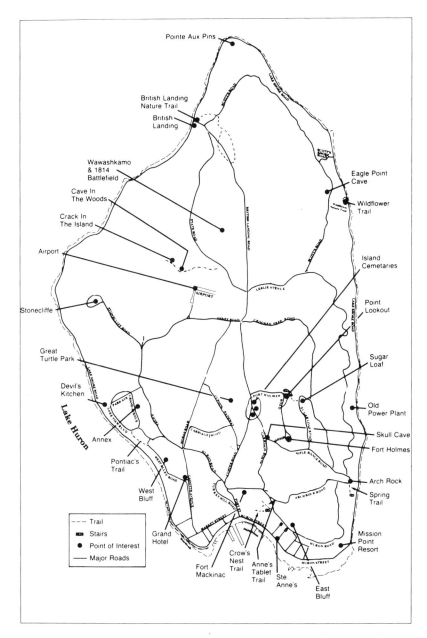

Major roads and attractions on Mackinac Island. (Courtesy of Bryce-Waterton Publications.)

TABLE I
Route #2

Segment	Distance (feet)	Roadway Surface	Dwell Time at Destination	Passengers Unload Here?
Dispatch Point	920	Good Pavement		
to	1337	Poor Pavement	3 Minutes	No
Great Turtle Park				
Great Turtle Park	4000	Poor Pavement		
to	435	Medium Pavement		
Cave-in-the-Woods/	1420	Poor Pavement	20 Minutes	Yes
Crack-in-the-Island	1797	Medium Pavement		
	2688	Poor Gravel		
Cave-in-the-Woods/				
Crack-in-the-Island	2669	Poor Gravel		
to	6255	Medium Pavement	5 Minutes	No
British Landing				
British Landing				
to	8911	Medium Pavement	30 Minutes	Yes
Eagle Point Cave/				
Wild Flower Trail				
Eagle Point Cave/	6240	Medium Pavement		
Wild Flower Trail	1336	Poor Pavement		
to	460	Medium Pavement	—	Yes
Dropoff Point	4460	Poor Pavement		
	1344	Good Pavement		

10.9 Phase (7): Model Validation

The validation process is of critical importance to every simulation project. Without insurance that the real world system being studied is accurately depicted by the model, the simulation's conclusions are worthless. DePorres began his validation process during the initial stages of the study. He used the following techniques to help "build in" validity:

1. *Observation.* Since the system being modeled was already in existence, DePorres was able to collect data directly through observation. The conclusions and assumptions used to build the model were all closely aligned to the real world system.

2. *Expert's Opinions.* DePorres was able to use the members of NMHC's staff to evaluate the assumptions and rules he was incorporating into the model.

3. *Statistical Testing.* DePorres used the proper methods of deriving the theoretical input data distributions. He collected empirical data and used goodness-of-fit tests to help develop the theoretical distributions.

4. *Direct Comparison.* The final and best validation tool DePorres had available was the direct comparison method. Some initial runs of the model would be

TABLE J
Route #3

Segment	Distance (feet)	Roadway Surface	Dwell Time at Destination	Passengers Unload Here?
Dispatch Point	900	Good Pavement		
to	888	Poor Pavement	15 Minutes	Yes
Island Cemetary	1782	Good Pavement		
Island Cemetary				
to	2235	Poor Pavement	10 Minutes	Yes
Point Look-Out				
Point Look-Out				
to	2240	Poor Pavement	3 Minutes	No
Fort Holmes				
Fort Holmes	445	Poor Pavement		
to	450	Medium Pavement	5 Minutes	No
Skull Cave				
Skull Cave				
to	4020	Good Pavement	15 Minutes	Yes
St. Anne's				
St. Anne's				
to	2673	Good Pavement	3 Minutes	No
Mission Point				
Mission Point	2650	Good Pavement		
to	435	Medium Pavement	10 Minutes	Yes
Arch Rock				
Arch Rock	420	Medium Pavement		
to	6691	Good Pavement		
Dropoff Point	450	Poor Pavement	—	Yes
	440	Good Pavement		

set up exactly as the system currently existed. The output data generated by the system would be compared to actual collected data. A confidence level could then be established to correlate the model to reality.

10.10 Phase (8): Concept Model Developed

Before beginning work on the detailed simulation model, DePorres wanted to take a quantitative look at the system using some concept modeling techniques. He decided to use Lotus 1-2-3 to analyze the carriage routes currently being used by NMHC. He wanted to determine carriage utilization and provide a quick answer to the question, "*Does NMHC have enough carriage capacity to realistically meet all its scheduled times?*"

TABLE K
Route #4

Segment	Distance (feet)	Roadway Surface	Dwell Time at Destination	Passengers Unload Here?
Dispatch Point	430	Good Pavement		
to	440	Poor Pavement	5 Minutes	No
Fort Mackinac	2675	Good Pavement		
Fort Mackinac				
to	2225	Good Pavement	20 Minutes	Yes
St. Anne's				
St. Anne's				
to	2673	Good Pavement	3 Minutes	No
Mission Point				
Mission Point	2690	Good Pavement		
to	3564	Medium Pavement	5 Minutes	No
Old Power Plant				
Old Power Plant	9805	Medium Pavement		
to	2711	Poor Pavement		
Dropoff Point	454	Medium Pavement	—	Yes
	4455	Poor Pavement		
	430	Good Pavement		

10.10.1 Assumptions

DePorres made the following assumptions for use in the development of a concept model:

1. The carriage tour operation lasts approximately 12 hours per day.
2. The required carriage count will be based on an 85% availability factor. This factor takes into account delay time in the stables and any other inefficiencies that exist in the system.
3. The time required for each route will be determined and multiplied by its number of daily repetitions. The time required to complete all routes will be added together to yield a "total carriage time required" figure.
4. Carriages are assumed to be available for dispatching immediately after completing a previous route. The stable delays are absorbed by the inefficiency factor in assumption 2 above.
5. The concept model will be developed using a Lotus 1-2-3 spreadsheet.
6. Each route will be broken down by the different roadway surfaces and will include passenger loading and unloading times, dwell times at each attraction, route distances, and speeds.
7. Passenger loading and unloading times will be based on the assumption that each passenger takes 45 seconds to board and an average of 8 passengers will be on each carriage.

TABLE L
Route #5

Segment	Distance (feet)	Roadway Surface	Dwell Time at Destination	Passengers Unload Here?
Dispatch Point to Great Turtle Park	434 / 1790	Good Pavement / Poor Pavement	5 Minutes	No
Great Turtle Park to British Landing	3570 / 435 / 7577	Poor Pavement / Medium Pavement / Poor Pavement	5 Minutes	No
British Landing to Eagle Point Cave	8920	Medium Pavement	15 Minutes	Yes
Eagle Point Cave to Old Power Plant	10695	Medium Pavement	5 Minutes	No
Old Power Plant to Arch Rock	3120	Medium Pavement	15 Minutes	Yes
Arch Rock to East Bluff	445 / 4900	Medium Pavement / Good Pavement	3 Minutes	No
East Bluff to Grand Hotel	7574	Good Pavement	5 Minutes	No
Grand Hotel to Dropoff Point	2770	Good Pavement	—	Yes

TABLE M
Dispatch Times of Every Route

Time	Route # 1	2	3	4	5
9:00 A.M.	X	X	X	X	X
10:00 A.M.	X		X		X
11:00 A.M.	X	X	X	X	X
12:00 P.M.	X		X		X
1:00 P.M.	X	X	X	X	X
2:00 P.M.	X		X		X
3:00 P.M.	X	X	X	X	X
4:00 P.M.	X		X		X
5:00 P.M.	X	X	X	X	X

	A	B	C	D	E	F
1	Route #1					
2						
3		Speed in		Dwell	Carriage	
4	Distance	Feet per	Time in	Time in	Load in	
5	in Feet	Minute	Minutes	Minutes	Minutes	
6	---	---	---	---	---	---
7	890	500	1.78			
8	890	300	2.97			
9	1785	500	3.57	3	0	
10	2228	500	4.46	3	0	
11	900	500	1.80			
12	850	100	8.50			
13	1865	300	6.22	15	12	
14	1336	300	4.45			
15	1778	400	4.45			
16	2673	200	13.37	10	12	
17	2673	200	13.37			
18	1800	400	4.50			
19	1113	300	3.71	3	0	
20	1788	300	5.96			
21	4010	500	8.02	0	6	
22	---	---	---	---	---	---
23	Totals		87.11	34	30	
24						
25						
26	Route #2					
27						
28		Speed in		Dwell	Carriage	
29	Distance	Feet per	Time in	Time in	Load in	
30	in Feet	Minute	Minutes	Minutes	Minutes	
31	---	---	---	---	---	---
32	920	500	1.84			
33	1337	300	4.46	3	0	
34	4000	300	13.33			
35	435	400	1.09			
36	1420	300	4.73			
37	1797	400	4.49			
38	2688	100	26.88	20	12	
39	2669	100	26.69			
40	6255	400	15.64	5	0	
41	8911	400	22.28	30	12	
42	6240	400	15.60			
43	1336	300	4.45			
44	460	400	1.15			
45	4460	300	14.87			
46	1344	500	2.69	0	6	
47	---	---	---	---	---	---
48	Totals		160.19	58	30	

Figure 10.3 Concept model written with Lotus 1-2-3.

Route #3

Distance in Feet	Speed in Feet per Minute	Time in Minutes	Dwell Time in Minutes	Carriage Load in Minutes
900	500	1.80		
888	300	2.96		
1782	500	3.56	15	12
2235	300	7.45	10	12
2240	300	7.47	3	0
445	300	1.48		
450	400	1.13	5	0
4020	500	8.04	15	12
2673	500	5.35	3	0
2650	500	5.30		
435	400	1.09	10	12
420	400	1.05		
6691	500	13.38		
450	300	1.50		
440	500	0.88	0	6
Totals		62.43	61	54

Route #4

Distance in Feet	Speed in Feet per Minute	Time in Minutes	Dwell Time in Minutes	Carriage Load in Minutes
430	500	0.86		
440	300	1.47		
2675	500	5.35	5	0
2225	500	4.45	20	12
2673	500	5.35	3	0
2690	500	5.38		
3564	400	8.91	5	0
9805	400	24.51		
2711	300	9.04		
454	400	1.14		
4455	300	14.85		
430	500	0.86	0	6
Totals		82.16	33	18

(*Figure 10.13 continued*)

```
101 Route #5
102
103                Speed in                    Dwell      Carriage
104     Distance  Feet per    Time in       Time in     Load in
105     in Feet   Minute      Minutes       Minutes     Minutes
106 ----------------------------------------------------------------
107         434       500        0.87
108        1790       300        5.97            5           0
109        3570       300       11.90
110         435       400        1.09            5           0
111        7577       300       25.26
112        8920       400       22.30           15          12
113       10695       400       26.74            5           0
114        3120       400        7.80           15          12
115         445       400        1.11
116        4900       500        9.80            3           0
117        7574       500       15.15            5           0
118        2770       500        5.54            0           6
119 ----------------------------------------------------------------
120 Totals                     133.52           53          30
121
122
123
124
125 Summary of Route Times
126
127     Route #     Time in # of Daily  Total Time
128               Minutes Repetitions  (Minutes)
129 -----------------------------------------------------------
130 Route #1       151.11          9     1359.97
131
132 Route #2       248.19          5     1240.93
133
134 Route #3       177.43          9     1596.91
135
136 Route #4       133.16          5      665.78
137
138 Route #5       216.52          9     1948.65
139 -----------------------------------------------------------
140 Totals                              6812.25
141
142
143 Total Route Time         6812.25 Minutes
144 Divided By                 60.00 Minutes Per Hour
145                        -----------
146                         113.54 Carriage Hours Required
147
148 Carriage Hours           113.54
149 Divided By                12.00 Operating Hours (Approximately)
150                        -----------
151                           9.46 Carriages Required
152
153 Carriages Required         9.46
154 Divided By                 0.85 Inefficiency Factor
155                        -----------
156                          11.13 Carriages Required
157
158
```

(Figure 10.13 continued)

8. Dwell times, distances, and speeds will be taken from the "Input Data Specification Document."
9. Specific dispatch times are not being considered by the concept model.

10.10.2 Model Listing

Figure 10.3 contains the spreadsheet model created by DePorres. He determined that 11.13 carriages were necessary to complete all scheduled repetitions of the five routes. Currently NMHC only operates nine carriages. To meet all the scheduled dispatches with only ten carriages, the system would have to be 94.6% efficient. DePorres felt this was an unrealistic figure and decided to start working on the detailed simulation model to strengthen his conclusions.

References and Reading

Henriksen, James O. 1981. "GPSS—Finding the Appropriate World-View." *Proc. 1981 Winter Simulation Conf.* (Atlanta, Dec. 9–11). (Oren, Delfosse, and Shub, eds.) SCS, San Diego, pp. 505–516.

Henriksen, James O., and Robert C. Crain. 1989. *GPSS/H User's Manual,* Third Edition. Wolverine Software Corporation, Annandale, Virginia.

Law, Averill M., and W. David Kelton. 1982. *Simulation Modeling and Analysis.* McGraw-Hill, New York.

Piljac, Thomas M., and Pamela A. Piljac. 1988. *Mackinac Island.* Bryce Waterton Publications, Portage, Indiana.

CHAPTER 11

Applying the Process: Part II

This chapter is a continuation of the example started in Chapter 10. This chapter steps through the final seven phases of a simulation project. These phases are as follows:

- Phase (9): Selection of a Language or Tool
- Phase (10): Construction of Model
- Phase (11): Model Verification
- Phase (12): Experimentation
- Phase (13): Output Analysis
- Phase (14): Generation of Output Report
- Phase (15): Logic Transfer

11.1   Phase (9): Selection of a Language or Tool

Professor Patrick DePorres had to make a decision and choose the software that he would use for creating a detailed model of the Northern Michigan Horse Company carriage tour system. He initially looked into both simulation languages and simulator packages. After doing a little research, he felt that no available simulators would accomplish what he desired. He decided to concentrate on general purpose simulation languages.

DePorres used a standard approach to the software evaluation process. The four steps in his procedure were:

1. Define needs of project
2. Research market
3. Compare available options
4. Select software

Step 1: Define Needs of Project

DePorres began the software selection process by analyzing the needs of the current simulation project and the anticipated needs of his future simulation projects. He did this by answering some questions.

1. *What will the frequency of future simulation work be? Will this be a one time project or will simulation be used regularly from now on?* The NMHC simulation will be a one time project. It will be maintained so that it can be modified and used for future analysis. However, the procedures used in this project and the experience gained will be applied to other problems requiring simulation. This simulation is not only for analyzing the system but also as a means of learning more about modeling.

2. *What type of system will be modeled? Is it unique in function?* A unique system is being modeled. That is why simulator packages have been ruled out. General purpose languages containing special "materials handling" modules may be adaptable to this application but are not desired.

3. *Who will be doing the simulation work?* DePorres would be doing the work. He was comfortable with his computer skills and desired to use a full power simulation language.

4. *What budgetary constraints exist?* DePorres had already obtained permission to use his employer's mainframe computer at the university and had access to several different modeling tools. So, budgetary constraints were not a major consideration for this project.

5. *Who will be using the results?* The results of the study would be used by DePorres as a means of analyzing his small company. The results of the study might be communicated at a simulation conference in a technical paper written by DePorres.

Answers to these questions help to start the software evaluation process.

Step 2: Research Market

Although a large and varied simulation market exists, DePorres is only concerned with the software currently available to him through the university.

Step 3: Compare Available Options

DePorres decided to develop a template to aid in the software package selection process. He started by generating a list of the attributes important to the simulation study (Figure 11.1).

DePorres used the evaluation template in Figure 11.2 to help in the software selection process. The weighting factors were subjectively developed from the attributes shown in Figure 11.1. The weighting factor is multiplied by the product score to produce a column of totals. These totals are added to give an overall numeric product score. The weighting factors range from 1 to 10, with 10 being most important.

1. This will be a one time simulation project, but the knowledge gained and techniques developed will be reused in other applications.
2. The system being modeled is somewhat unique.
3. DePorres himself will be doing the work. His skills as a programmer and an analyst will be helpful.
4. Software cost is not an issue. The software must, however, be available on the university mainframe.
5. Results will be used by DePorres. Animation is not important to the study.

Figure 11.1 Attribute list.

	Weighting Factor		Product Score		Total
User friendliness	2	X	____	=	____
Software capability	10	X	____	=	____
Ease of use	3	X	____	=	____
Power	8	X	____	=	____
Output reports	6	X	____	=	____
Ease of debugging	8	X	____	=	____
Statistics	7	X	____	=	____
Customer support	8	X	____	=	____
Training	5	X	____	=	____
Documentation	10	X	____	=	____
Vendor stability	8	X	____	=	____
Application specific modules	1	X	____	=	____
			Total product score =		____

Figure 11.2 Software evaluation template.

Step 4: Select Software

DePorres used the template to evaluate four simulation language products that were maintained by the university. He chose GPSS/H as being most suited to his current application. The template for GPSS/H is shown in Figure 11.3.

11.2 Phase (10): Construction of Model

DePorres began building the detailed model of the Northern Michigan Horse Company. He used the GPSS entities shown in Table 11.1 to represent different parts of the system.

11.2.1 General Flowchart

The flowcharts shown in Figures 11.4 through 11.8 depict the general operation of the GPSS/H program developed by DePorres. It is important to remember that transactions may be simultaneously processing in different parts of the model.

	Weighting Factor		Product Score		Total
User friendliness	2	X	5	=	10
Software capability	10	X	10	=	100
Ease of use	3	X	4	=	12
Power	8	X	10	=	80
Output reports	6	X	7	=	42
Ease of debugging	8	X	7	=	56
Statistics	7	X	6	=	42
Customer support	8	X	10	=	80
Training	5	X	8	=	40
Documentation	10	X	7	=	70
Vendor stability	8	X	10	=	80
Application specific modules	1	X	0	=	0
		Total product score		=	612

Figure 11.3 GPSS/H template score.

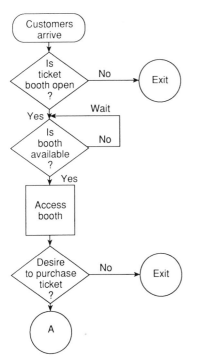

Figure 11.4 Customer arrival logic.

TABLE 11.1
GPSS Entities and Other Information Used in Model

Time Units		All Times Are Expressed in Seconds
TRANSACTIONS	ROUTE TENDER	One transaction is generated every simulated day for the specific function of notifying the system each time a route is scheduled to be dispatched.
	CUSTOMER GROUPS	Transactions representing a group of potential customers are created approximately every five minutes while the system runs.
	CARRIAGES	A specific number of transactions representing the carriages are generated for use during the simulation.
	TIMING	A transaction is generated every 3600 seconds to decrement the 'START' count.
FACILITIES	TBOOTH	Represents ticket booth server (resource).
QUEUES	TBOOTH	Waiting line statistics, customers waiting for service from ticket booth resource.
	DISPTCH	Customer waits from time of ticket purchase until scheduled dispatch time of carriage tour.
STORAGES	DSPTCH	Storage (capacity one). Only allows one carriage to be called simultaneously. Prevents multiple carriages from being assigned to the same route.
	NORT3	Used to count the number of potential customers leaving the system because their group was unable to be scheduled on a specific route at a specific time.
	NOTCK	A counter to keep track of the number of potential customers that leave the system without ever buying tickets because of price, competition, or other unknown reasons.
	NORT1	Counter keeping track of the number of customers leaving the system because the rest of the carriage tours in the day do not have sufficient capacity to accommodate their group.
	NORT2	Counter tracking the number of customers leaving the system because all repetitions of a specific route could not accommodate their group.
	DISPT1	Counter keeping track of the number of customers actually boarding a carriage.
	REFUN	Counter keeping track of the number of irate customers demanding a refund for their ticket.
	WAITC	Storage used to keep track of the amount of time customers wait for a carriage when it is late for its scheduled dispatch.

TABLE 11.1
(Continued)

Time Units		All Times Are Expressed in Seconds
	STABLE	A storage representing the stable area where unused carriages are stored.
	HMCARR	A storage that allows only &NUMCAR carriages in the system.
FUNCTIONS	GRSIZE	Returns a value that represents the size of a group of customers that wants to access the ticket booth.
	WPERSON	Describes the personality type that dominates a group of customers. This parameter determines the likelihood of a group demanding a ticket refund.
	PERSONT	The amount of time a person will wait before demanding a refund (based on personality type).
	WTALK	Describes how talkative the leader of each group of customers is.
	ROUTEZ	Returns the desired first choice route selection of each customer.
	ALTP	Returns one of three alternate plans of action if a customer group cannot get their first choice route.
USER CHAINS	DSPTCH	User chain to hold route dispatches that have been scheduled but have not yet occurred.
GROUPS	DSPTCH	Group that holds the transaction representing the current route to be dispatched. Allows transaction to be scanned.
	STABLE	Group that holds the transaction numbers of all carriages.
BOOLEAN VARIABLES	RTFUL1	Checks to see if the desired route has room for this group of customers (GROUTE section of code).
	RTFUL2	Checks to see if the desired route has room for this group of customers (SMRT section of code).
	WAITL	Checks to see if customer group can stop waiting for a late carriage to arrive.
FULLWORD MSAVEVALUES	TIMERT	Holds scheduled departure times for all repetitions of each route.
	ROUTE1	Contains carriage route #1 information including distances, speed, dwell times, and load/unload info.

(continues)

TABLE 11.1
(*Continued*)

Time Units		All Times Are Expressed in Seconds
	ROUTE2	Contains carriage route #2 information including distances, speed, dwell times, and load/unload info.
	ROUTE3	Contains carriage route #3 information including distances, speed, dwell times, and load/unload info.
	ROUTE4	Contains carriage route #4 information including distances, speed, dwell times, and load/unload info.
	ROUTE5	Contains carriage route #5 information including distances, speed, dwell times, and load/unload info.
HALFWORD MSAVEVALUES	RCAPAC	Contains a current count of the remaining passenger capacity of each repetition of each scheduled route.
	DCAR	Contains a '1' for each repetition of a route that has been dispatched.
	GOCAR	Contains a '1' for carriage that has all its passengers loaded to go. Used as a flag for releasing loaded carriages.
FULLWORD PARAMETERS	GSIZE	Size of customer group represented by transaction.
	PERSON	Contains the personality type for each group.
	TALK	Contains the talkativeness factor for each group.
	RETURN	Contains block number for transactions returning from subroutines.
	ROUTE	Number of route being taken.
	PLAN	Alternate plan for transactions being denied their first choice routes.
	INDX	Used to index through different repetitions of the same route.
	DRTTIM	Dispatch time for customer's selected route.
	NUMPAS	Number of passengers on a carriage.
	TIME	Used in advance blocks for a delay time.
INTEGER &VARIABLES	CARHLD	Maximum carriage capacity.
	I	Index variable.
	J	Index variable.
	MOSTRT	Highest number of repetitions of any particular route.
	NRUNS	Used as an index in a control statement.
	NUMCAR	Number of carriages available to system.

TABLE 11.1

(Continued)

Time Units		All Times Are Expressed in Seconds
	NUMRTS	Number of routes being run by NMHC.
	RUNSD	Number of sample simulations run (control statement variable).
INTEGER &ARRAYS	CARCNT(9)	Used to count passengers boarding a carriage. Subscripted by route number.
	DRTRN(9)	Current repetition of each route to be dispatched. Subscripted by route number.
	DTRT(9)	Next departure time for each route. Subscripted by route number.
	NUMRT(9)	Number of different segments in each route array. Subscripted by route number.
	RDPRTN(9)	Number of daily repetitions of each route. Subscripted by route number.
	SPDDEV(9)	Standard deviation of each carriage speed used. Subscripted by roadway type.
	SPEED(5)	Speeds that carriage travels on each roadway type. Subscripted by roadway type.

11.2.2 GPSS/H Code

Figure 11.9 contains a listing of the GPSS/H program written for NMHC.

11.3 Phase (11): Model Verification

DePorres used two verification techniques to assure that his simulation program was performing as expected. These two methods were prevention and appraisal.

11.3.1 Prevention

Preventative verification strives to insure that the simulation has been created in a way that will minimize errors. DePorres had been practicing this technique throughout his model development process. Two methods of preventative verification that he used were the careful documentation of his model and a structured programming approach.

11.3.2 Appraisal

Verification techniques used to check or appraise the programming after it has been coded are called appraisal verification techniques. Several appraisal methods used by DePorres follow:

Running the System under Simplified Conditions DePorres checked much of the program by forcing certain variable parameters to values that would enable

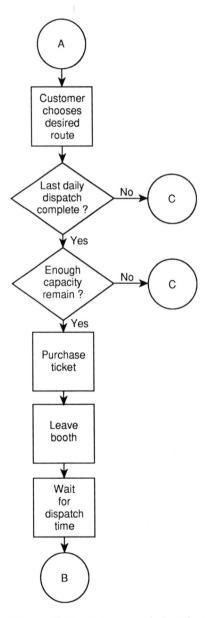

Figure 11.5 Customer purchases ticket for selected route.

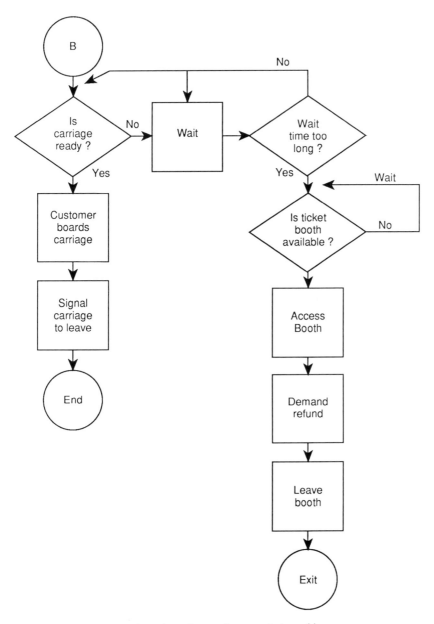

Figure 11.6 Customer boards carriage or becomes irate and leaves.

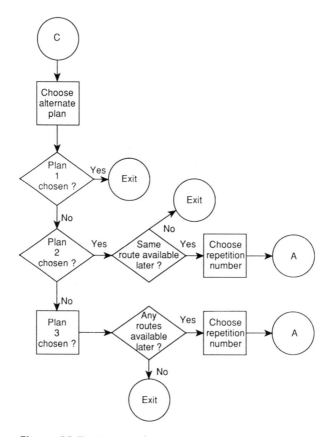

Figure 11.7 Customer chooses alternate plan of action when desired route is unavailable.

him to predict the course of action selected by affected transactions. If the courses of action did not match what was expected, he would look for errors.

Checking System State DePorres would stop the simulation at different points in time and check the transaction flows and statistics. If something seemed out of the ordinary, he would investigate it more thoroughly.

Apply Common Sense to Output Reports One of the best methods of verification is the use of common sense. If something in an output report looks unusual or out of place, it probably is. Because of his prior experience, DePorres was able to use this appraisal extensively.

11.4 Phase (12): Experimentation

Having verified that the model runs properly, the next step in the simulation process is the experimentation phase (production runs). Initially DePorres wanted to determine how many carriages would be required to keep the number

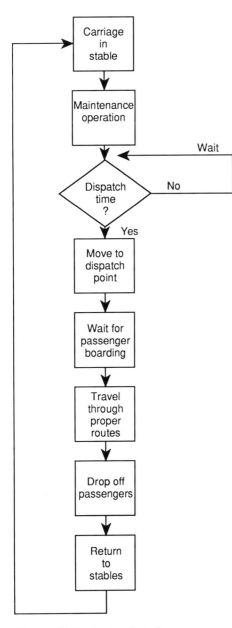

Figure 11.8   Carriage logic flows.

```
*===========================================================*
*     Northern Michigan Horse Company Simulation            *
*===========================================================*
*
* AMPERVARIABLE DECLARATIONS
*
        INTEGER    &DTRT(9)      ' NEXT DEPARTURE TIME FOR THIS (ROUTE)
        INTEGER    &DRTRTN(9)    ' CURRENT REPETITION OF ROUTE DISPATCHED
        INTEGER    &RDPRTN(9)    ' # OF DAILY REPETITIONS OF EACH ROUTE
        INTEGER    &CARCNT(9)    ' COUNT OF PASSENGERS ON BOARD
        INTEGER    &NUMRTS       ' NUMBER OF DIFFERENT ROUTES
        INTEGER    &MOSTRT       ' MOST REPETITIONS IN ANY ROUTE
        INTEGER    &CARHLD       ' CARRIAGE CAPACITY
        INTEGER    &SPEED(5)     ' CARRIAGE SPEEDS
        INTEGER    &SPDDEV(5)    ' STANDARD DEVIATIONS OF SPEEDS
        INTEGER    &NUMRT(9)     ' NUMBER OF SEGMENTS IN EACH ROUTE
        INTEGER    &NUMCAR       ' NUMBER OF CARRIAGES IN SYSTEM
        INTEGER    &I            ' INDEX VARIABLE FOR READING IN DATA
        INTEGER    &J            ' INDEX VARIABLE FOR READING IN DATA
        INTEGER    &NRUNS        ' NUMBER OF RUNS INDEX (CONTROL)
        INTEGER    &RUNSD        ' NUMBER OF RUNS DESIRED
*
DSPTCH STORAGE    1             ' DEFINE THE SIZE OF DSPTCH TO BE ONE,
*                               ' LIMITS CALLS FOR CARRIAGE
*                               ' DISPATCHES TO ONE AT A TIME
*===========================================================*
*
*        INITIALIZE VARIABLES
*
        LET        &NUMRTS=5    ' NUMBER OF DIFFERENT ROUTES AVAILABLE
*
        LET        &CARHLD=10   ' NUMBER OF PASSENGERS PER CARRIAGE
*
        LET        &RDPRTN(1)=9  ' NUMBER OF REPETITIONS OF ROUTE 1
        LET        &RDPRTN(2)=5  ' NUMBER OF REPETITIONS OF ROUTE 2
        LET        &RDPRTN(3)=9  ' NUMBER OF REPETITIONS OF ROUTE 3
        LET        &RDPRTN(4)=5  ' NUMBER OF REPETITIONS OF ROUTE 4
        LET        &RDPRTN(5)=9  ' NUMBER OF REPETITIONS OF ROUTE 5
*
        LET        &SPEED(1)=500 ' SPEED ON GOOD PAVEMENT
        LET        &SPEED(2)=400 ' SPEED ON MEDIUM PAVEMENT
        LET        &SPEED(3)=300 ' SPEED ON POOR PAVEMENT
        LET        &SPEED(4)=200 ' SPEED ON GRAVEL
        LET        &SPEED(5)=100 ' SPEED ON POOR GRAVEL
*
        LET        &SPDDEV(1)=36 ' STD DEV FOR SPEED 1
        LET        &SPDDEV(2)=28 ' STD DEV FOR SPEED 2
        LET        &SPDDEV(3)=18 ' STD DEV FOR SPEED 3
        LET        &SPDDEV(4)=10 ' STD DEV FOR SPEED 4
        LET        &SPDDEV(5)=4  ' STD DEV FOR SPEED 5
*
        LET        &MOSTRT=9     ' MOST REPETITIONS IN ANY ROUTE
*
        LET        &RUNSD=1      ' NUMBER OF RUNS (DAYS) TO BE SIMULATED
*===========================================================*
* MATRIX DEFINITIONS AND INITIALIZATIONS
*
* NUMBER OF UNRESERVED PLACES ON EACH REPETITION OF ALL ROUTES
* -  ROW INDEXED BY ROUTE #
* -  COLUMN INDEXED BY REPETITION NUMBER OF EACH ROUTE
RCAPAC MATRIX     H,&NUMRTS,&MOSTRT
*
* ALL REPETITIONS OF EACH ROUTE CAN HOLD TEN PASSENGERS
* -  ROW INDEXED BY ROUTE #
* -  COLUMN INDEXED BY REPETITION NUMBER OF EACH ROUTE
        INITIAL    MH$RCAPAC(1-&NUMRTS,1-&MOSTRT),&CARHLD
```

Figure 11.9 GPSS/H program.

```
*==========================================================*
*
* THE SCHEDULED DEPARTURE TIMES OF EACH REPETITION OF ALL ROUTES
* -  ROW INDEXED BY ROUTE #
* -  COLUMN INDEXED BY REPETITION NUMBER OF EACH ROUTE
TIMERT MATRIX     X,&NUMRTS,&MOSTRT
*==========================================================*
*
* TRUE WHEN ROUTE IS ACTUALLY DISPATCHED
* -  ROW INDEXED BY ROUTE #
* -  COLUMN INDEXED BY REPETITION NUMBER OF EACH ROUTE
DCAR   MATRIX     H,&NUMRTS,&MOSTRT
*==========================================================*
*
* TRUE WHEN ROUTE IS LOADED AND CARRIAGE SHOULD GO
* -  ROW INDEXED BY ROUTE #
* -  COLUMN INDEXED BY REPETITION NUMBER OF EACH ROUTE
GOCAR  MATRIX     H,&NUMRTS,&MOSTRT
*==========================================================*
*
* HOLDS INFORMATION CONCERNING EACH CARRIAGE ROUTE
* FIELD 1 : DISTANCE OF CURRENT SEGMENT
* FIELD 2 : ROADWAY TYPE
* FIELD 3 : ATTRACTION DWELL TIME AFTER CURRENT SEGMENT
* FIELD 4 : 'TRUE' IF PASSENGER UNLOADING AFTER CURRENT SEGMENT
* EACH ROW REPRESENTS A SEGMENT IN THE ROUTE
ROUTE1 MATRIX     X,20,4
ROUTE2 MATRIX     X,20,4
ROUTE3 MATRIX     X,20,4
ROUTE4 MATRIX     X,20,4
ROUTE5 MATRIX     X,20,4
*==========================================================*
*
* DEFINE EXTERNAL INPUT FILE
INDAT FILE        'INDAT.DAT'
*
* READ CARRIAGE ROUTE INFORMATION IN FROM EXTERNAL FILE
      GETLIST     FILE=INDAT,&NUMRT(1) 'NUMBER OF SEGMENTS IN ROUTE 1
      GETLIST     FILE=INDAT,((MX$ROUTE1(&I,&J),&J=1,4),&I=1,&NUMRT(1))
*
      GETLIST     FILE=INDAT,&NUMRT(2) 'NUMBER OF SEGMENTS IN ROUTE 2
      GETLIST     FILE=INDAT,((MX$ROUTE2(&I,&J),&J=1,4),&I=1,&NUMRT(2))
*
      GETLIST     FILE=INDAT,&NUMRT(3) 'NUMBER OF SEGMENTS IN ROUTE 3
      GETLIST     FILE=INDAT,((MX$ROUTE3(&I,&J),&J=1,4),&I=1,&NUMRT(3))
*
      GETLIST     FILE=INDAT,&NUMRT(4) 'NUMBER OF SEGMENTS IN ROUTE 4
      GETLIST     FILE=INDAT,((MX$ROUTE4(&I,&J),&J=1,4),&I=1,&NUMRT(4))
*
      GETLIST     FILE=INDAT,&NUMRT(5) 'NUMBER OF SEGMENTS IN ROUTE 5
      GETLIST     FILE=INDAT,((MX$ROUTE5(&I,&J),&J=1,4),&I=1,&NUMRT(5))
*==========================================================*
* FUNCTION DEFINITIONS
*
* DESCRIBES THE SIZE OF EACH GROUP OF PEOPLE COMING TO THE TICKET BOOTH
GRSIZE  FUNCTION    RN2,D10
0.03,1/0.52,2/0.75,3/0.89,4/0.96,5
0.98,6/0.99,7/0.9975,8/0.9990,9
1.0,10
*==========================================================*
*
* DESCRIBES WHICH PERSONALITY TYPE DOMINATES EACH GROUP
WPERSON FUNCTION    RN3,D5
0.03,1/0.11,2/0.70,3/0.91,4/1.0,5
*==========================================================*
```

(*Figure 11.9 continued*)

255

```
*
* DESCRIBES THE LENGTH OF TIME A PERSON WILL WAIT BEFORE
* FOR A LATE CARRIAGE BEFORE DEMANDING A REFUND
PERSONT FUNCTION    PF$PERSON,C5
1,0/2,600/3,1200/4,2400/5,36000
*=========================================================*
*
* DESCRIBES HOW TALKATIVE THE LEADER OF EACH GROUP IS
WTALK   FUNCTION    RN4,D4
0.12,300/0.47,120/0.83,60/1.0,0
*=========================================================*
*
* DESCRIBES THE FREQUENCY WITH WHICH CUSTOMERS INITIALLY CHOOSE ROUTES
ROUTEZ  FUNCTION    RN5,D5
0.20,1/0.40,2/0.60,3/0.80,4/1.0,5
*=========================================================*
*
* THE PERCENT OF PASSENGERS CHOOSING EACH ALTERNATE
* PLAN OF ACTION WHEN THEIR PREFERRED ROUTE IS FULL
ALTP    FUNCTION    RN6,D3
0.75,1/0.94,2/1.0,3

*=========================================================*
*
* SYNONYM DECLARATIONS
ALT1    SYN         1       ' ALTERNATE PLAN 1
ALT2    SYN         2       ' ALTERNATE PLAN 2
ALT3    SYN         3       ' ALTERNATE PLAN 3
TRUE    SYN         1       ' BOOLEAN TRUE
FALSE   SYN         0       ' BOOLEAN FALSE
SEVERE  SYN         1       ' SEVERE PERSONALITY TYPE
*=========================================================*
*
* TRANSACTION PARAMETERS DECLARED
GSIZE   EQU         1,PF    ' SIZE OF CUSTOMER GROUP TRANSACTION DEPICTS
PERSON  EQU         2,PF    ' PERSONALITY TYPE
TALK    EQU         3,PF    ' TALKATIVENESS FACTOR
RETURN  EQU         4,PF    ' STORES BLOCK NUMBER FOR SUBROUTINE RETURN
ROUTE   EQU         5,PF    ' NUMBER OF ROUTE
PLAN    EQU         6,PF    ' NUMBER OF ALTERNATE PLAN IF ROUTE FULL
INDX    EQU         7,PF    ' USED TO INDEX THROUGH REPETITIONS OF ROUTE
DRTTIM  EQU         8,PF    ' DISPATCH TIME FOR CUSTOMER'S ROUTE
NUMPAS  EQU         9,PF    ' NUMBER OF PASSENGERS ON CARRIAGE
TIME    EQU         10,PF   ' ADVANCE TIME PARAMETER
*=========================================================*
* MACRO DEFINITION SECTION
*
* ROUTET MACRO TO MAKE ROUTE CHANGES AND 'WHAT-IF' EASIER
* # A - TIME OF 1ST DISPATCH FOR THIS ROUTE ;
* # B - TIME OF 2ND DISPATCH FOR THIS ROUTE ;
* # C - TIME OF 3RD DISPATCH FOR THIS ROUTE ;
* # D - TIME OF 4TH DISPATCH FOR THIS ROUTE ;
* # E - TIME OF 5TH DISPATCH FOR THIS ROUTE ;
* # F - TIME OF 6TH DISPATCH FOR THIS ROUTE ;
* # G - TIME OF 7TH DISPATCH FOR THIS ROUTE ;
* # H - TIME OF 8TH DISPATCH FOR THIS ROUTE ;
* # I - TIME OF 9TH DISPATCH FOR THIS ROUTE :
* # J - ROUTE NUMBER
* PUT ZEROS IF DISPATCH NOT BEING USED
*
ROUTET STARTMACRO                   START MACRO CODE
*
        GENERATE    43201,,0,,,10PF GENERATE A TRANSACTION TO
*                                   'TEND' THE ROUTE
*
        PRIORITY    100             GIVE TENDER A HIGH PRIORITY
*                                   TO AVOID TIMING PROBLEMS
```

(Figure 11.9 continued)

256

```
        MSAVEVALUE  TIMERT,#J,1,#A,MX    LOAD UP ROUTE'S DISPATCH TIME MATRIX
        MSAVEVALUE  TIMERT,#J,2,#B,MX
        MSAVEVALUE  TIMERT,#J,3,#C,MX
        MSAVEVALUE  TIMERT,#J,4,#D,MX
        MSAVEVALUE  TIMERT,#J,5,#E,MX
        MSAVEVALUE  TIMERT,#J,6,#F,MX
        MSAVEVALUE  TIMERT,#J,7,#G,MX
        MSAVEVALUE  TIMERT,#J,8,#H,MX
        MSAVEVALUE  TIMERT,#J,9,#I,MX
*
        ASSIGN      1,1,PF               INITIALIZE PF1 FOR USE AS A COUNTER
*
        ASSIGN      ROUTE,#J,PF          GET ROUTE ASSIGNMENT
*
        BLET        &DTRT(#J)=MX$TIMERT(#J,PF1)    SET DTRT FOR THIS ROUTE
*                                        TO DISPATCH TIME PER
*                                        INDEXED REPETITION
*
        TEST NE     &DTRT(#J),0,*+7      MAKE SURE THIS DISPATCH IS VALID
*
        BLET        &DRTRTN(#J)=PF1      SET DRTRTN TO CURRENT REPETITION
*                                        NUMBER FOR THIS ROUTE
*
        ADVANCE     &DTRT(#J)-C1         WAIT UNTIL SCHEDULED DISPATCH TIME
*
        SPLIT       1,CARRD              SIGNAL CARRIAGES THAT A DISPATCH
*                                        TIME HAS ARRIVED
*
        ASSIGN      1+,1,PF              GET READY FOR NEXT REPETITION OF ROUTE
*
        TEST LE     PF1,&MOSTRT,*+2      MAKE SURE LAST REPETITION HAS NOT BEEN
*                                        EXCEEDED
*
        TRANSFER    ,*-7                 CONTINUE LOOPING THROUGH ALL REPETITIONS
*                                        OF ROUTE
*
        BLET        &DRTRTN(#J)=0        LAST REPETITION OF ROUTE IS SCHEDULED TO
*                                        BE DISPATCHED
*
        TERMINATE                        ROUTE TENDER IS COMPLETE WITH DUTIES
*
        ENDMACRO                         END THE MACRO
*========================================================*
*
*       MACRO TO MOVE CARRIAGE THROUGH SEGMENT IN ROUTE
*       ALSO PERFORM PASSENGER LOAD/UNLOAD AND DWELL TIME IF REQUIRED
*       #A = MATRIX TO BE ACCESSED BY MACRO (MX$ROUTE1....MX$ROUTE5)
DROUTE STARTMACRO
*
*       TRAVEL TIME TO MOVE THROUGH SEGMENT
        ASSIGN      TIME,#A(PF$INDX,1)/_
                    RVNORM(7,&SPEED(#A(PF$INDX,2)),_
                    &SPDDEV(#A(PF$INDX,2)))*60,PF
*
        TEST G      PF$TIME,0,*-1        IF TRAVEL TIME IS LESS
*                                        THAN 0 GET NEW SAMPLE
*
        ADVANCE     PF$TIME              DELAY TRAVEL TIME
*
        TEST E      #A(PF$INDX,4),TRUE,*+2    IS UNLOADING REQUIRED AT
*                                        THIS POINT
*
        ADVANCE     PF$NUMPAS*RVTRI(8,30,45,70)    DO PASSENGER UNLOAD
*
        TEST NE     PF$INDX,&NUMRT(PF$ROUTE),DRPPNT    IS CARRIAGE AT DROP OFF
*                                        POINT?
*
```

(Figure 11.9 continued)

257

```
          ADVANCE     #A(PF$INDX,3)                      DWELL TIME PASSES (IF
*                                                        ANY EXISTS)
*
          TEST E      #A(PF$INDX,4),TRUE,*+2             DO PASSENGERS NEED TO
*                                                        BE RELOADED?
*
          ADVANCE     PF$NUMPAS*RVTRI(8,30,45,70)        RELOAD TIME PASSES
*
          ENDMACRO                                       MACRO IS ENDED
*============================================================*
* SET-UP ROUTE DISPATCH TIMES WITH ROUTET MACRO CALLS
*
*         ROUTE #1 DISPATCH TIMES
ROUTET MACRO       3600,7200,10800,14400,18000,21600,25200,_
                   28800,32400,1
*============================================================*
*         ROUTE #2 DISPATCH TIMES
ROUTET MACRO       1800,9000,16200,23400,30600,0,0,0,0,2
*============================================================*
*         ROUTE #3 DISPATCH TIMES
ROUTET MACRO       3600,7200,10800,14400,18000,21600,25200,_
                   28800,32400,3
*============================================================*
*         ROUTE #4 DISPATCH TIMES
ROUTET MACRO       1800,9000,16200,23400,30600,0,0,0,0,4
*============================================================*
*         ROUTE #5 DISPATCH TIMES
ROUTET MACRO       3600,7200,10800,14400,18000,21600,25200,_
                   28800,32400,5
*============================================================*
*              POTENTIAL CUSTOMERS APPROACH TICKET BOOTH        *
*============================================================*
*
          GENERATE    RVEXPO(8,300),,,,,,10PF            CREATE POTENTIAL CUSTOMERS
*
          TEST LE     C1,32400,EXIT                      MAKE SURE TICKET BOOTH IS
*                                                        STILL OPEN
*
          ASSIGN      GSIZE,FN$GRSIZE,PF                 TRANSACTION REPRESENTS THIS
*                                                        MANY PEOPLE
*
          ASSIGN      PERSON,FN$WPERSON,PF               CUSTOMER/GROUP HAS THIS
*                                                        PERSONALITY TYPE
*
          ASSIGN      TALK,FN$WTALK,PF                   CUSTOMER/GROUP IS THIS
*                                                        TALKATIVE
*
          QUEUE       TBOOTH,PF$GSIZE                    CUSTOMER/GROUP WAITS FOR
*                                                        ACCESS TO TICKET BOOTH
*
          SEIZE       TBOOTH                             BOOTH IS ACCESSED
*
          DEPART      TBOOTH,PF$GSIZE                    CUSTOMER/GROUP LEAVES QUEUE
*
          ADVANCE     PF$TALK                            CUSTOMER TALKS TO BOOTH
*                                                        ATTENDANT
*
          TRANSFER    .87,NOTCKT,*+1                     87% OF ARRIVING CUSTOMER/
*                                                        GROUPS ATTEMPT TO BUY A
*                                                        TICKET
*
          TRANSFER    SBR,GROUTE,RETURN$PF               TRY TO ASSIGN ROUTE AND
*                                                        DEPARTURE TIME TO GROUP
*
          ADVANCE     RVNORM(7,25,3)+3*PF$GSIZE          TICKET PURCHASE TIME
*
```

(*Figure 11.9 continued*)

```
        RELEASE    TBOOTH                  CUSTOMER/GROUP LEAVES TICKET
*                                          BOOTH
*
        QUEUE      DISPTCH,PF$GSIZE        CUSTOMER WAITS FOR SCHEDULED
*                                          DEPARTURE TIME
*
        TEST GE    PF$DRTTIM-C1,0,*+2      IF CARRIAGE HAS BEEN "JUST
*                                          DISPATCHED" (DURING TICKET
*                                          PURCHASE) RUN TO DISPATCH GATE
*                                          QUICKLY
*
        ADVANCE    (PF$DRTTIM-C1)+60       LET TIME ADVANCE UNTIL
*                                          DISPATCH TIME ARRIVES (+ TRAVEL
*                                          TIME TO STABLE)
*
        DEPART     DISPTCH,PF$GSIZE        LEAVE THE "WAIT FOR SCHEDULED
*                                          DISPATCH" QUEUE
*
        TRANSFER   ,SDSPCH                 MOVE TRANSACTION TO SCHEDULED
*                                          DISPATCH SEGMENT OF CODE
*
EXIT    TERMINATE                          TICKET BOOTH CLOSED

*================================================================*
*    SUBROUTINE ATTEMPTING TO ASSIGN CUSTOMERS TO A ROUTE        *
*================================================================*
*
GROUTE  ADVANCE
*
        ASSIGN     ROUTE,FN$ROUTEZ,PF      CUSTOMER INQUIRES ABOUT
*                                          DESIRED ROUTE
*
        TEST NE    &DRTRTN(PF$ROUTE),0,ALTPLN  IF LAST REPETITION OF THIS
*                                          ROUTE HAS BEEN DISPATCHED,
*                                          TAKE AN ALTERNATE COURSE OF
*                                          ACTION
*
*    BOOLEAN VARIABLE THAT CHECKS TO SEE IF REMAINING CAPACITY TO
*    ACCOMMODATE THE ENTIRE GROUP EXISTS
RTFUL1  BVARIABLE  (MH$RCAPAC(PF$ROUTE,&DRTRTN(PF$ROUTE)) PF$GSIZE)'GE'0
*
        TEST E     BV$RTFUL1,TRUE,ALTPLN   IF CAPACITY DOES NOT EXIST,
*                                          TAKE AN ALTERNATE COURSE OF
*                                          ACTION
*
*    CAPACITY DOES EXIST, ASSIGN GROUP WITH A DISPATCH TIME
        ASSIGN     DRTTIM,MX$TIMERT(PF$ROUTE,&DRTRTN(PF$ROUTE)),PF
*
*    RESERVATIONS FOR GROUP BY DECREMENTING REMAINING CAPACITY COUNT
MSAVEVALUE RCAPAC-,PF$ROUTE,&DRTRTN(PF$ROUTE),PF$GSIZE,H
*
        ASSIGN     INDX,&DRTRTN(PF$ROUTE),PF  SET INDX TO REPETITION NUMBER
*                                          OF ROUTE SELECTED
*
        TRANSFER   ,PF$RETURN+1            ROUTE HAS BEEN SELECTED,
*                                          RETURN FROM SUBROUTINE
*============================================================*
*
ALTPLN  ADVANCE                            SEGMENT TO DETERMINE WHAT CUSTOMER
*                                          WILL DO IF DESIRED ROUTE IS NOT
*                                          AVAILABLE
*
        ASSIGN     PLAN,FN$ALTP,PF         CHOOSE A NEW PLAN OF ACTION
*
        TEST NE    PF$PLAN,ALT3,NORTO      LEAVE SYSTEM
*
```

(*Figure 11.9 continued*)

259

```
       TEST NE    PF$PLAN,ALT2,SMRT          SAME ROUTE LATER
*
       TRANSFER   ,RMRTS                     CHOOSE A DIFFERENT REMAINING ROUTE
*==================================================================*
*
NORTO  ADVANCE                               CUSTOMER DECIDES TO LEAVE BECAUSE
*                                            SPECIFIC ROUTE IS NOT AVAILABLE
*
       ENTER      NORT3,PF$GSIZE             COUNT NUMBER OF CUSTOMERS LEAVING
       LEAVE      NORT3,PF$GSIZE             FOR THIS REASON
*
       RELEASE    TBOOTH                     RELEASE TICKET BOOTH
*
       TERMINATE                             LEAVE SYSTEM
*==============================================================*
*
SMRT   ADVANCE                               CUSTOMER WISHES TO TAKE
*                                            SAME ROUTE LATER.IF NOT
*                                            AVAILABLE LEAVE SYSTEM
*
       TEST NE    &DRTRTN(PF$ROUTE),0,NORTS  MAKE SURE ALL REPETITION
*                                            OF THIS ROUTE ARE NOT
*                                            DISPATCHED
*
       ASSIGN     INDX,&DRTRTN(PF$ROUTE)+1,PF  ASSIGN INDEX TO THE NEXT
*                                            REPETITION OF DESIRED ROUTE
*
       TEST LE    PF$INDX,&RDPRTN(PF$ROUTE),NORTS MAKE SURE THIS IS NOT PAST
*                                            THE LAST REPETITION OF THIS
*                                            ROUTE
*
*      BOOLEAN VARIABLE CHECKS TO SEE IF SUFFICIENT CAPACITY
*      REMAINS TO ACCOMMODATE GROUP ON THIS REPETITION OF DESIRED ROUTE
RTFUL2 BVARIABLE  (MH$RCAPAC(PF$ROUTE,PF$INDX)-PF$GSIZE)'GE'0
*
       TEST E     BV$RTFUL2,FALSE,RTFND      IF CAPACITY EXISTS, GOTO
*                                            ROUTE FOUND SEGMENT
*
       ASSIGN     INDX+,1,PF                 CAPACITY DOES NOT EXIST TRY
*                                            NEXT REPETITION OF THIS ROUTE
*
       TEST G     PF$INDX,&RDPRTN(PF$ROUTE),*-2  MAKE SURE ALL REPETITIONS
*                                            HAVE NOT BEEN CHECKED ALREADY
*
       TRANSFER   ,NORTS                     NO REPETITIONS OF DESIRED
*                                            ROUTE AVAILABLE, LEAVE SYSTEM
*==============================================================*
*
RMRTS  ADVANCE                               CUSTOMER DECIDES TO TAKE
*                                            ANY AVAILABLE REPETITION
*                                            OF ANY ROUTE
*
       ASSIGN     ROUTE,1,PF                 START CHECKING FOR CAPACITY
*                                            WITH ROUTE #1
*
       TEST NE    &DRTRTN(PF$ROUTE),0,NLOOP  MAKE SURE LAST REPETITION
*                                            OF THIS ROUTE HAS NOT BEEN
*                                            DISPATCHED
*
       ASSIGN     INDX,&DRTRTN(PF$ROUTE),PF  START INDEXING THROUGH
*                                            REPETITIONS WITH NEXT
*                                            PENDING DISPATCHES
*
       TEST E     BV$RTFUL2,FALSE,RTFND      MAKE SURE CAPACITY EXISTS,
*                                            IF SO GOTO SEGMENT "ROUTE
*                                            FOUND"
```

(*Figure 11.9 continued*)

260

```
NLOOP   ASSIGN      ROUTE+,1,PF                             LOOP THROUGH TO CHECK ALL
        TEST LE     PF$ROUTE,&NUMRTS,*-4                    ROUTES
*
        ASSIGN      INDX,&DRTRTN(PF$ROUTE)+1,PF             NO ROUTES PENDING DISPATCH
*                                                           ARE AVAILABLE, "CHECK ONE
*                                                           TIME" INDEX IS INCREMENTED
*                                                           ONE TIME SLOT BACK
*
RRETRY  ASSIGN      ROUTE,1,PF                              ALL ROUTES START
*                                                           IN POSITION ONE
*
RETRY   TEST LE     PF$INDX,&RDPRTN(PF$ROUTE),RETRY2        MAKE SURE REPETITION OF
*                                                           ROUTE BEING CHECKED EXISTS
*
        TEST NE     &DRTRTN(PF$ROUTE),0,RETRY2              MAKE SURE ALL REPETITIONS
*                                                           OF THIS ROUTE ARE NOT
*                                                           DISPATCHED
*
        TEST E      BV$RTFUL2,FALSE,RTFND                   MAKE SURE CAPACITY EXISTS
*                                                           FOR GROUP IF SO GOTO ROUTE
*                                                           FOUND
*
RETRY2  ASSIGN      ROUTE+,1,PF                             TRY NEXT ROUTE
*
        TEST G      PF$ROUTE,&NUMRTS,RETRY                  MAKE SURE ROUTE EXISTS
*
        ASSIGN      INDX+,1,PF                              TRY BACK ONE MORE TIME SLOT
*
        TEST G      PF$INDX,&MOSTRT,RRETRY                  MAKE SURE THIS ROUTE HAS
*                                                           NOT HAD ALL REPETITIONS
*                                                           DISPATCHED
*
        TRANSFER    ,NORT                                   NO CARRIAGES TOURS ARE
*                                                           AVAILABLE, CUSTOMER LEAVES
*                                                           SYSTEM
*===========================================================*
*
RTFND   ADVANCE                                             CUSTOMER GROUP FINDS ROUTE
*                                                           WITH CAPACITY
*
        ASSIGN      DRTTIM,MX$TIMERT(PF$ROUTE,PF$INDX),PF   GET DISPATCH TIME
*
        MSAVEVALUE  RCAPAC ,PF$ROUTE,PF$INDX,PF$GSIZE,H     MAKE RESERVATIONS
*                                                           BY DECREMENTING
*                                                           CAPACITY COUNTER
*
        TRANSFER    ,PF$RETURN+1                            RETURN FROM SUBROUTINE
*===========================================================*
*
NOTCKT  ADVANCE                                             CUSTOMER GOES TO TICKET BOOTH BUT
*                                                           DECIDES NOT TO BUY
*
        ENTER       NOTCK,PF$GSIZE                          KEEP COUNTER OF CUSTOMERS THAT LEAVE
        LEAVE       NOTCK,PF$GSIZE                          THE SYSTEM WITHOUT ATTEMPTING TO BUY
*
        RELEASE     TBOOTH                                  RELEASE TICKET BOOTH
*
        TERMINATE                                           LEAVE SYSTEM
*===========================================================*
*
NORT    ADVANCE                                             CUSTOMER GOES TO TICKET BOOTH BUT
*                                                           DECIDES NOT TO BUY AFTER FINDING ALL
*                                                           ROUTES ARE TOO FULL TO ACCOMMODATE
*                                                           GROUP
*
```

(*Figure 11.9 continued*)

261

```
        ENTER       NORT1,PF$GSIZE           KEEP COUNTER OF CUSTOMERS THAT LEAVE
        LEAVE       NORT1,PF$GSIZE           SYSTEM
*
        RELEASE     TBOOTH                   RELEASE TICKET BOOTH
*
        TERMINATE                            LEAVE SYSTEM
*============================================================*
*
NORTS   ADVANCE                              CUSTOMER DECIDES NOT TO BUY AFTER
*                                            FINDING PARTICULAR SET OF ROUTES ARE
*                                            TOO FULL TO ACCOMMODATE GROUP
*
        ENTER       NORT2,PF$GSIZE           KEEP COUNT OF CUSTOMERS LEAVING
        LEAVE       NORT2,PF$GSIZE
*
        RELEASE     TBOOTH                   RELEASE TICKET BOOTH
*
        TERMINATE                            LEAVE SYSTEM
*============================================================*
*
SDSPCH  ADVANCE                              SCHEDULED DISPATCH TIME HAS
*                                            ARRIVED
*
        TEST E      MH$DCAR(PF$ROUTE,PF$INDX),TRUE,ZWAIT    IS CARRIAGE AVAILABLE
*                                            FOR BOARDING?
*
ZCARR   ENTER       DISPT1,PF$GSIZE          A STATISTIC TO REPRESENT
        LEAVE       DISPT1,PF$GSIZE          CUSTOMER BOARDING IS TABULATED
*
        ADVANCE     PF$GSIZE*RVTRI(8,30,45,70)  DELAY TO REPRESENT CUSTOMER
*                                            BOARDING TIMES
*
* KEEP TRACK OF THE NUMBER OF PASSENGERS ON THE CARRIAGE
        BLET        &CARCNT(PF$ROUTE)=&CARCNT(PF$ROUTE)+PF$GSIZE
*
        TEST GE     &CARCNT(PF$ROUTE),&CARHLD-_
                    (MH$RCAPAC(PF$ROUTE,PF$INDX)),*+3 IF THIS IS THE LAST
*                                            PASSENGER GROUP TO BOARD,
*                                            DROP THROUGH
*
        BLET        &CARCNT(PF$ROUTE)=0      ALL ON BOARD: RESET COUNTER
*
        MSAVEVALUE  GOCAR,PF$ROUTE,PF$INDX,TRUE,MH  SIGNAL CARRIAGE THAT IT CAN
*                                            GO!
*
        TERMINATE                            CUSTOMER TRANSACTIONS NO
*                                            LONGER NEEDED IN MODEL
*============================================================*
*
REFUND  ADVANCE                              IRATE CUSTOMERS ENTER THE
*                                            TICKET REFUND SUBROUTINE
*
        ENTER       REFUN,PF$GSIZE           COUNT THE NUMBER OF CUSTOMERS
*                                            DEMANDING A REFUND
*
        MSAVEVALUE  RCAPAC+,PF$ROUTE,PF$INDX,PF$GSIZE,H  LESS PEOPLE TO BOARD
*                                            THE CARRIAGE
*
        SEIZE       TBOOTH                   USE THE TICKET BOOTH RESOURCE
*
        ADVANCE     RVNORM(7,46,4)+3*PF$GSIZE  EACH CUSTOMER GROUP TAKES TIME
*                                            TO RECEIVE REFUNDS
*
        ADVANCE     PF$TALK                  SOME CUSTOMERS TAKE TIME TO
*                                            CHEW OUT THE BOOTH ATTENDANT
*
```

(*Figure 11.9 continued*)

```
        RELEASE   TBOOTH                          EX-CUSTOMERS LEAVE TICKET BOOTH
*
        LEAVE     REFUN,PF$GSIZE                  REFUND OPERATION COMPLETE
*
        TERMINATE                                 CUSTOMERS LEAVE SYSTEM
*=======================================================*
*
ZWAIT   ADVANCE                                   ALTHOUGH DISPATCH TIME HAS
*                                                 ARRIVED, NO CARRIAGE IS
*                                                 AVAILABLE
*
        TEST NE   PF$PERSON,SEVERE,REFUND         PEOPLE WITH 'SEVERE'
*                                                 PERSONALITIES GET MAD AND GO
*                                                 FOR A REFUND
*
        ASSIGN    PERSON,FN$PERSONT+C1,PF         A MAXIMUM WAITING TIME IS
*                                                 ASSIGNED TO EACH CUSTOMER GROUP
*
        ENTER     WAITC,PF$GSIZE                  WAIT TIME IS MEASURED
*
*       CUSTOMERS WAIT UNTIL THEIR PATIENCE LIMIT IS REACHED OR UNTIL
*       A CARRIAGE ARRIVES
WAITL   BVARIABLE PF$PERSON'LE'C1+MH$DCAR(PF$ROUTE,PF$INDX)'E'TRUE
        TEST E    BV$WAITL,TRUE
*
        LEAVE     WAITC,PF$GSIZE                  CUSTOMER LEAVES THE WAITING
*                                                 STATISTIC
*
        TEST E    MH$DCAR(PF$ROUTE,PF$INDX),TRUE,REFUND   IF A CARRIAGE IS
*                                                 AVAILABLE BOARDING
*                                                 BEGINS, OTHERWISE A
*                                                 REFUND IS DEMANDED
*
        TRANSFER  ,ZCARR                          CUSTOMER GOES TO
*                                                 BOARD THE CARRIAGE
*=======================================================*
*
CARRD   ADVANCE                                   CARRIAGE DISPATCH IS DESIRED
*
        ASSIGN    INDX,PF1,PF                     INDICATE WHICH REPETITION OF
*                                                 THE ROUTE IS DESIRED
*
        LINK      DSPTCH,FIFO,CARRD2              KEEP EXTRA TRANSACTIONS ON A USER
*                                                 CHAIN
*
CARRD2  ENTER     DSPTCH                          ALLOW ONE DISPATCH TO BE PENDING
*                                                 AT ANY GIVEN TIME (STORAGE
*                                                 CAPACITY = 1)
*
        JOIN      DSPTCH                          JOIN A GROUP SO DISPATCH TRANSACTION
*                                                 CAN BE "SCANNED" BY CARRIAGE
*                                                 TRANSACTION
*
        GATE SE   DSPTCH                          WAIT UNTIL CARRIAGE TRANSACTION
*                                                 LEAVES DSPTCH INDICATING THAT THE
*                                                 "CALL FOR A DISPATCH" HAS BEEN
*                                                 SERVICED
*
        VLINK     DSPTCH,CARRD2,1                 NEXT DISPATCH TRANSACTION IS
*                                                 ALLOWED TO LEAVE CHAIN
*
        REMOVE    DSPTCH                          SCAN COMPLETE SO TRANSACTION CAN
*                                                 REMOVE ITSELF FROM THE GROUP
*
        TERMINATE                                 TRANSACTION IS DELETED FROM
*                                                 SIMULATION
```

(Figure 11.9 continued)

```
*=================================================================*
*          CARRIAGES AND ROUTE LOGIC SEGMENT                      *
*=================================================================*
*
        GENERATE    0,0,0,20,,10PF          CREATE REQUIRED NUMBER OF CARRIAGES
*
        ENTER       HMCARR                  ALLOW ONLY A CERTAIN NUMBER OF
*                                           CARRIAGES INTO THE SYSTEM
*
        PRIORITY    50                      ASSIGN CARRIAGE A HIGHER PRIORITY
*                                           THAN A CUSTOMER TRANSACTION
*
STABLE  ENTER       STABLE                  CARRIAGE IN THE STABLE AREA
        JOIN        STABLE
*
        ADVANCE     RVTRI(8,250,300,500)    WHEN IN STABLE A CARRIAGE REMAINS
*                                           AROUND 5 MINUTES BEFORE BEING
*                                           ELIGIBLE FOR DISPATCH
*
        GATE SNE    DSPTCH                  WAIT FOR A ROUTE DISPATCH TIME TO
*                                           OCCUR
*
        SCAN MIN    DSPTCH,ROUTE$PF,,ROUTE$PF,ROUTE$PF   OBTAIN ROUTE AND
        SCAN MIN    DSPTCH,ROUTE$PF,,INDX$PF,INDX$PF     REPETITION FROM
*                                                        DISPATCHING TRANSACTION
*
        LEAVE       STABLE                  CARRIAGE LEAVES STABLE AREA
*
        LEAVE       DSPTCH                  TELL DISPATCHING TRANSACTION THAT
*                                           ITS DUTY IS DONE
*
        ADVANCE     RVTRI(8,50,60,300)      MOVE TO DISPATCH POINT
*
*
        MSAVEVALUE DCAR,PF$ROUTE,PF$INDX,TRUE,MH   TELL PASSENGERS THAT
*                                                  CARRIAGE IS READY FOR
*                                                  BOARDING
*
*       ASSIGN THE CARRIAGE A NUMBER OF PASSENGERS
        ASSIGN      NUMPAS,&CARHLD-(MH$RCAPAC(PF$ROUTE,PF$INDX)),PF
*
        TEST NE     PF$NUMPAS,0,DRPPNT      MAKE SURE PASSENGERS HAVE SIGNED UP
*                                           TO GO ON TRIP. IF NONE RETURN TO
*                                           STABLE
*
        TEST E      MH$GOCAR(PF$ROUTE,PF$INDX),TRUE   TELL SYSTEM THAT THE
*                                                     CARRIAGE IS "GOING"
*
        ASSIGN      INDX,0,PF                         INDX PARAMETER IS RESET
*=================================================================*
*
NXMOV   ASSIGN      INDX+,1,PF              CARRIAGE MOVES ALONG THROUGH ITS ROUTE
*
        TEST E      PF$ROUTE,1,NXMOV1       CARRIAGE IS ON ROUTE #1
DROUTE  MACRO       MX$ROUTE1
*
NXMOV1  TEST E      PF$ROUTE,2,NXMOV2       CARRIAGE IS ON ROUTE #2
DROUTE  MACRO       MX$ROUTE2
*
NXMOV2  TEST E      PF$ROUTE,3,NXMOV3       CARRIAGE IS ON ROUTE #3
DROUTE  MACRO       MX$ROUTE3
*
NXMOV3  TEST E      PF$ROUTE,4,NXMOV4       CARRIAGE IS ON ROUTE #4
DROUTE  MACRO       MX$ROUTE4
*
NXMOV4  TEST E      PF$ROUTE,5,NXMOV        CARRIAGE IS ON ROUTE #5
DROUTE  MACRO       MX$ROUTE5
```

(Figure 11.9 continued)

```
*
        TRANSFER    ,NXMOV                    TRAVEL THROUGH NEXT SEGMENT IN ROUTE
*===============================================================*
*
DRPPNT  ADVANCE                               PASSENGERS HAVE BEEN DROPPED
*
        ADVANCE     RVTRI(8,50,60,300)        CARRIAGE MOVES TO STABLE
*
        TRANSFER    ,STABLE                   CARRIAGE ARRIVES AT STABLE AREA
*===============================================================*
*                   TIMING TRANSACTION SECTION                  *
*===============================================================*
        GENERATE    3600          ' EVERY 3600 SECONDS (1 HR)
        TERMINATE   1             ' DECREMENT START COUNT
        START       12            ' RUN FOR A TWELVE HOUR DAY
        END                       ' SIMULATION ENDED
*===============================================================*
```

(*Figure 11.9 continued*)

```
*===============================================================*
*                   TIMING TRANSACTION SECTION                         *
*===============================================================*
        GENERATE    3600              ' EVERY 3600 SECONDS (1 HR)
        TERMINATE   1                 ' DECREMENT START COUNT
*
*       NUMBER OF RUNS (DAYS) TO BE SIMULATED
        LET         &RUNSD=1
*
*       RUN EXPERIMENTS WITH 8 THROUGH 16 CARRIAGES
        DO          &NUMCAR=8,16,1
*
*       EACH NEW CARRIAGE COUNT ALLOWS ONE MORE CARRIAGE
*       TRANSACTION TO BECOME ACTIVE
        STORAGE     S$HMCARR,&NUMCAR
*
*       DO 100 REPETITIONS FOR EACH CARRIAGE COUNT
        DO          &NRUNS=1,&RUNSD,1                '&RUNSD = 100
*
*       CLEAR OUT STATS
        RESET
        INITIAL     MH$RCAPAC(1-&NUMRTS,1-&MOSTRT),&CARHLD
        INITIAL     MH$GOCAR(1-&NUMRTS,1-&MOSTRT),0
        INITIAL     MH$DCAR(1-&NUMRTS,1-&MOSTRT),0
*
*       TWELVE HOUR DAYS
        START       12,NP             ' RUN FOR TWELVE HOURS
*
        ENDDO
        ENDDO
        END
*=========================================================*
```

Figure 11.10 Control statements required for desired simulation runs.

of dispatch delays to an acceptable minimum. To do this, he decided to run 100 repetitions for each carriage count from 8 through 16. (Each repetition represents one day of carriage tour operation.) The control statements shown in Figure 11.10 were added to the model to produce the desired output.

11.5 Phase (13): Output Analysis

After running the series of experiments, DePorres loaded the model's output data into a Lotus 1-2-3 spreadsheet. This facilitated the process of analyzing the results (Figure 11.11). He used the output data to arrive at an average number of

	A	B	C	D	E	F	G	H	I	J	K	L
1	Number of Tickets Refunded Due to Carriage Delays											
2												
3	Run					Number of Carriages						
4	Number		8	9	10	11	12	13	14	15	16	
5												
6	1		52	48	9	10	2	6	7	6	8	
7	2		50	14	5	14	8	13	5	7	4	
8	3		61	23	16	21	4	9	9	3	4	
9	4		60	34	11	0	3	3	12	10	9	
10	5		59	24	0	9	6	14	7	9	7	
11	6		64	6	19	4	5	7	7	3	4	
12	7		61	26	20	0	8	2	4	2	2	
13	8		59	12	6	2	8	4	6	11	2	
14	9		89	29	8	3	2	1	19	10	8	
15	10		99	9	15	10	10	4	12	5	4	
16	11		97	28	5	11	6	18	12	12	4	
17	12		50	27	4	5	5	7	2	0	3	
18	13		64	16	18	15	0	9	4	5	3	
19	14		58	27	10	6	0	3	2	7	7	
20	15		43	26	17	11	7	5	3	2	2	
21	16		74	18	3	6	0	0	4	2	5	
22	17		53	17	8	7	13	6	4	7	14	
23	18		108	45	2	4	9	13	6	6	7	
24	19		53	21	30	3	10	10	4	2	2	
25	20		60	32	15	8	3	5	7	14	8	
26	21		66	27	20	13	8	12	9	14	6	
27	22		57	35	10	10	12	7	5	6	8	
28	23		41	23	14	8	6	2	9	8	4	
29	24		38	10	14	7	9	2	17	11	11	
30	25		38	26	4	4	4	2	22	5	9	
31	26		22	33	5	9	11	3	13	3	0	
32	27		39	30	8	16	4	0	7	9	7	
33	28		30	24	20	4	6	8	2	2	0	
34	29		23	5	2	10	5	12	7	12	9	
35	30		38	12	4	5	8	0	13	5	5	
36	31		28	22	6	2	4	2	8	4	2	
37	32		51	14	8	7	6	0	4	6	2	
38	33		45	19	11	7	2	6	4	0	4	
39	34		55	33	8	6	11	6	4	12	9	
40	35		36	5	9	4	12	6	8	0	0	
41	36		51	48	4	0	15	0	5	6	4	
42	37		6	14	9	9	1	4	18	15	9	
43	38		52	44	6	9	22	13	4	2	15	
44	39		55	14	8	6	5	0	7	5	10	
45	40		56	42	20	9	2	6	8	10	14	
46	41		24	35	9	5	16	3	11	6	16	
47	42		49	25	11	5	6	11	3	5	4	
48	43		29	64	5	20	3	15	2	17	22	

Figure 11.11 Lotus 1-2-3 spreadsheet containing initial results of the NMHC detailed simulation.

49	44	47	39	22	5	7	0	18	7	6
50	45	81	17	7	19	10	2	5	12	8
51	46	59	14	16	6	11	4	8	4	6
52	47	67	19	6	10	14	0	9	7	4
53	48	33	30	2	12	11	4	9	4	8
54	49	19	31	7	4	4	9	13	5	17
55	50	41	29	9	12	11	3	15	8	6
56	51	38	15	3	4	10	14	2	2	17
57	52	25	7	3	6	11	8	3	9	10
58	53	37	11	18	17	8	8	8	12	0
59	54	53	39	8	6	7	0	10	2	9
60	55	44	38	0	2	17	10	11	6	8
61	56	25	15	4	10	7	7	5	10	4
62	57	63	27	2	2	3	8	9	4	0
63	58	37	21	4	11	12	3	0	4	4
64	59	66	44	15	14	9	19	5	4	7
65	60	38	30	11	10	9	9	0	3	9
66	61	51	34	18	13	5	5	7	13	6
67	62	41	22	7	5	0	4	9	5	2
68	63	76	13	12	7	4	12	0	3	9
69	64	60	18	13	5	7	2	4	2	15
70	65	33	38	9	12	10	5	8	2	3
71	66	44	14	28	2	9	18	7	14	12
72	67	41	22	19	0	2	4	4	6	9
73	68	58	29	7	2	2	10	14	0	8
74	69	55	22	6	23	0	6	4	9	4
75	70	63	12	19	4	11	0	10	5	7
76	71	53	15	5	8	0	10	0	10	8
77	72	28	16	7	8	0	8	8	5	4
78	73	53	13	7	4	6	4	13	2	9
79	74	22	27	4	16	7	15	7	9	7
80	75	23	43	6	4	11	4	10	4	2
81	76	16	21	4	9	10	4	6	0	6
82	77	40	26	9	0	4	2	0	0	2
83	78	28	38	19	6	6	12	3	4	4
84	79	74	24	5	6	4	12	7	2	0
85	80	45	7	9	14	10	4	11	2	13
86	81	70	20	3	20	9	6	5	11	0
87	82	39	13	11	0	2	7	1	19	19
88	83	33	15	15	2	3	8	2	5	2
89	84	13	3	8	2	12	5	2	11	2
90	85	31	22	14	6	5	10	0	11	4
91	86	63	46	3	2	5	3	4	7	7
92	87	42	61	22	13	6	3	13	15	0
93	88	44	39	15	6	7	4	7	12	6
94	89	32	33	2	20	13	2	3	7	12
95	90	31	26	8	5	9	3	8	8	5
96	91	40	11	5	0	5	11	19	12	9
97	92	105	33	9	3	2	6	0	0	2
98	93	44	36	11	10	3	8	0	4	7
99	94	26	26	2	4	5	7	4	2	6
100	95	48	40	8	9	9	11	0	17	7
101	96	34	27	4	8	0	4	4	13	0
102	97	43	76	0	5	0	5	5	5	0
103	98	51	18	10	3	2	6	12	9	3
104	99	49	14	4	3	4	7	13	6	6
105	100	34	16	2	2	8	5	7	5	3
106	--
107	Average	47.9	25.4	9.4	7.5	6.7	6.3	7.0	6.7	6.3
108	Refunds									

(Figure 11.11 continued)

| STORAGE | AVG-UTIL-DURING | | | ENTRIES | AVERAGE | CURRENT | PERCENT | CAPACITY | AVERAGE | CURRENT | MAXIMUM |
	TOTAL TIME	AVAIL TIME	UNAVL TIME		TIME/UNIT	STATUS	AVAIL		CONTENTS	CONTENTS	CONTENTS
DSPTCH	.046	.000	.000	37	53.365	AVAIL	100.0	1	.046	0	1
NORT3	.000	.000	.000	2	.000	AVAIL	100.0	2147483647	.000	0	2
NOTCK	.000	.000	.000	34	.000	AVAIL	100.0	2147483647	.000	0	7
NORT2	.000	.000	.000	9	.000	AVAIL	100.0	2147483647	.000	0	7
DISPT1	.000	.000	.000	260	.000	AVAIL	100.0	2147483647	.000	0	7
REFUN	.000	.000	.000	8	163.165	AVAIL	100.0	2147483647	.030	0	6
WAITC	.000	.000	.000	225	112.508	AVAIL	100.0	2147483647	.586	0	26
HMCARR	1.000	.000	.000	11	43200.000	AVAIL	100.0	11	11.000	11	11
STABLE	.000	.000	.000	47	3509.949	AVAIL	100.0	2147483647	3.819	10	11

| FACILITY | --AVG-UTIL-DURING-- | | | ENTRIES | AVERAGE | CURRENT | PERCENT | SEIZING | PREEMPTING |
	TOTAL TIME	AVAIL TIME	UNAVL TIME		TIME/XACT	STATUS	AVAIL	XACT	XACT
TBOOTH	.316			109	125.335	AVAIL	100.0		

QUEUE	MAXIMUM CONTENTS	AVERAGE CONTENTS	TOTAL ENTRIES	ZERO ENTRIES	PERCENT ZEROS	AVERAGE TIME/UNIT	$AVERAGE TIME/UNIT	QTABLE NUMBER	CURRENT CONTENTS
TBOOTH	7	.356	313	204	65.2	49.181	141.225		0
DISPTCH	56	21.008	268	14	5.2	3386.298	3572.945		0

Figure 11.12 GPSS/H standard output for a selected run.

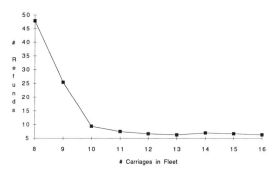

Figure 11.13　Refunds versus fleet size.

refunded tickets for each carriage count from 8 to 16. Figure 11.12 contains the standard GPSS/H output for a run of the model with 11 carriages.

11.6　Phase (14): Generation of Output Report

DePorres decided to create a graphic representation of the information he obtained from the simulation. Figure 11.13 shows that increasing the number of carriages from 8 to 11 significantly reduces the number of ticket refunds. After 11 carriages, the number of refunds levels off. Adding more carriages after this point has a minimal effect on the number of refunds.

11.7　Phase (15): Logic Transfer

The purpose of running a simulation is to obtain knowledge that can be applied in a real world system. Phase 15 in a simulation project involves making sure that this knowledge is properly communicated or transferred from the model to the real system.

DePorres transferred the simulation logic by making a decision to upgrade the current operation from 9 carriages to 11. Using 11 carriages is consistent with his findings that this number is required to reduce ticket refunds to a "steady-state" number.

11.8　Summary

Chapters 10 and 11 have given a brief overview of what is involved with completing a simulation project. The detailed simulation illustrated in Chapter 11 shows how a model might be created and some of the different scenarios that might be run by an analyst to aid in investigating a system. Many runs and experiments, in addition to the ones shown, would normally be conducted in an actual simulation study. The process demonstrated in these chapters should not be construed as a comprehensive, definitive simulation project. Rather, it should be looked upon as an example of the thought process and types of activities involved with performing a simulation.

Index